THE RISKY BUSINESS OF EDUCATION POLICY

The Risky Business of Education Policy focuses commentary and analysis on some of the most pressing policy challenges facing public school educators and those invested in a healthy, vibrant public-school system. This book shares insights and makes recommendations from leading scholar-practitioners, namely from educational leadership and science education, on ways to ponder, navigate, and challenge serious policy issues. The chapters present important policy topics and critical analysis of the topics from the authorial perspective of experienced educators leading the preparation of future school leaders and teachers.

Through fast paced, user-friendly chapters, contributors grapple with an education reform policy issue of the day, reflecting what is contentious territory while wading through it. These educational researchers also make evidence-informed practical recommendations for educators and policymakers on how to better approach the policy challenges presented, so public education can be improved for all children. Each chapter contains stimulating ideas, useful information, and practical tips for school practitioners, higher education faculty, and constituent groups.

Christopher H. Tienken, EdD, is an Associate Professor of Education Leadership, Management, and Policy. He is the author of more than 85 publications whose recent books include *Cracking the Code of Education Reform: Creative Compliance and Ethical Leadership* (Corwin Press, 2020) and *The School Reform Landscape Reloaded: More Fraud, Myth, and Lies* (Rowman & Littlefield, 2021).

Carol A. Mullen, PhD, is Professor of Educational Leadership and Policy Studies, Virginia Tech, and a US Fulbright scholar alumnus. She has authored over 240 articles and chapters and 28 academic books, including *Canadian Indigenous Literature and Art* (Brill, 2020); *Revealing Creativity* (Springer, 2020); *Creativity Under Duress in Education?* (Springer, 2019); and *Handbook of Social Justice Interventions in Education* (Springer, 2021).

KAPPA DELTA PI CO-PUBLICATIONS

Experiencing Dewey, Second Edition
Insights for Today's Classrooms
Edited by Donna Adair Breault, Rick Breault

The Power of Teacher Leaders
Their Roles, Influence, and Impact
Edited by Nathan Bond

Education Policy Perils
Tackling the Tough Issues
Edited by Christopher H. Tienken, Carol A. Mullen

Creativity and Education in China
Paradox and Possibilities for an Era of Accountability
Carol A. Mullen

Star Teachers of Children in Poverty, 2nd Edition
Martin Haberman, Maureen D. Gillette, Djanna A. Hill

Reframing the Curriculum
Design for Social Justice and Sustainability
Susan Santone

The New Teacher's Guide to Overcoming Common Challenges
Curated Advice from Award-Winning Teachers
Edited by Anna M. Quinzio-Zafran, Elizabeth A. Wilkins

The Risky Business of Education Policy
Edited by Christopher H. Tienken, Carol A. Mullen

THE RISKY BUSINESS OF EDUCATION POLICY

Edited by Christopher H. Tienken and Carol A. Mullen

First published 2022
by Routledge
605 Third Avenue, New York, NY 10158

and by Routledge
2 Park Square, Milton Park, Abingdon, Oxon OX14 4RN

Routledge is an imprint of the Taylor & Francis Group, an informa business

© 2022 Kappa Delta Pi

The right of Kappa Delta Pi to be identified as the author of the editorial material, and of the authors for their individual chapters, has been asserted in accordance with sections 77 and 78 of the Copyright, Designs and Patents Act 1988.

All rights reserved. No part of this book may be reprinted or reproduced or utilised in any form or by any electronic, mechanical, or other means, now known or hereafter invented, including photocopying and recording, or in any information storage or retrieval system, without permission in writing from the publishers.

Trademark notice: Product or corporate names may be trademarks or registered trademarks, and are used only for identification and explanation without intent to infringe.

Library of Congress Cataloging-in-Publication Data
Names: Mullen, Carol A. editor. | Tienken, Christopher editor.
Title: The risky business of education policy / edited by Christopher H. Tienken, Carol A. Mullen.
Description: New York, N.Y. : Routledge, [2022] | Includes bibliographical references and index.
Identifiers: LCCN 2021011375 (print) | LCCN 2021011376 (ebook) | ISBN 9780367622466 (paperback) | ISBN 9780367622480 (hardback) | ISBN 9781003108511 (ebook)
Subjects: LCSH: Education and state. | Public schools. | Educational change. | Privatization in education. | Business and education.
Classification: LCC LC71 .R57 2022 (print) | LCC LC71 (ebook) | DDC 379--dc23
LC record available at https://lccn.loc.gov/2021011375
LC ebook record available at https://lccn.loc.gov/2021011376

ISBN: 978-0-367-62248-0 (hbk)
ISBN: 978-0-367-62246-6 (pbk)
ISBN: 978-1-003-10851-1 (ebk)

DOI: 10.4324/9781003108511

Typeset in Bembo
by Taylor & Francis Books

Christopher H. Tienken:
For Gabriella and Francesca—keep dreaming out loud. Voi andate avanti.

Carol A. Mullen:
For Bill—wishing you "Double Happiness" in love and life

CONTENTS

Acknowledgments   *ix*
Preface   *x*
Foreword   *xiv*

1 Corporate Networks' Grip on the Public School Sector and Education Policy   1
  Carol A. Mullen

2 Neoliberalism as a Policy Ventriloquist: Deconstructing the Discourse of Corporate America for Its Public Schools   23
  Fenwick W. English

3 Threats to Meaningful Reform of Civic Education   40
  Patricia H. Hinchey and Pamela J. Konkol

4 *Brown versus Board* Did Not Work: Finding a New Pathway to Educational Justice   57
  Ryan W. Coughlan

5 Charter Schools' Impact on Public Education: Theory versus Reality   72
  Julia Sass Rubin and Mark Weber

6 OECD, PISA, and Globalization: The Influence of the International Assessment Regime   88
  Svein Sjøberg

7 Students as the Missing Actor in Education Reform 113
   Yong Zhao and Jim Watterston

8 "*We Come from Everywhere*": Innovating Bi/Multilingual
   Principal Preparation Programs 128
   Soribel Genao

9 Evaluating the Different SIDES of Education Policies: A
   Practical Policy Analysis Framework for School Leaders 142
   Christopher H. Tienken

Contributor Biographies *159*
Index *162*

ACKNOWLEDGMENTS

We appreciate the invitation to produce a new edited book and work with leading policy educators of our choosing whose chapter contributions are important and informative as well as impactful.

We are grateful to Routledge/Taylor & Francis and Kappa Delta Pi (KDP) for their continued partnership in the formation and sponsorship of this book. With their mutuality and highly responsive publishing timeline, we were provided outstanding managerial assistance. With gratitude, we wish to again thank Kathie-Jo Arnoff, former Director of Publications of KDP, the International Honor Society in Education, for her outstanding work on the original version of this book and Michelle Melani, Director of Knowledge Integration for KDP, for her support and encouragement throughout the process of creating this book. We also appreciate the detailed copyediting of this book by Jane Fieldsend, a publishing professional.

Anonymous peer reviewers of this book provided encouraging comments and statements to the effect that the book remains current with more recent policy changes and discussion of the rising complexities in education. They also like that the book is both theoretical and practical, and intellectual yet accessible to its readers.

PREFACE

Risky business. To us, these two words best describe the current education policy landscape for school leaders and those aspiring to lead schools. Controversial issues—like the corporatization of education, school segregation, proliferation of charter schools, international competitiveness, and the overall degradation of democracy and democratic education—grab mainstream press headlines and attract policymakers' attention at all levels. We believe all such issues deserve the close attention of school leaders and their advocacy with respect to equitable and socially just education for underserved student populations and marginalized communities.

Our primary purpose with this coedited book, *The Risky Business of Education Policy*, is to focus commentary and analysis on some of the most pressing policy issues facing public school educators and those invested in striving for a healthy, vibrant public school system. Another purpose is to share insights and make recommendations from leading scholar-practitioners, namely from educational leadership and science education, on ways to ponder, navigate, and confront serious policy challenges.

For this volume, we assembled an accomplished group of thought-leaders to pierce the veil on some of the most provocative issues facing education policy-making today. Each of the nine chapters presents an important policy topic and critical analysis of a pertinent education reform policy issue from the authorial perspective of experienced educators leading the preparation of future school leaders and teachers.

Contributors of the fast-paced, user-friendly chapters essentially grapple with an education reform policy issue of the day, reflecting what is contentious territory while wading through it. These educational researchers also make evidence-informed practical recommendations for educators and policymakers on how to better approach the policy challenges presented so that public education can be improved for all children. Each chapter contains stimulating ideas, useful information, and practical tips for school practitioners and constituent groups more generally.

Every contributing author brings national and international education and research experience to the conversation. And they all leverage deep knowledge of the policymaking environment to drill down beneath the headlines. The contributors use their experiential lens to examine ongoing tensions between ideologically driven education reform policy and empirical research results to offer a critical review, casting a laser-like focus on current policy perils and recommendations for education policy and practice. A common goal we share is endeavoring to look more deeply and comprehensively at what dwells below the surface of education policy and the influences that impact public education.

In Chapter 1, Carol A. Mullen, Virginia Tech, USA, takes evidence-based aim at the corporatization of public education. She tackles corporate network proliferation in the public school sector and rapid erosion of capital. She contends that a major policy problem confronting professional educators in schools and universities is that public education is being abandoned as a public service in the United States. In a world where corporate network proliferation erodes the capital of these schools, the meaning of formal education becomes distorted. For-profit corporations insert/assert themselves as the caretaker of an ethos of public service for the greater good. In this critical analysis, public education and education policy are conceived of as an intricate, morphing network. The connections Mullen traces among markets reveal the neoliberal movement's takeover of public education and public resources. What unfolds is the view of a powerful, surging market wherein one curriculum is adopted. An effect is the disenfranchising of underserved groups by such forces as the momentous financial push by private enterprise into the public sector and the influence of foundations over federal policies.

In Chapter 2, Fenwick W. English, Ball State University, USA, examines major precepts of neoliberalism and managerialism in maintaining influence and continuing dominance in how schools should be led and to what ends their existence should be directed. Early proponents of neoliberalism and managerialism did not often call them by their names, instead opting to advance ideas and solutions for the educational and financial problems they were supposed to solve. English explains that although neoliberal and managerial actions were visible and debated, the beliefs they embodied were often neither disclosed nor made public. His metaphors of ventriloquist and dummy illustrate how neoliberalism and managerialism's positive sounding language mask their true identities and hide anti-democratic assumptions within ideologies that work to de-legitimate public service.

Patricia H. Hinchey, Professor Emerita, Penn State University, USA, and Pamela J. Konkol, Concordia University, USA, tackle the struggles facing educators who try to engage in comprehensive civic education in Chapter 3. For decades educators and other stakeholders have been alarmed by survey after survey indicating that many American citizens lack even rudimentary knowledge of civics and participate in few civic activities, including voting. Recently, diverse efforts to improve civic education have grown, including requiring high school students to take the U.S. citizenship exam and promoting pedagogical strategies known collectively as action civics. Success of such efforts depend on countering threats to civic education that the authors dissect.

In Chapter 4, Ryan Coughlan, Molloy College, USA, explores how policy and law have failed to advance school desegregation in the face of campaigns, some hidden, to maintain the status quo that privileges White Americans. Along with identifying the value of school integration and root causes of the United States' failure to desegregate its schools, Coughlan also calls for action to make progress on this issue. Building on the work of advocates and scholars, he underscores the reality that desegregation alone is insufficient if we hope to achieve educational justice for all students.

Julia Sass Rubin and Mark Weber, Rutgers University, USA, rebut the argument that charter schools improve public education by creating competition that encourages local public schools to up their game to retain and attract students and the funding associated with them (Chapter 5). This theory, however, is built on problematic assumptions about charter schools and the kind of competition they create; the students who attend charter and traditional public schools; and student performance and how to measure it. In this chapter, the authors also examine the validity of those assumptions, drawing on extensive research to assess the impact of charter schools on students, district public schools, and communities.

In the sixth chapter, Svein Sjøberg, University of Oslo, Norway, challenges the emergence of the global educational reform movement where the Organization of Economic Co-operation and Development (OECD), through its Programme for International Student Assessment (PISA) project, has become the key driver. Sjøberg's details of PISA extend to an appraisal from different perspectives. Most important is his critique of the political and normative nature of PISA as an instrument for standardizing and globalizing education and for treating children as human capital. As argued, many PISA results are problematic and intriguing: PISA scores are unrelated to educational resources although mainstream research across the globe suggests that resources do influence achievement, funding, class size, school leadership, and similar factors. PISA scores are also at odds with best teaching practices in the classroom, notably, active teaching methods, inquiry-based instruction, and computer technology.

Yong Zhao, University of Oregon, USA, and Jim Watterston, University of Melbourne, Australia, remind us that students are rarely considered actors in education reforms. Instead, they are typically treated as the recipients of reform efforts lacking agency. However, as they argue, students are the real owners of learning. In Chapter 7, the authors propose to treat students as such. They discuss why students should be the owners of their learning and how schools and teachers can help them develop the mindset and skills to own their learning. According to Zhao and Watterston, personalized learning is not sufficient. Education, like learning, should be personalized, and students should be shaping their learning, not having it "done" to them.

In Chapter 8, Soribel Genao, CUNY-Queens College, USA, takes up the advocacy of a more intentionally driven principal preparation of education leaders in bi/multilingual schools and communities in New York City. Under CR 154–2.3(d) (2), school districts in which the sum of each school's annual estimate of enrollment of English Language Learners (ELLs) equals 20 or more ELLs of the same grade level, all of whom have a home language other than English, shall provide enough bilingual education programs in the district the following school year. This is an important juncture whereby teachers, principals, superintendents, teacher education programs, and officials must work to make bilingual education a reality.

In the ninth and final chapter, Christopher H. Tienken, Seton Hall University, USA, proposes a policy analysis framework known as SIDES that school leaders can use to conduct an initial scan of education policies at the school level. The framework directs attention to, and focuses on, ways that education policies influence students, instruction and curriculum, democratic principles, equity, and social justice within schools. Reflective questions, provided for school leaders, enable the framework to be thoughtfully used as a practical tool. Steering away from an academic treatise on policy evaluation, Tienken offers a hands-on approach to the SIDES intended for school use.

Whether you are a policy professional, educator, researcher, or another stakeholder interested in public education such as a parent, student, or community group, the chapters in this volume offer evidence-based information and ideas for action. Without a voice, children are vulnerable, unrecognized policy actors—they do not have a presence in the halls of power, the backrooms where some education policies are made, or even, in many cases, their own classrooms and schools. So, adults have a very serious duty to advocate on behalf of policy ideas, backed by informed professional judgment and demonstrated evidence, that protect children and advance their best interests. In the final analysis, it is the responsibility of all education stakeholders to facilitate a quality public school experience for future generations. We believe this collection will help in that individual and collective effort.

Readers are encouraged to contact us with feedback on the ideas and content presented and make suggestions for a future edition on education policy.

Christopher H. Tienken and Carol A. Mullen

FOREWORD

Education Policy Reform: A Tale of Haunting

> The way of the ghost is haunting, and haunting is a very particular way of knowing what has happened or is happening. Being haunted draws us affectively … into the structure of feeling of a reality we come to experience, not as cold knowledge, but as a transformative recognition … the forces in our lives that we usually try to ignore or forget, but never totally leave us alone.
>
> (Jacobs, 2007, p. 7)

Let me begin by stating the obvious, the education policymaking that has taken place in the United States since the late 1980s has been scary. Terrifying, really—like a string of bad horror films—full of ghosts, zombies, vampires, and shapeshifters. As I write this Foreword to Tienken and Mullen's *The Risky Business of Education Policy*, we have not yet arrived at the end of the movie. I fear the neoliberal education policy "monsters" might yet continue to appear at the federal level (Giroux, 2010) and leap out to try to take down the public education system into the bowels of hell. Indeed, now more than any other moment in recent history, time feels "out of joint," as Hamlet described in Shakespeare's (n.d.) beloved ghost story *Hamlet*. With this sentiment in mind, I frame my ideas around the theme of ghosts and haunting. I concur with Haiven (2020) that capitalism, cast in this book during the neoliberal era, always requires a narrative of "revenge" by the ruling elite upon the "Other," using fabricated threats to justify the need for oppression in the name of "progress" (see Arundhati (2014) for more on this theme). It is no coincidence that most ghost and horror stories involve revenge, or an avenging of past wrongs. Therefore, Derrida's (1994) concept of "hauntology" becomes an apt metaphor for exploring the perilous landscape of revengeful neoliberal polices. Hauntology illustrates the return and persistence of beliefs and practices that "haunt" like specters for good and for ill.

Full of ghost stories and cautionary tales, *The Risky Business of Education Policy* includes visitations from those that warn with spectral clarity about how and why we must proceed with bravery and caution. It is also a book with ideas for how all of those with an interest in public education might escape from the house of horrors and defeat the monster.

The policy stories cast in the chapters are set in haunted landscapes with "restless and troubled spirits" (Hepburn, 2020, para. 4). We, as readers, make our way through an abandoned democracy of zombie political rhetoric (Giroux, 2010). I read this book as if I were reading Dicken's (1812–1870/1995) *A Christmas Carol* in that I saw ghosts of free-market policies past, present, and future. The contributing authors expertly describe how policy ghosts "wreak self-destructive vengeance on human life" (Haiven, 2020, p. 38) by commodifying and standardizing education in ever-widening international circles. Finally, the authors raise some specters that foretell of both a peril and promise of alternatives to the policy perils they detail. Chapters contain recommendations for how education leaders can become ghostbusters, if you will, and turn the tide of policy perils at school and at national levels.

However, haunting isn't always devised as a "bad" thing. It is also possible to consider that "nothing died, it just got buried" (Daspit, 1999, p. 71). The rise, and subsequent effects, of neoliberal education policies explored in these chapters indicate a message both of angst *and hope*. The authors examine what (or who) "got buried" only to rise and haunt with an avenging eye to right the wrongs of oppression, notably White supremacy. We hear the voices of students rising up, "haunting" the graveyard of dead policies and demanding change.

A common thread through each section of the book is the notion of public education itself for a common good. Oftentimes I hear the authors whispering the dreaded question, *Is public education really dead?* This question is followed by *Can we re-animate and re-create it in the likeness of equity, diversity, and justice that we imagine it can become?* In each chapter you will be visited by specters of lost futures, showing us how "(D)espite everything, that we don't have to live as we presently do" (Whyman, 2019, para 5). These apparitions foretell of a public education built not upon revenge of a dead neoliberalism, but of an "avenging imaginary" (Haiven, 2020) created by postcolonial alternatives to the horrors wrought by colonial and corporatist forms of capitalism.

Ghosts of the Past and Revenge

Just as in Shelley's *Frankenstein* (1818/1994), education policies of the 20th and 21st centuries are ghostly stories of "revenge" (Haiven, 2020) in which capitalism wreaks retribution upon marginalized bodies and lives to justify its domination. A legacy of punitive practices like zero tolerance discipline, high stakes testing, and the philosophy of eugenics all use data to terrorize students and schools. Such practices especially demonize students and communities of color where "these experiences, these *ghosts*—so often unresearched, unrecognized, unvalidated … rob a student's will to persevere and sap their very humanity and dignity" (Benson, 2019, para 3). Centuries of neoliberal education reform from dejure racial segregation to colonizing Black communities via charter schools have left us in an educational ghost town of deadening specters of student agency and engagement.

Ghosts of the Present

One way to think of current neoliberal dominance in education policies and practices is as a haunting of what is commonly referred to as "colonialism 2.0"—a globalizing entity which mobilizes free-market economic ideology and 21st-century technologies to re-colonize communities populated by people of color and disenfranchised White populations. Education in these spaces is embedded within broader concentric circles of inequality, such as the global failure to deliver humane responses to COVID-19, revealing how "the ghosts of colonialism are haunting" us still (Karan & Khan, 2020, para 1).

Mullen's (Chapter 1) exploration of the corporate connections with the Common Core reminds me of *Rolling Stone* contributor Matt Tabbi's (cited in Giroux, 2010) description of the "blood lust" of neoliberal policies (which, for the purposes of *The Risky Business of Education Policy* includes education policies) as a "great vampire squid wrapped around the face of humanity, relentlessly jamming its blood funnel into anything that smells like money" (p. 1). This is an equally fitting description for the role that the World Bank plays in global efforts as noted by English (Chapter 2). In Shelley's classical tale, Victor claims, "I succeeded in discovering the cause of generation and life … I became myself capable of bestowing animation upon lifeless matter" (p. 57). Monsters are analogous to surplus human capital, the other-than-human or sometimes post-human entities that haunt the borderland between our colonial worlds and what might be possible otherwise.

Matt Taibbi, a writer for Rolling Stone, has aptly described as "a great vampire squid wrapped around the face of humanity, relentlessly jamming its blood funnel into anything that smells like money."

Future Ghosts

"Future-haunting" describes neoliberalism's turn toward globalized surveillance via the international assessment machine (Sjøberg, Chapter 6) and corporate economic control. In this future, free market progress is no longer measured by efficiency of manual labor on the factory lines, or output of sales or production. It relies on abstract "bodies" of data for social engineering and profiteering. For example, Sjøberg illustrates how PISA data in Norway are used by the Organisation for Economic Co-operation and Development (OECD) to invest in a "future life" (p. 95) aimed at benefiting global corporations by justifying reduced investments in public services and "ignoring the national priorities set for our school system" (p. 92), and reinvent policies designed for "future economic conpetitiveness" (p. 89). Bodies of students—valued as commodities for their data production—are harnessed by the Programme for International Student Assessment ("PISA") creators who are "blatantly claiming that they have identified the critical skills necessary for future life, for all humans on the planet" (p. 91).

Such policies reveal the chasm between those with access and privilege within the global testing paradigm, and those without—colonized and disenfranchised (surplus) persons. Also revealed is how students and teachers (like the monster in *Frankenstein*) are all little more than body parts harvested for re-assemblage. As such, "[they] will eventually emerge like a ghost from its machine—to destroy its makers and the whole of humanity" (Haselby, 2017, para 2). In the impending epoch of the Global Education Reform Movement, one could become a social "ghost" so to speak. The validation of one's existence could disappear in the flick of a keystroke.

A Cautionary Tale of Absence and Possibility

I worry that society is ringing the death-knell for public education. We might justifiably concur in a society where "a third of Americans can name all three branches of government, a quarter can name one, and a fifth of the population cannot name any" (Hinchey & Konkol, Chapter 3, p. 41) that we are surrounded by zombies, created by the hollowing out of public education with almost a half century of neoliberal education policy. The absence of widespread civic knowledge is matched by the absence of critical engagement with decolonial histories, which have been "buried," but hopefully are not dead. We are haunted by the continued absence of scholars and students of color in schools and universities. Future ghosts remind us that we also remain haunted by a resurgence of globalized colonial politics, a return to racist divisions, and near-exclusions of decolonial voices in scholarship and policies.

But, as I noted in the beginning, "Nothing died, it just got buried" (Daspit, 1999, p. 71). Not all ghosts should be exorcised—some hauntings are necessary. In *The Risky Business of Education Policy*, it could be said that the authors call for a policy séance, invoking what Saleh-Hanna (2015) describes as the "ghosts through whom we can locate the abusive and morally bankrupt nature of structural race relations as they manifest through the violent race-making and land-grabbing conquests of colonialism" (p. 1). So, while haunting reminds us of what may have been lost or deadened, it also speaks to a resurgence of possibility through "sustained collective action" (Haiven, 2020, p. 192). Ultimately, hauntology is "founded on our ability to imagine a world better than the one we presently have"; it follows that, "if capitalist realism represents the attempt to take our political imagination away from us, then hauntology can do the work to get it back" (Whyman, 2019, para. 5).

Viewing this book as a cautionary tale with less fear and with more hope, the authors argue for transformative solutions by which we may avert a dying future. Instead, as Giroux (2010) argues, we can fight *and win* "against an apocalyptic zombie politics and its accompanying culture of fear, its endless spectacles of violence that promote airtight forms of domination" (p. 5). Here we are in a pandemic world confronting life and death, and a liminal reality between neoliberalism and postcolonialism. In these moments—where past and future collide—cracks and fissures create spaces for horror *and* promise. We can, as Jacobs (2007) suggests, "deliberately investigate these ghosts … learn to take control over troubling memories" and perhaps "turn destructive haunting into something more enabling" (p. 7).

Specters always appear delivering a message. The question is, do we *see* them? And, *are we listening*?

Morna McDermott McNulty, PhD
Professor
Towson University
College of Education, Department of Elementary Education

References

Arundhati, R. (2014). *Capitalism: A ghost story*. Haymarket Books.
Benson, T. (2019). Chasing ghosts: Racism and U.S. education. *The Blog of Harvard Education Publishing*. www.hepg.org/blog/chasing-ghosts-racism-and-us-education.
Daspit, T. (1999). "Nothing's died; it just got buried": Theory as exhumation, as duty dance (for Thomas Wayne Daspit and Mandy Jo Delcambre). *Counterpoints*, 90, 71–78.
Derrida J. (1994). *Specters of Marx*. Routledge.
Dickens, C. (1812–1870/1995). *A Christmas carol and other stories*. Modern Library.
Giroux, H. (2010). Zombie politics and other late modern monstrosities in the age of disposability. *Policy Futures in Education*, 8. doi:10.2304/pfie.2010.8.1.1.
Haiven, M. (2020). *Revenge capitalism: The ghosts of empire, the demons of capital, and the settling of unpayable debts*. Pluto Press.
Haselby, S. (2017). Godmother of intelligences. *Aeon*. https://aeon.co/essays/what-frankensteins-creature-can-really-tell-us-about-ai.
Hepburn, C. (2020). *Ghosts in a time of Covid-19*. Edinburgh University Press: Blog. https://euppublishingblog.com/2020/05/01/ghosts-in-a-time-of-covid-19/.
Jacobs W. R. (2007). *Ghostbox: A memoir*. iUniverse, Inc Press.
Karan, A., & Kahn, M. (2020, May 29). Opinion: *The ghosts of colonialism are haunting the worlds responses to the pandemic*. [Blog]. Ghosts and Soda: Stories of Life in a Changing World. National Public Radio. www.npr.org/sections/goatsandsoda/2020/05/29/862602058/opinion-the-ghosts-of-colonialism-are-haunting-the-worlds-response-to-the-pandem.
Saleh-Hanna, V. (2015). Black feminist hauntology: Re-memory the ghosts of abolition? *Champ Penal*, 12. https://journals.openedition.org/champpenal/9168?lang=en.
Shelley, M. (1818/1994). *Frankenstein* (3rd ed.). Dover.

Shakespeare, W. (n.d.). *Hamlet, prince of Denmark.* (B. Mowat & P. W. Werstine, Eds.). The Folger Shakespeare. https://shakespeare.folger.edu/shakespeares-works/hamlet#line-1.3.0.

Whyman, T. (2019). The ghosts of our lives. *New Statesman.* www.newstatesman.com/politics/uk/2019/07/ghosts-our-lives.

1
CORPORATE NETWORKS' GRIP ON THE PUBLIC SCHOOL SECTOR AND EDUCATION POLICY

Carol A. Mullen

In this chapter, I address corporate networks' grip on the public school sector and education policy. Corporations have a pervasive, often hidden, influence in education policy, and practice (Moeller, 2020; Mullen, 2017; Tienken, 2020). In actuality, "American corporate leadership is an extraordinary, well-financed, determined group of corporate millionaires and billionaires that are financing a self-serving, destructive doctrine on school leaders and public education in America" (English, 2014, p. 51). Public education in the United States and around the world needs to be defended against neoliberal policy making, as does our right as taxpaying citizens to keep public schools public. Well-intentioned people are trying to improve public schools in the education policy environment. But they are hampered without support from activists and policy actors. Committed educators and stakeholders are hitting a wall, so to speak: "The only pathways they can see are too often ones prescribed and scripted by others," meaning that they lack the freedom to use their expertise and capacities to develop learner-centered programs (Bogotch & Shields, 2014, p. 2).

By *neoliberalism*, I am referring in this chapter to the political forces that control our lives, including in the educational sphere. These forces encompass "global capitalism, the economic ideological stances of free-market competition, and the privatization of state social services" in the context of "the rise … of neoliberal foundations and think tanks that privatize and commodify public spaces" (Mullen et al., 2013, p. 182; also, Ball, 2012).

Purpose

Here I grapple with complexities and nuances involved in the marketization or commodification, also known as the market takeover, of the public education

DOI: 10.4324/9781003108511-1

sector in the United States. Three questions stem from my purposes to reveal dynamics of special interest groups and their influence on public schools and education policy:

1. What networks and entities are driving current school reform in the United States, and how are they functioning within, and affecting, the public education enterprise?
2. Whose interests are served by extracting revenues, labor pools, and services from the nation's public school system?
3. What are the implications of the Common Core State Standards (CCSS); National Governors Association Center for Best Practices & Council of Chief State School Officers (NGA & CCSSO, 2010) for social democracy and social justice in education?

I use the original concept "Public Education, Inc." to frame the neoliberal takeover of public education and marketing of schooling as a commodity from which profiteers and some entrepreneurs benefit economically and politically. I connect various markets to evoke a picture of these dynamics. Because the markets and their influence are largely invisible, linking for-profit corporations and their supporting cast is a complicated task. A proliferating number of neoliberal corporations, councils, think tanks, and sponsors that favor free-market education reforms co-opt public school rhetoric, control curriculum, and pocket profits.

Feigning a concerned stake in public education and democracy, these entities, including for-profit lobbyists, in some cases directly influence or make education policy and curriculum, disguising their true intentions. According to Berliner and Glass (2014), the American Legislative Exchange Council (ALEC) is in the business of treating public education as a business by influencing education policy reforms that give parents choice; by proposing schemes that claim to make schools more accountable, transparent, and efficient; and by paving the way for public funds to be redirected to private or semi-private education options. ALEC favors charter schools that make money for private management firms, not public schools that spend public money on public services (Ravitch, 2013). Prisons and tobacco are examples of other business priorities that overshadow ALEC's interest in education. By lobbying "politicians to attach free-market reforms to state education laws" (p. 8), ALEC ventures to turn private prisons into big business by landing severer punishments for criminals. In the same way, they have turned schools into a marketplace.

Identifying the existence of Public Education, Inc. serves as a mechanism for forcing uncomfortable truths into the open about the influence of corporate agendas on public education policy. This provocative conception of public education as a tool to generate profits for the private sector provides a medium for equipping educators with ideologies and evidence needed to claim a greater stake in the public school sector and exert greater influence on policy making.

Moreover, Public Education, Inc. should elicit a collective moral outcry against the destruction of public education.

I have organized this chapter by (a) introducing my concept of Public Education, Inc. as a jolt for anyone who wants public schools to thrive; (b) describing markets' commodification of public schools; (c) summarizing CCSS as a policy issue of high relevance; (d) identifying this policy issue in broad terms, drawing on select literature in curriculum studies, educational leadership, and sociology; (e) addressing why key stakeholders should care about the issue; and (f) ending with a call to action.

Public Education, Inc. Concept

Public Education, Inc. allows me to critically speak to the dire situation of U.S. public schools. I do not see all corporations as automatically bad or somehow conspiring against public education. And I do not see entrepreneurial leadership as inherently wrong-headed or aimed at undermining public schooling or higher education. Those who authentically work to achieve social benefits as social entrepreneurs may be contributing positively to public education, but this is not my topic. Many educators use the services of corporations and have codependent relationships with them in roles as customers and investors.

Military–Industrial Complex

The military–industrialization of 21st-century American society provided a playbook for Public Education, Inc. by laying the groundwork for public schools to be sold to the highest bidder. The U.S. Department of Defense Education Activity (DoDEA, 2012), under the Office of the Secretary of Defense, adopted the CCSS as did 43 states and the District of Columbia. The DoDEA, a federally operated school system, prepares children of military families for education in America, Europe, and the Pacific by operating many schools in 11 foreign countries. Attention is on a prescription for science in addition to language arts and math.

Government agencies like the DoDEA are supported with taxpayers' dollars, yet their neoliberal ideologies and marketing tactics favor the private sector over public service. Taxpaying citizens, concerned about the health of public education, should want to know and do more to protect the legacy and future of public education: "The transfer of public funds to private management and the creation of thousands of deregulated, unsupervised, and unaccountable schools have opened the public coffers to exploitation by large and small entrepreneurs" (Ravitch, 2013, p. 4). Abuses of power in the misuse of the public school sector is a common refrain in the education policy domain.

Public Education, Inc. is a by-product of the "military–industrial complex" President Eisenhower (1961) coined in his farewell speech. He alluded to a "compelling" military–industrial need for the nation to "create a permanent armaments industry of vast proportions," arguing against the risks involved in "emergency improvisation of national defense." Yet Eisenhower admitted that military spending was out of line compared to other priorities: "We annually spend on military security more than the net income of all United States' corporations." This admission made a domain comparison between the military world and the corporate world, in effect establishing an alliance. Additionally, he disclosed the high-priority investment of the government in the military and impact of that investment on increasing the wealth of U.S. corporations.

Eisenhower (1961) also alluded to "misplaced power" and its "total influence" on all sectors of society. Although he did not specify public education or repercussions for schools (or university-based teacher and leader preparatory programs), it seemed presaged. Today's reigning megacorporations, Pearson Education, Google, and Microsoft among them, have invaded public school systems like a military campaign. They overpower the agency of schools to serve constituents and communities, and remold them to the self-serving, profiteering interests of the market economy. Arguably, Eisenhower's speech revealed a neoliberal thrust. Profiting in the corporate structure by developing unneeded arms and ammunition has grave consequences for public education and its sustainability around democratic values and the common good.

Not all readers may be aware of the extent to which the corporate takeover of public schools has been occurring or its historic context, fueling my decision to tackle this topic. Readers may wonder what the moving pieces are, how they fit together, and what the possibilities are for new leadership in the roles of policy actor and advocate. To this end, Bogotch and Shields (2014) discussed the blindsiding of educators and education leaders who are "often swallowed up by dominant business and governmental interests which today often represent global, corporate, and capitalistic ... interests gone awry" (p. 2).

As public school activists believe, corporations invade schools and destroy their integrity and the capacity of school people to do their jobs. The military take on this equation is very real, although from another perspective. James Heintz (2011) of the Political Economy Research Institute explained that heavy investment from the federal government in the military deprived the nation's schools of financial support, robbing them of much-needed improvements in poor infrastructure. Michigan schools' horrendous sanitary problems are among the countless examples.

Referencing governmental military investments and real costs to public schools, Heintz's (2011) analysis is directed at the financial investment in the military since the 9/11 terrorist attack and the U.S. wars in Afghanistan and Iraq. Total military assets rose significantly starting in that time to "$1,245 billion ($1.2 trillion) by the end of 2009—an increase of $341 billion" (p. 4). Importantly, Heintz concluded that "these capital investments [could have been] made in U.S. education infrastructure" (p. 4). Without the investment of public assets in makeshift schools, the costs of the wars show up as dilapidated facilities in high-poverty areas, compounding the health and safety of poor children.

Outside-In Rewiring

In the modern-day military–industrial complex, public education leadership and policy are being rewired from the outside-in by external interest groups. Consider the Broad Foundation, Uncommon Schools, Success Academy, Teach For America—all corporately organized controlling giants. Just as we are being changed from the outside, we, the taxpaying citizens, are being altered from the inside by colleagues, supervisors, entrepreneurial leaders, and a new crop of neoliberal leaders trained by the corporate giants they quickly come to represent.

Critical awareness among educators, leaders, and professors means understanding such prevailing educational dynamics and doing something about them. People we know at work moonlight with marketeers (who sell goods and services in public schools and advocate for public schools to be made into a marketplace, e.g., Gates, 2009) and benefit financially while, importantly, fundamentally changing education's value system. Yet it is those working in public schools whose jobs are on the line and whose schools are in jeopardy—they are the ones being pressured by accountability policies and measures of student performance, and they are the ones being penalized when expectations set by policies fall short (English, 2014; Ravitch, 2013).

It should not escape our notice that we, the taxpaying public, are being conditioned to humanize corporations and see them as valuable education leaders and stakeholders, in effect giving them greater latitude to colonize schools. By not protesting, we fall prey to the subliminal rewiring of citizens by our highest federal court: "The U.S. Supreme Court has decreed [that] corporations are people too. And as a person, a corporation has plenty of self-interest in the forms of revenues and stock prices" (Berliner & Glass, 2014, p. 6).

Anthropomorphizing corporations by making them out to be benevolent friends and even saviors—in keeping with Gates's (2009) accusatory rhetoric of school failure and messianic messages of corporate intervention—disrupts our ability to spot the bullying tactics that propel market invasions of schools. The hostage-taking of the public education sector should motivate wanting to know how public schools are being exploited for their revenues, services, and labor.

Zapping School Agency

As social services become increasingly privatized, schools lose their power and agency for protecting the common good: "The school system is an agency that should exist to support and protect the local service" (Westbury, 2008, p. 3). Westbury's concern was that schools can lose sight of this reality. Cheating on standardized tests is a phenomenon reflecting the shortsightedness of school leaders who fear the negative repercussions of failing to meet the narrowly prescribed expectations of student achievement and school success (English, 2014).

Many leading education specialists argue a two-pronged perspective: (a) There exists a critical mass of influential decision makers and entities in American society; and (b) there is "misplaced power" (ironically, Eisenhower's own words in 1961) in the erosion of the core mission, common good, local control, and democratic goals of the public education system. Some entrepreneurs—among them the very powerful corporatist Bill Gates (2009)—claim that these are the same ideals that engineer their vision. Supporters of Gates would say that his interventions improve public schools, whereas critics adamantly disagree; social justice proponents have reached a boiling point (English, 2014).

The right-wing, wealthy elite—corporations and individuals alike—and legislators have bought into the myth that America's public schools are hopeless, dismal failures. Berliner and Glass (2014) drove home this point: "Organized private interests" spread "modern myths about schools," such as public education is inferior to private education, and "stand to gain from widespread belief in the myths" (p. 7).

Power in the industrial, capitalist market economy of the day is associated with free unregulated markets, competition, and property holdings, not membership in society or good intentions (Bogotch & Shields, 2014). Greed is the golden pretense of improving schools, but in reality money and power are at stake: "The lure of making money is a powerful motivator for these agencies to promote standardization and to take steps to remain in power"—"public school defenders are fighting back" (English, 2010, p. xii).

Being Whipped into Shape

Gates (2009), a celebrated hero in this campaign to infiltrate public schools, has insisted that public schools be subjected to the curricular control of outsiders like policymakers, corporations, and agencies. Accordingly, public schools have been bought and sold (English, 2014), and turned into profitable warehouses selling goods and services. With momentum, entrepreneurs rationalize the failure of public schools, paving the way for intervention from outside "experts" and their unchecked conversions. Gates brokered the control of the public school sector by "promot[ing] unproven school reforms" like the CCSS, intent on "boost[ing] international test scores to reclaim the United States' rightful place at the top … —a position we never held" (Berliner & Glass, 2014, p. 17).

Falling prey, high-poverty schools lack the power to take a stand in their own best interests (English, 2014). Many times, these schools have come under mayoral control or the authority of mayor-appointed school boards. Justice-oriented values of public education, such as the democratization of education and self-governance without interference from external entities, have eroded: "Business values are not appropriate to drive American education," advocates of social justice protest, even though citizens would support "the most efficient use of the taxpayer dollar in the public schools. But that is not an educational core value … . Democracy is not efficient" (Tienken, 2021, p. 68).

Educating poor and disenfranchised children so they can succeed as contributing members of society is a hallmark of democracy. Markets are ostensibly efficient, making them seductive to stakeholders but perilous to those like students with special needs requiring non-standardized services. School leaders and parents are being misled by Gates's claim that K–12 public schools are simply too expensive to operate, having lost sight of the fact that in a democratic society we do not institutionalize children with disabilities—instead, we support them and fund special education (Berliner & Glass, 2014).

"Modern corporations," argued Berliner and Glass (2014), "are beginning to view the public schools as ripe for picking big profits" (p. 6). A functional/instrumental role, not educative role, of service provider feeds marketing companies' appetite for operationalizing schools as targets of economic gain (English, 2010, 2014; Ravitch, 2013). Conservative pundit William J. Bennett who was U.S. secretary of education (during the Reagan administration) received millions from the U.S. Department of Education (USDOE) under the name K12, Inc., a private company he cofounded (English, 2010). The illusion of being a sponsor of K–12 public education and imitating this system using a company name, but in reality debasing its cherished ideals, serves only to compound the moral bankruptcy Heintz (2011) described.

Megacorporations like Pearson Education are powerhouses, accessing and controlling delivery and evaluation services to the public education sector; their exploitation of the country's public schools is unprecedented. It's challenging to identify all of the influential policy pundits and marketeers, as well as to unearth their connections to one another. In fact, it has proven exhausting to try and unravel how these networked players manage to mimic the rhetoric of education reform for their own ends. Moreover, it is labor intensive to assemble the many puzzle pieces only to realize that the power grid is made of quicksand. We are stuck. A nimble machine, it extends beyond the federal government to a shadow government operating right under our feet.

Policy Issue: A Single Market for the CCSS

The CCSS initiative and the accompanying technology-based products to implement it or its second generation of revised state standards, and its related testing products, are driven by Public Education, Inc. Entrepreneurs wielding political power require the use of imported tests, services, and products that, at least hypothetically, align with the standards (Brass, 2014; Ravitch, 2013). In a single market, "the adoption of only one form of curriculum is an example of symbolic power" that disempowers some groups; "It is a myth that any new set of standards that imposes only one type of curriculum will reduce the achievement gap when the gap is built into the system itself" (Papa et al., 2012, pp. 45–46).

Wielding "symbolic power," the CCSS initiative is heavily funded, reflecting the private sector's momentous financial push for implementation in the public sector. As Wexler (2014) described, an elite network of megacorporations supports the CCSS, which itself "is funded by the richest private foundations in the country," primarily the Gates Foundation and the Broad Foundation (p. 52). Wexler, like other researchers, draws attention to how these foundations exercised influence over the policies of the past Obama presidential administration.

Federal Backing Gives Weight

The CCSS was state adopted, but it is misleading to stop there. The federal weight and nationwide networking were rife during its development. Consider the widespread influence of the Council on Foreign Relations (CFR) Task Force, which reworked its stated mission of national security to send the urgent message that education in America is not only a dismal failure, but also a national security issue. The Task Force formed a partnership with the federal government and private industry to expand the CCSS's influence (Blumenfeld, 2012) and spread the military–industrialization of the United States. Aligned with the CFR, the U.S. Department of Defense, through its DoDEA field activity branch, colonizes the children of military families on a grand global scale with its strong endorsement and use of the CCSS.

Yet Jones and King (2012) insisted that the CCSS was not a "national curriculum" violating state and local control of education or placing constitutional limits on the federal government's influence over curriculum and pedagogy. Their logic was misleading and dangerous, and so was the demarcation. Those who make the argument invoking constitutional limitations obscure how the CCSS works to discipline classroom practice and, moreover, force radical shifts in the governance of public education in the United States (English, 2014).

Hence the CCSS did not pop up out of nowhere as a heavily financed policy initiative. The underlying ideologies and practices of corporate accountability and standardization have been inextricably meshed with federal legislation in education that has existed for more than 20 years (Bracken, 2013). As Wexler (2014) explained, policy reform has led to the involvement of the Gates and Broad Foundations, which set in motion the corporate reforms of the CCSS, and their second generation spawn under the auspices of revised state curriculum content standards, standardized testing, and CCSS predecessors (e.g., No Child Left Behind Act of 2001 [NCLB] and adequate yearly progress).

Ravitch (2013) unpacked how "national standards and national assessments created a national marketplace for products" (p. 181). "Equity investors" acted on ideas to make money after Race to the Top was launched. Businesses began developing "technological resources, hardware, and online curricula for the new national standards [CCSS]. National standards and national assessments created a national marketplace for products" (p. 181). According to Ravitch (2013), a consultant predicted that public school officials would be put in the position of wanting to receive assistance from businesses, worrying that if the CCSS tests turned out to be as rigorous as promoted, students and schools would look bad.

Neoliberal Public Enemies

English (2010) "outed" neoliberal public enemies, ranking Eli Broad America's number 1 enemy of public education, with his multimillion dollar funding and "top-down corporate takeover of urban school systems" (p. 67). Broad has not promoted credible academic educators. Lacking knowledge of the education field, the leaders (noneducators) "are beholden to efficiency management tactics and simplistic economic models," and they "discourage innovation and privatize formerly non-commodified public spheres while failing to bring about the dramatic improvements they advertise" (p. 67). Also, the Broad approach does not offer anything new, and its curriculum and purported experts are kept hidden.

Public enemy number 2 in English's (2010) lexicon is Arne Duncan, former U.S. Secretary of Education, whose ideology and practice were driven by the neoliberal agenda that directs the Democratic and Republican parties, with presidential administrations endorsing it just as much as any Republican and right-wing think tank. Additional enemies like former U.S. Assistant Secretary of Education Chester E. Finn Jr. and former U.S. Secretary of Education William Bennett, have ties to the neoliberal agenda that commodifies public schools through the CCSS. Bennett channeled millions from the USDOE through K12, Inc., his private online education company (English, 2010). The irony of the entrepreneurial coopting of "K12" does not go unnoticed.

Further elucidating the marketeers' policy grip in the United States, the most influential agencies in education—the National Governors Association (NGA), Achieve, and CCSSO—are all backers of the CCSS (Bracken, 2013; English, 2014), in addition to the USDOE (Wexler, 2014). Networked powerhouses such as "Achieve, Inc., the Business Roundtable, the U.S. Chamber of Commerce, the Gates Foundation, and a host of other business-oriented organizations supported the CCSS" (Tienken, 2021, p. 115). One outcome of the CCSS was a prescription for the curriculum and assessment of the language arts and math as subjects, with science (and who knows what else) to follow, and for which public education's resources are being expended.

Here is some background on the three agencies that back the CCSS—"Common Core":

1. NGA is a trade association that has nothing to do with governors (Bracken, 2013).
2. Achieve, also Achieve, Inc., is "a private contractor" that was created by NGA and quickly completed the "NGA/CCSSO standards-development process" (Tienken & Orlich, 2013, p. 107). Achieve (2008) presents itself as a cutting-edge, empirically grounded think tank. This is another example of how marketeers cleverly disguise themselves as legitimate researchers.
3. CCSSO is among the forces behind the CCSS standards aimed at "form[ing] the core curriculum of every public school program, driv[ing] another stronger wave of high-stakes testing, and thus becom[ing] student selection criteria for K–12 programs" (Title I services, etc.) (Tienken & Orlich, 2013, p. 107).

Neoliberal Business Networks

Neoliberalism relies heavily on networks as a conduit for penetration of the public school sector. Ball (2012) encouraged researchers to do a "more careful tracing of policy networks that underpin the global expansion of neoliberal ideas" and "descriptions of circulatory systems that connect policy regimes" (pp. 2–3). A deep understanding of the connections among corporate networks and their dynamics will guide educators to empower themselves to act.

Educators documented the Common Core's networks in relation to connections and impact: Moore (as cited in Downey, 2013) concluded, "It is a private club [in which] these people all know each other." McDermott-McNulty's (2013) depiction of the network, on which Figure 1.1 is based, is thought-provoking.

This visual illustration identifies some key players and their connections in today's education policy environment, specifically regarding the overflow of networks supporting the CCSS movement. In my opinion, it is an intriguing instructional exhibition. The reigning neoliberal worldview is operationalized as a power grid of brokers dealing not with human beings, their lives and teaching–learning complexities, but with decontextualized services and products declared necessary for improving public education.

CCSS Ploys and Bedfellows

Not surprisingly, the states were financially pressured to comply with the CCSS. Wexler (2014) argued that they were indeed "coerced into adopting the standards through federal grants and … [NCLB] waivers" (p. 52). From this angle, Jones and King's (2012) viewpoint seems simplistic, not sufficiently attuned to the federal government's politics and role as a colossal market cooperative.

An NGA brief suggested that the political workings and intentions of governmental marketeers are not even all that covert anymore (Nielson, 2014). Consider that the NGA announced that it will use "the bully pulpit" to make states comply with the CCSS-aligned tests (p. 2). Nielson rationalized that this action would ensure rigor in the Washington-based bullying tactics that permeate the attitude and actions of powerhouse networks—oddly enough, revealing NGA's machinations while concealing them.

So, who partnered with whom to benefit financially from the CCSS and associated education products? Wayne Washington (as cited in Downey, 2013) responded by "outing," among others, a conglomerate network with key players—Achieve, Inc.—as "a Washington, D.C.-based nonprofit group" funded by "corporate titans" like "Microsoft" to write the standards. He disclosed the networked connections to administrations and partnerships, as well as Achieve, Inc.'s executives' average salary in 2011 of $198,916 and $263,800 as "the company's president, former Clinton administration official Michael Cohen"; further, "the Partnership for Assessment of

Corporate Networks' Grip 11

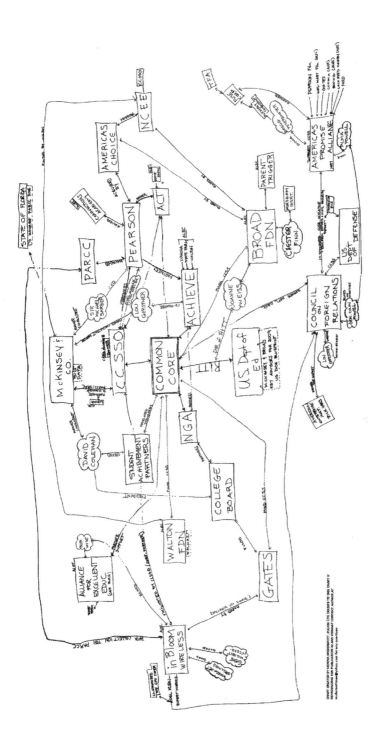

FIGURE 1.1 Who Created Common Core? A Working Flow Chart
McDermott-McNulty (2013) created this illustration to educate her college students about real ways neoliberalism takes over public education. She credits Karen Bracken as the image's originator. Used with permission.

Readiness for College and Careers [PARCC] and Smarter Balanced [received] $346 million in federal education grants to create ... standardized tests tied to Common Core" (as cited in Downey, 2013). The rich get richer and their shadow governments help them campaign on their own behalf.

Lacking Empirical Evidence

Proliferating changes in the policy reform landscape have come about without proper vetting and testing by school leaders, teachers, and parents (Zhao, 2014). The CCSS was implemented in most states in 2014–2015, with one justification being that it is a "godsend" to academically struggling K–12 schools (Wexler, 2014). Tienken (2012) added the crucial perspective that "large social programs" like the CCSS "should have research to support them prior to being released large-scale on the public. That research should be independent .... Neither of those things happened in this case" (p. 154).

Basic expectations for rigor in curricular programming have long been established by education researchers. Certainly, many educators would disagree with this analysis, given the assumptions of rigor in the development of standards for math and the English language arts (see Darling-Hammond et al., 2014; Jones & King, 2012). However, like Brass (2014) whose criticism of the CCSS targets curricular and diversity issues pertaining to the reading standards, Tienken (2012), among other critics, contended that curricular uniformity does not prepare children well; in actuality, reliance on "one set of standards" is "dangerously naïve and professionally irresponsible" (p. 154).

Money-Making Markets

Education markets make money hand over fist. Achieve's executives' incomes are but one toxin in this polluted sea. The resulting education crisis has enabled "state-led" intervention through "the provision of CCSS-based tests (PARCC and Smarter Balanced), prepackaged materials developed by educational publishers" (Brass, 2014, p. 24). About the politics driving education policy and testing, educators have protested that "There is a huge economic interest in the [CCSS] as ... companies stand to gain with a host of prepackaged products ready to sell for the new market created by the new curriculum" (Papa et al., 2012, pp. 45–46). After buying McGraw-Hill and other publishers, Pearson Education had them retain their names; in a shadow government, one motive is to conceal one's monopoly (Bracken, 2013).

In the current education policy environment dominated by product-packaged solutions, the teacher is a consumer of new technologies who has been rewired to use the tests and services. Market domination cheats teachers of their curricular autonomy and expertise, and their independent thinking and professionalism.

Private Sector Profits

Networked powerhouse connections across America suggest that conservative and progressive forces alike forged partnerships in creating the standards and publicizing them (Ball, 2012; Bracken, 2013). Thus, CCSS is *not* a philanthropic endeavor, despite declarations to that effect. It's disconcerting that "the private sector has developed and established the CCSS with considerable federal support" (Brass, 2014, p. 24), which is a refrain in the literature. Brass's fiscal breakdown of private sector profits animates an undeniable picture of greed: "The $350 million of federal funding for CCSS-aligned tests represent a small portion of the $4.35 billion in economic stimulus money ... distributed ... to develop and promote the standards" (p. 24).

Just think about how the federal dollars have been used. Most of it, Brass (2014) explained, has gone "to subsidize entrepreneurs, testing companies, and the educational technology sector to displace the curricular and pedagogical leadership of elected public representatives ... at the public's expense" (p. 24).

Even while such corporate identifications can be made and interconnections traced, the market conversion of education is neither a linear narrative nor a transparent operation. Rather, as I have metaphorized (Mullen, 2017), this mechanistic force consists of many moving parts across corporate structures and within educational systems; it works in and against schools and citizens.

A single market that is actually a reform movement of cataclysmic proportions, the CCSS initiative, with all of its neoliberal trappings, made it possible for contractors, for-profit and not-for-profit alike, to make more money doing business with public schools; contractors also benefit from related political opportunities (Brass, 2014). Savage et al. (2014) opined that the CCSS movement raises questions about the extent to which today's reforms can be considered public or democratic. The binary between Democratic and Republican ideologies disappears in the neoliberal thirst for money and power.

Corporate titan CORE has wielded its financially draining demands upon schools. The CCSS is big business: Just scrutinize the CORE (2013) web pages. Add up the costs from its suite of implementation tools (curriculum analysis templates, lesson planning/design templates, and observation rubrics). "CORE" has been described by educator McDermott-McNulty as "a profit-driven vehicle that collects ... funding to deliver goods and services they advertise as 'necessary' to implement education policies (like CCSS) that their [partners] lobbied to create in the first place." And she added that "corporate hijacking of public education at its worst" is entangled in CORE (personal communication, September 28, 2014).

Neoliberalism and Marketization

To Ball (2012), neoliberalism values money, power, and markets, and neoliberalist actions subject the state to markets and advance "self-interest" over the common good and "well-being." Regarding the "common good and social protection," these "concerns have been given less focus and the market [is being] valued over the state" (B. Lingard, 2009, p. 18; cited in Ball, 2012, p. 2). Curricular and other school practices are reorganized around a romantic image of free enterprise where the playing field is about accumulating capital and making profits (English, 2014).

Another take on neoliberalism is Wexler's (2014) concern that the reform business enterprise as a collective undermines struggling children and youth, higher education, and the arts. Apple (2014) asserted that market-based policy reforms are part of the neoliberal agenda that presents schools as broken and needing outside intervention. Berliner and Glass (2014) and Ravitch (2013) argued that marketeers and policy reformers try to manipulate the public and government into trusting this worldview. Persistent rhetoric around failing schools has turned public perception sour. Without independent, critical agency, reformers have converted public schools into markets that are supposedly in the business of repairing and renewing curriculum.

Although I am presenting public education as invaded, public schools have not literally been "incorporated" like a company. The idea behind my pushback is that schools are being consumed and converted at a rapid rate by free-market influenced ideas, fed by the sway of neoliberal ideology. Children's lives, teachers' work, and leaders' responsibilities reflect investment opportunities for marketeers and consultants, not only inside the burgeoning education industry, but also within sites of learning. Schools are looking like the markets controlling them these days, and entrepreneurs disguised as educators promote creeds favoring the greater good while funneling the riches their way.

Corporate Thinning of Democracy

A growing body of literature in education critiques neoliberal education reform motivated by turning public education into a marketplace steeped in the market logic of competition (e.g., Apple, 2011; Ball, 2012; Mullen et al., 2013; Mullen, 2017; Tienken, 2021). Describing democracies as "thick" or "thin" is social justice language taken from Ball (2012) and Apple (2014) in their analyses of the effect of markets on schools and education policy. Representing only a "thin" segment of public interests, dominant groups are powerful, complex, and invisible in their work, sponsoring "a network of foundations, think tanks, consultants, entrepreneurs, and corporations" (Ball, 2012, p. xxii).

The success of "these networks" goes beyond "their connections, money, and ideological sophistication," Ball (2012) expounded, "because in many instances state-centric policies are *not* successful or have left a vacuum because of their absence" (p. xxii). An example Ball gave of this networked marketing reality is the overtaking of under-resourced state schools and overly bureaucratized ones by India's chains of private schools; a "thickly democratic public sphere" needs to be defended, he reasoned, paving the way for "a radical egalitarian politics of redistribution, recognition, and representation" (p. xxii).

Also convinced that we are witnessing powerful neoliberal networks in the corruption of public education, Apple (2014) argued that markets' "'thin' forms of democracy" (p. xx) and consumption practices are outstripping the "thick democracy" (p. 193) evidenced by citizen participation in promoting democratic schooling. Grounded in his communications with parties in different countries, Apple sent the "SOS" that perceptions of public education are being distorted and rationalized as wholly and uniformly inadequate to the point of needing private sector intervention.

Neoliberal networks' cooperative bedfellows have been found in schools, districts, colleges, universities, states, and elsewhere. This helps explain why the corporatization and marketization of public schools is the new normal. One serious effect is "bankrupting" democracy and its values for advancing the common good (Apple, 2011). Because profits are of paramount importance and people enable the education marketplace to thrive, public schools are constantly being exploited with resources. Just think about how "robotic" curricular circuitry can be seen all around the country with people serving as test givers, test takers, consumers, product implementers, service providers, and cooperative agents.

To elucidate, the problem is not "contracting or outsourcing to private groups by public schools [as this] has always been commonplace" (Miron, 2008, p. 340). Schools have commonly purchased food from providers, leased buses, and so forth. For many years, though, as Miron explained, "A new form of contracting has occurred, one that involves contracting out the complete operation of public schools to private operators" (p. 340), including student recruitment—a practice, Miron considered "controversial." Companies, exempt from legal responsibility, can operate without being (fully) seen. Miron's (2008) justifications indicate that for-profit marketeers are not required to adhere to "public laws on transparency [as these] do not cover private companies"; also, school and public officials have become increasingly dependent on private contractors' services. Additionally, evidence is weak for arguing that private companies are more efficient than public schools and have better outcomes: "The only studies that suggest positive performance levels by private contractors are conducted by or commissioned by the private companies themselves" (Miron, 2008, p. 340; e.g., Achieve [a private contractor], 2008).

Giroux's (2014) analysis targets U.S. lobbyists' control of elected representatives and promotion of interests from megacorporations and the financial sector. The "superrich" buy the policies and laws they need to regulate the economy. They introduce vast inequality by "leveraging full use of Americans' wealth and resources—there is more at stake here than legalized corruption, there is the arrogant dismantling of democracy and the production of policies that extend ... suffering [and hardship]" (p. 7). The market's "sovereignty" over "democratic governance" (p. 8) means that public schools' agency (and legacy) is to play second fiddle.

Linguistic Gaming Ploys

A new age of colonization seems evident—every which way we turn, neoliberal markets have colonized public school sectors. Democracy gets drained. Habermas's (1985) view of influential groups is that they control "interactions" and behaviors, including speech, which leverages influence over attitudes and actions. Familiar terms like *democracy, equality, freedom, justice,* and *rigor* are an entrepreneurial strategy. These have made their "way into the lexicon of education reform," including the CCSS for which the claim is that they were "'based on rigorous content'" (Tienken, 2020, p. 56). Educational language is circulated by networks and through interaction; widely advertised, game-changing rhetoric, once instilled, is normalized (see Achieve, Inc., 2008; CORE, 2013).

This usurpation of the democratic mindset and inherent speech patterns weakens the democratic public sphere, Apple (2014) explained: "Long-term and creative ideological work in the media and elsewhere" replaces "'thick' meanings of democracy grounded in full collective participation [with] 'thin' understandings where democracy is reduced to choice on a market" (p. xxi). "Dominant groups," Ball (2012) observed, "attach their policies and practices to the elements of good sense" (not only the bad in human lives) (p. xxii). In this way, they not only mimic educators' terminology but also use clever word plays that seem reasonable and wise.

Language powerfully serves as both an example of commodification and a highly influential phenomenon. Words (*democracy,* etc.) signifying public education are eviscerated by for-profit markets (Apple, 2011). Core democratic values (liberty, equality, justice, equity, responsible leadership, etc.) at the heart of public education have been manipulated, along with our capacity for imbuing them with meaning and holding true to their integrity. They have taken our "core" and repurposed it for their own ends.

Metacorporations and other marketeers even use educators' words, filling them with their own meanings. "Borrowed" terms like *achievement, core, partnership, assessment, readiness, careers, college,* and *growth* are salient in the school–university marketplace. Take *achievement,* for example. It was coopted when Achieve, Inc. was founded in 1996 at the National Education Summit by governors and business leaders. The Summit is a partner of the Education Trust, Thomas B. Fordham Institute, and National Alliance of Business to launch the American Diploma Project. In 2010 the CCSS were released, and Achieve, Inc. partnered with the NGA and CCSSO on the initiative, hiring consultants. Achieve, serving as project management partner for the PARCC, manages the state-led development of the K–12 Next Generation Science Standards (released in 2013).

Achieve, Inc., is a vigorous tendril-climbing network. Not only that, it's a shadow government fueled by the standardizing of learning within public schools using tests that ostensibly reflect a common core of English and math knowledge and skills (e.g., Achieve, 2008). But these approaches undercut school agency in curriculum making; struggling schools are penalized when teachers deemed "incompetent" are removed. Such actions are antithetical to the core value of thoughtfully building human and intellectual capital for a global society (English, 2014; Firestone, 2014).

Importantly, Cuban (2013) criticized megacorporations as failed experiments, largely because they overlook classroom and school context and because they are not, as English (2014) argued, democratic agencies committed to children's well-being. Blind to school culture and context, business entrepreneurs can only pretend to know people's daily struggles and successes.

And they cannot know the finer points about high-quality teacher performance. Take Firestone's (2014) point about the kinds of empirical and observational feedback uniquely cultivated by schools: "Teachers need quick, fine-grained feedback that does not encourage gaming the system, and such feedback seems unlikely to come from the state" (p. 105). Relying on well-honed expertise, feedback is the purview of educators. Promises from U.S. states of empirical observation to be carried out by skilled observers are empty to Firestone.

Taking Back Public Education

Public schools together with aspiring teacher and leader preparation programs speak to a triple reality: "mounting corporate pressures," the erosion of democracy, and "social movement building" (Anyon, 2014, p. 170). To public school defenders I say that we need to band together to urge educators and constituents, importantly policymakers, to work as a collective to re-create and repossess educational institutions. We need to help our communities understand how markets dominate their domains and impact lives through CCSS and other top-down reforms.

As educators, we can empower ourselves to imagine a different future for public education through consciousness raising, policy initiatives, and social movements. A tighter connection is needed between school leadership research and the practices of school personnel, but also with advocacy, in that professional staff in school systems have the access to local communities and constituents (Westbury, 2008). The staff who have leadership responsibility for reclaiming their agency include superintendents, school principals, and teachers.

We must take back public education by educating ourselves as to the challenge itself and by "resisting and fighting for democracy and keeping public education public" (English, 2014, p. 51). U.S. President Trump and his goal of "patriotic education" arguably stoked "hatred and division" by, as but one example, mounting a defense against "critical race theory, which holds that the founding of the U.S. is inextricable from slavery and racism, with their impacts still reverberating today" (Benveniste & Disis, 2020, para. 2). Proclaiming that he will "educate people" about the "real history of our country," Trump said that the new conglomerate TikTok Global was a deal he was making (unconfirmed by TikTok's Chinese executives) for which he called upon "$5 billion fund" to avert

American schools and universities from "being overrun by 'radical' teachers bent on destroying 'our children' with "Marxist doctrines" (para. 1).

When we "follow the money," reverberances in education policy and practice grow louder. Concerning the CCSS and other policies in the wake, Wexler (2014) cited implications for higher education programs: "The new teacher certification reform called edTPA follows the top-down, corporate formula, with the not-so-hidden agenda of disrupting the authority and autonomy of university education programs"; under the umbrella of "data-driven assessment, the CCSS and corporate views of accountability have made their way into the new certification and licensure process"; evaluation of teacher candidates will be based on CCSS-aligned "certification tests" and data from "Pearson Corporation" (p. 55). Can public education remain a public good? By revealing *and* disrupting corruptive practices that seem to be rapidly multiplying, we can defend public education and help it to reclaim its rightful place.

Organizing for Action

We must assess the damage neoliberal solutions—like testing and more funding for more testing—impose on public education. What values will children, youth, and aspiring teachers and leaders be inculcated to have? These days, the message is that math, science, and being globally competitive matter most. The arts and humanities, and the pathways they provide for becoming fully engaged, empathetic citizens and leaders are being lost (Wexler, 2014; Zhao, 2014). School stakeholders can make a difference by advocating against capitalist greed and for a public education that serves all children. This vision for transformational leadership has been described by district superintendents attempting to effect change (Kelleher & Van der Bogert, 2006).

Public school educators, and their constituents and defenders, can build awareness about the effects of neoliberalism and corporate networking on schools by considering these steps:

- Use Figure 1.1 for team building and instructional purposes to educate one another on how the neoliberal power grid functions.
- Identify the sponsors (e.g., publishers) of curricular materials from your district and ask critical questions about who they are. Then make connections among the networks they represent and the ways in which your own domain underwrites them.
- Use this book to generate a reading list that gives your team a better understanding of pertinent education policy issues and real costs involved for schools, especially for disadvantaged populations.
- Conduct seminars/workshops on education policy and corporate networks, and school empowerment and local control to increase team awareness and potency; choose materials that provoke thinking. Raise consciousness about

how programs and people, ideas and language, are being marketed, measured, and packaged (i.e., commodified).
- Discuss how your control over curriculum can be matched by the level and type of agency you desire, and how your school-community can be better protected.
- Make bold assertions based on your discoveries about what you have determined as public needs for education and pathways for moving your constituents in that direction.

We need to challenge one another to question the dominant political wisdom. What is our responsibility for countering the for-profit, anti-intellectual mindset that damages sectors and people? How do we transform education into that which honors the public school mission? Debates like this one put power grids under a microscope, and potentially expose the sneak attacks that subvert authentic teaching and learning. The spirit of public service needs to thrive and education for the common good must benefit all children.

Public Education, Inc., my device, calls on stakeholders to mindfully attend to the corporatization of the public education sphere and impact of special interest groups on schools and policy—hence the moniker "Inc." Satire has given me leverage for prying open Pandora's Box of greedy corporate forces and bedfellows. A goal is to spark consciousness of the corporate siege of public education and what actions can be taken by and on behalf of schools.

The critical voices cited reveal that profiteers are much more robustly controlling symbolic and real forms of power than is generally recognized. And they are waging a forceful, deliberate, and long-term seizure of public education. To education researchers, I am pointing out that while some of the sources reviewed make the case, others understate or even circumvent the issues. The magnitude and influence of corporate marketization on public school sectors are largely unknown to some academics while others support the market-based reforms.

Market appropriations of education spur large-scale social injustice. Public education needs citizens who care about public schools to think critically and act persuasively on behalf of the common good and every child's future. The Black Lives Matter (BLM) movement has wielded an activist consciousness and new crop of policy actors. A game-changer, BLM's confrontation of White supremacy is rapidly influencing the status quo. Black Lives Matter at School, formed by educators and students, seeks to dismantle systemic racism in education systems. Also in 2020, as another example, Buffalo Public Schools emerged as a race-conscious policy actor by incorporating BLM into its elementary curriculum. The BLM spirit and ideology are finding expression in K–12 schools where opponents of high-stakes standardized testing, the CCSS, and other top-down reforms resist White supremacy and anti-Blackness. As coalitions and new curriculum organized for racial justice empower actors, especially students of color, corporate networks' tight grip on public education and education policy may loosen, if not wane. To maintain or reclaim power, wouldn't neoliberal reformers have to rescript themselves as human rights champions of the BLM vision of racially just schooling?

My intent has been to force the sheer scope of this reality into the light of day. Hopefully, readers will explore the issues and draw additional conclusions for themselves and take action.

References

Achieve, Inc. (2008, July 31). *Out of many, one: Toward rigorous common core standards from the ground up*. www.achieve.org/OutofManyOne.
Anyon, J. (2014). *Radical possibilities: Public policy, urban education, and a new social movement* (2nd ed.). Routledge.
Apple, M. W. (2011). Democratic education in neoliberal and neoconservative times. *International Studies in Sociology of Education*, 21(1), 21–31.
Apple, M. W. (2014). *Official knowledge: Democratic education in a conservative age* (3rd ed.). Routledge.
Ball, S. J. (2012). *Global education inc.: New policy networks and the neo-liberal imaginary*. Routledge.
Benveniste, A., & Disis, J. (2020, September 21). *Trump wants the TikTok deal to pour $5 billion into "real history" education. It's not that simple*. CNN Business. https://edition.cnn.com/2020/09/20/business/trump-education-fund/index.html.
Berliner, D. C., & Glass, G. V. (Eds.). (2014). *50 myths & lies that threaten America's public schools: The real crisis in education*. Teachers College Press.
Blumenfeld, S. (2012, July 27). CFR task force calls for education reform. *The New American*. www.thenewamerican.com/reviews/opinion/item/12235-cfr-task-force-calls-for-education-reform.
Bogotch, I., & Shields, C. M. (Eds.). (2014). Introduction: Do promises of social justice trump paradigms of educational leadership? In I. Bogotch & C. M. Shields (Eds.), *International handbook of educational leadership and social (in)justice* (pp. 1–12). Springer.
Bracken, K. (2013, April 18). *Common core: Subversive threat to education*. Presentation at the Chattanooga TEA Party meeting. www.youtube.com/watch?v=0X0EFeH25bw.
Brass, J. (2014). Reading standards as curriculum: The curricular and cultural politics of the common core. *Journal of Curriculum and Pedagogy*, 11(1), 23–25.
CORE. (2013). *Data charts*. www.corelearn.com/Results/Data-Charts.html.
Cuban, L. (2013). *Inside the black box of classroom practice: Change without reform in American education*. Harvard Education Press.
Darling-Hammond, L., Wilhoit, G., & Pittenger, L. (2014). Accountability for college and career readiness: Developing a new paradigm. *Education Policy Analysis Archives*, 22(86), 1–38. https://epaa.asu.edu/ojs/article/view/1724/1334.
Downey, M. (2013, Aug. 25). Common core as a brand name. Who is making money off the new standards? *Atlanta Journal-Constitution*. www.ajc.com/weblogs/get-schooled/2013/aug/25/common-core-brand-name-who-making-money-new-standa.
Eisenhower, D. D. (1961, January 17). *Farewell radio and television address to the American people* ("Military-industrial complex speech"). presidency.ucsb.edu/documents/farewell-radio-and-television-address-the-american-people.

English, F. W. (2010). The ten most wanted enemies of American public education's school leadership. *NCPEA Education Leadership Review*, 5(3). http://cnx.org/content/m34684/latest.

English, F. W. (2014). *Educational leadership in the age of greed: A requiem for res publica*. NCPEA Press.

Firestone, W. A. (2014). Teacher evaluation policy and conflicting theories of motivation. *Educational Researcher*, 43(2), 100–107.

Gates, B. (2009, July 21). A bold new vision for education. Address at the National Conference of State Legislatures, Philadelphia. www.gatesfoundation.org/Media-Center/Speeches/2009/07/Bill-Gates-National-Conference-of-State-Legislatures-NCSL.

Giroux, H. A. (2014). *Neoliberalism's war on higher education*. Haymarket Books.

Habermas, J. (1985). *The theory of communicative action: Vol. 2. Lifeworld and system: A critique of functionalist reason* (T. McCarthy, Trans.). Beacon Press.

Heintz, J. (2011, June). *Military assets and public investment*. http://costsofwar.org/sites/default/files/articles/31/attachments/Heintzmilitaryassets.pdf.

Jones, A. G., & King, J. E. (2012). The Common Core State Standards: A vital tool for higher education. *Change: The Magazine of Higher Learning*, 44(6), 37–43.

Kelleher, P., & Van der Bogert, R. (Eds.). (2006). Voices for democracy: Struggles and celebrations of transformational leaders. *Yearbook of The National Society for the Study of Education*, 105(1), 1–9. Blackwell.

McDermott-McNulty, M. (2013, August 25). Common core developers—a private club you are not in. [Blog post]. http://perdidostreetschool.blogspot.com/2013/08/common-core-developers-private-club-you.html.

Miron, G. J. (2008). The shifting notion of "publicness" in public education. In B. S. Cooper, J. G. Cibulka, & L. D. Fusarelli (Eds.), *Handbook of education politics and policy* (pp. 338–349). Routledge.

Moeller, K. (2020). Accounting for the corporate: An analytic framework for understanding corporations in education. *Educational Researcher*, 49(4), 232–240.

Mullen, C. A. (2017). What are corporate education networks? Why ask questions? *Kappa Delta Pi Record*, 53(3), 100–106.

Mullen, C. A., English, F. W., Brindley, S., Ehrich, L. C., & Samier, E. A. (2013). Neoliberal issues in public education [Guest edited 2-volume issue]. *Interchange: A Quarterly Review of Education*, 43(3) and 43(4), 181–377.

National Governors Association Center for Best Practices & Council of Chief State School Officers. (2010). *Common Core State Standards*. www.corestandards.org.

Nielson, K. (2014, April 3). *Trends in state implementation of the Common Core State Standards: Making the shift to better tests* [Brief]. National Governors Association. www.nga.org/files/live/sites/NGA/files/pdf/2014/1404NGACCSSAssessments.pdf.

Papa, R., English, F. W., Davidson, F., Culver, M., K., & Brown, R. (2012). *Contours of great leadership: The science, art, and wisdom of outstanding practice*. Rowman & Littlefield.

Ravitch, D. (2013). *Reign of error: The hoax of the privatization movement and the danger to America's public schools*. Vintage Books.

Savage, G. C., O'Connor, K., & Brass, J. (2014). Common Core State Standards: Implications for curriculum, equality and policy. *Journal of Curriculum and Pedagogy*, 11(1), 18–20.

Tienken, C. H. (2012). The Common Core State Standards: The emperor is still looking for his clothes. *Kappa Delta Pi Record*, 48(4), 152–155.

Tienken, C. H. (2020). *Cracking the code of education reform: Creative compliance and ethical leadership*. Corwin.

Tienken, C. H. (2021). *The school reform landscape reloaded: More fraud, myths, and lies*. Rowman & Littlefield.

Tienken, C. H., & Orlich, D. C. (2013). *The school reform landscape: Fraud, myth, and lies*. Rowman & Littlefield.

U.S. Department of Defense Education Activity. (2012, June 5). *DoDEA schools to adopt Common Core State Standards*. www.dodea.edu/newsroom/pressreleases/06052012.cfm.

Westbury, I. (2008). Curriculum in practice. In F. M. Connelly, M. F. He, & J. Phillion (Eds.), *The SAGE handbook of curriculum and instruction* (pp. 1–4). Sage.

Wexler, A. (2014). Reaching higher? The impact of the Common Core State Standards on the visual arts, poverty, and disabilities. *Arts Education Policy Review*, 115(2), 52–61,

Zhao, Y. (2014). *Who's afraid of the big bad dragon? Why China has the best (and worst) education in the world*. Jossey-Bass.

2
NEOLIBERALISM AS A POLICY VENTRILOQUIST

Deconstructing the Discourse of Corporate America for Its Public Schools

Fenwick W. English

Introduction

An ideology has no voice, but it speaks in the policies and actions undertaken by those who traffic in it. The ideology of neoliberalism is like a ventriloquist. It only becomes manifest when the ventriloquist's dummy speaks, manifested through written policies and legislative action. Weiner (2005) observed, "Neoliberalism is an economic, political, and cultural system that requires a certain level of political docility, social cynicism, and economic fatalism on behalf of its constituencies to maintain its hegemony" (p. 17). He completes his definition by also saying "neoliberalism is a conservative ideology, hostile to democratic control of power, privilege, and authority. Its conservatism finds meaning in its attack on public oriented projects, like public education" (p. 23).

Too often the actions taken by those who work within the ideology spark reaction and conflict by those who are affected without ever really understanding the master narrative, i.e., the ventriloquist at work. Mullen (2016) has referred to the presence of this ideology serving as a kind of "shadow government" (p. 34). Diamond (2020) underscored the nature of the silent assumptions and interests behind the ideology of neoliberalism by noting that, "so few of the leaders and policymakers credited with advancing the neoliberal project … ever even used the term" (p. 108).

Even as neoliberalism has been involved in myriad projects, causes, initiatives, and policies Mason (2015) cautioned us about when he observed that "It is easy to miss the fact that … the destruction of labour's bargaining power … was the essence of the entire project: it was a means to all the other ends." This observation meant that "Neoliberalism's guiding principle [was] not free markets, nor fiscal discipline, not sound money, nor privatization and offshoring—not even globalization. All these things were byproducts or weapons of its main endeavor to remove organized labor from the equation" (pp. 91–92).

Mason's identification of the principle objective of neoliberalism re-orders an understanding of its manifestations in the contemporary political landscape. It does help explain the unwavering antipathy of neoliberal advocates against teacher unions. The alleged friendly view of the teacher unions is one reason the highly educated scholar and educator Linda Darling-Hammond was not selected to be the U.S. Secretary of Education by the Obama administration (Ravitch, 2010, p. 22). Neoliberal precepts and antidotes to "reforming" public education are used and accepted in both political parties, and Darling-Hammond's work was panned by pundits, reformers, and politicians on both sides of the aisle.

So what is Neoliberalism?

Defining neoliberalism is about as difficult as defining liberalism. Rosenblatt (2019) said,

> For some, liberalism refers to the Lockean idea of individual rights and free markets; for others, it means the welfare state. In many parts of the world, being liberal in colloquial parlance means favouring "small government," while in the US it means favouring "big government."
>
> *(p. 77)*

Trujillo and Douglass Horsford (2020) defined *neoliberalism* as, "A system of political, economic, and cultural beliefs, norms, and practices that favour free-market capitalism and a deregulated state role in the provision of public goods, like education" (p. 17).

While some writers classify neoliberalism as a theory (Harvey 2009, p. 2) in the light of Popper's (1959) distinction that for something to be a "theory" in the scientific sense, it had to be able to have its assertions subject to being falsified. If it failed that test, it was just a narrative, no better and no worse than others that could not be disproven. So for a theory to be accepted as scientific, the proponent had to be able to state ahead of time how it could be shown to be falsified. If the advocates could not so stipulate, then empirical data were useless in proving or disproving any theory, and theory itself was non-scientific.

So neoliberalism is the belief (i.e., ideology), that "the market is the most effective (or least irrational) method of distributing goods and resources, and the role of the state should be limited to the maintenance of necessary order, legality, and stability" of the market (Barker, 2002, p. 369). Weiner (2005) indicated, "neoliberalism represents a 'nonsystemic' system; that is, an ideological system of language, thought, and behavior that detests … and … wants to destroy … collective structures which may impede the pure market" (p. 16).

Although neoliberalism makes a claim that it is centered in economics and rationality, Hamowy (2011), one of its major advocates, confessed that it couldn't be totally logical:

> The rationalist who desires to subject everything to human reason is thus faced with a major dilemma. The use of reason aims at control and predictability. But the process of the advance of reason rests on freedom and the unpredictability of human action. Those who extol the power of human reason usually see only one side of the interaction of human thought and conduct in which reason is at the same time used and shaped. They do not see that, for advance to take place, the social process from which the growth of reason emerges must remain free from its control. There can be little doubt that man [sic] owes some of his greatest success in the past to the fact that he has *not* [italics in the original] been able to control social life.
>
> (p. 15)

Hayek and Friedman: Two Major Prophets of Neoliberalism

There were two major figures in the intellectual definition and spread of neoliberalism. The first was Friedrich Hayek (1899–1992). Hayek was an Austrian–British economist, awarded the Nobel Prize in 1974 as well as the Presidential Medal of Freedom in 1991 from President George H. W. Bush. Also, President Ronald Reagan indicated that Hayek was one of a few individuals who most influenced his personal philosophy.

While spending some time in America at the University of Chicago, Hayek met Milton Friedman (1912–2006) who subsequently became the second prophet and outspoken advocate of free markets as part of the ideology of neoliberalism. Cassidy (2009) summarized Friedman's contribution by noting that "[He] furnished conservative politicians with a consistent and well-articulated set of ideas and policy proposals" (p. 72).

Friedman's landmark book *Capitalism and Freedom* (1962) was the political equivalent of Martin Luther nailing his 95 Theses on the Castle Church's door in Wittenberg, Germany, in 1517. While Luther was opposed to the Church selling indulgences and excesses of the clergy, Friedman was opposed to all but a tiny fragment of government regulation and viewed social programs as excesses and indulgences of government overreach. He argued for the "United States to do away with Social Security, progressive income taxes, free public high schools, the minimum wage, housing and highway subsidies, and health care, even for the elderly" (Madrick, 2011, p. 42). Friedman began the neoliberal assault on government regulations and any policies that created monopolies and worked against individuals being able to exercise maximum freedom in the marketplace.

The withdrawal or stunting of government support for the less well off in America, Britain, and other countries where the implementing of neoliberal policies was pursued relentlessly was, according to many economists, the major propellant to the huge gaps in inequality that are so obvious and blatant today (see Stiglitz, 2010). Bourdieu (1999) indicated that the overall result of the pursuit of neoliberal notions has produced "the destruction of the idea of public service" (p. 182).

In 2004, Henry Giroux wrote his prescient book *The Terror of Neoliberalism*. His purpose was to help educators and others understand the nature of neoliberalism because

> it has to be named and critically understood before it can be critiqued. The common-sense assumptions that legitimate neoliberalism's alleged historical inevitability have to be unsettled and then engaged for the social damage they cause at all levels of human existence.
>
> *(p. xxv)*

Giroux (2004) was appalled by neoliberal ideology, with its ongoing emphasis on deregulation and privatization that led to an all-out attack and devaluation of the public good. He objected to the neoliberal position when he pointed out that "Public services such as health care, childcare, public assistance, education, and transportation are now subject to the rules of the market" (p. 46).

> Bourdieu (1999) similarly opined that:
>
> It is understandable that minor civil servants, and more especially those charged with carrying out the so-called "social" functions, that is, with compensating, without being given all the necessary means, for the most intolerable effects and deficiencies of the logic of the market—policemen and lower-level judges, social workers, educators and even, more and more in recent years, primary and secondary school teachers—should be abandoned, if not disowned outright, in their efforts to deal with the material and moral suffering that is the only certain consequence of this economically legitimated Realpolitik.
>
> *(p. 183)*

In an Op-Ed piece in *The New York Times*, Appelbaum (2020) observed that the implementation of neoliberalism has

> been an experiment on a grand scale, and the results are depressingly clear. Growth has slowed, and much of the available gains have been pocketed by a small minority of very wealthy Americans. The shareholding class keeps getting richer; the rest of the nation is falling behind.
>
> *(p. A22)*

The cascading wealth gap was the result of such policies.

The rise of such inequality in a society was also related to health, social problems and policies. In fact, Wilkinson and Pickett (2010) concluded in their studies of equality that

> If you want to know why one country does better or worse than another, the first thing to look at is the extent of inequality. There is not one policy for reducing inequality in health or the educational performance of school children, and another for raising national standards of performance. Reducing inequality is the best way of doing both.
>
> *(pp. 29–30)*

Neoliberalism's Discursive Seven Core Pillars of Belief

The silent scaffolding that links the ventriloquist to the dummy are seven tenets that provide the ideological web for the enactment of the neoliberal ideology in education (English & Papa, 2018):

1. Economic and political freedoms are connected.
2. Pure political freedom is sabotaged by monopolies.
3. Professional associations and unions compromise economic exchange.
4. The role of government is to create markets and simultaneously restrict their regulation.
5. Government policies and watchdogs work against creativity.
6. Destruction of existing institutional relationships is a sign of progress.
7. Erasure or diminution of any mechanism seeking to foster social justice.

(pp. 4–9)

Core Pillar 1: Economic and Political Freedoms Are Connected

The first pillar of neoliberal belief begins with a utopian vision regarding individual freedom in any given social setting and balancing its status against the role of government. As Friedman and Friedman (1990) wrote, "In a society whose participants desire to achieve the greatest possible freedom to choose as individuals, as families, as members of voluntary groups, as citizens of an organized government, what role should be assigned to government?" (p. 28). Following this conjecture they wrote, "Restrictions on economic freedom inevitably affect freedom in general" (p. 67).

According to neoliberal belief, open competition is the best antidote against most of the ills that plague American society, but it will only work if individuals are free to choose. There have to be two existing conditions that make this utopia of open competition work: (1) choice over all aspects of human life and (2) no or very little governmental interference or restrictions in how those choices can be made. The situation that permits both of these conditions to exist is *a free market*, meaning a non-regulated market. Thirty years earlier it was Milton Friedman (1962) who pointed out that "the great threat to freedom is the concentration of power" (p. 2); as government becomes centralized and grows in its authority and reach, it becomes too powerful. Too much power becomes a threat to freedom itself, so "Government power must be dispersed" (p. 3).

Bourdieu (1999) averred that

> by making economic liberalism the necessary and sufficient condition of political freedom, neoliberals assimilate state interventionism to "totalitarianism" ... [and] by associating efficiency and modernity with private enterprise, and archaism and inefficiency with the public sector ... they identify "modernization" with the transfer into the private sector of the public services with the most profit potential.
>
> *(p. 182)*

The result is "the destruction of the idea of public service" (p. 182).

Core Pillar 2: Political Freedom Is Compromised by Monopolies

In his landmark 1962 book *Capitalism and Freedom*, Friedman wrote, "Monopoly implies the absence of alternatives and thereby inhibits effective freedom of exchange" (p. 28). Monopolies were inherently evil, even if created by the state for the protection of its citizens. One neoliberal economist wrote, "A monopolist is an implicit thief, because his possession of market power leads to the exchange of commodities at prices that do not reflect social scarcities" (DeLong, 1990, pp. 601–618 as cited in Madrick, 2011, p. 35).

A classic method of creating a monopoly in education by government (state and federal) is in the creation of standards linked to licensure: in education, transportation, and even air quality. Friedman claimed that eventually stagnation sets in and progress is blocked. So, the antidote to this probability is the free market, which not only optimizes individual choice, but also acts as a deterrent against the power of state to expand its authority. Behind this claim lies the assumption that the free market will drive quality up and eliminate mediocrity and through its dynamism refresh competition and avoid stagnation. The dynamic open market, which is the place for competitive capitalism to flourish, "promotes political freedom because it separates economic power from political power, and in this way enables one to offset the other" (Friedman, 1962, p. 9).

Core Pillar 3: Professional Associations and Unions Compromise Economic Exchange

Friedman and Friedman (1990) were also opposed to licensing of certain occupations, writing,

Today you are not free to offer your services as a lawyer, a physician, a dentist, a plumber, a barber, a mortician, or engage in a host of other occupations, without first getting a permit or license from a government official.

(p. 66)

Beginning with the premise that true political freedom could only exist for a person when free to choose among alternatives, Friedman said that bad doctors or bad teachers would be driven from the marketplace over time. The trouble with licensing of professionals was that it created a monopoly. And as it did so it denied a citizen an unfettered choice. The idea was that uncompromised political freedom could only exist when there was an absolute open and unregulated market. The reality of dealing with a constant flow of bad actors was left to the market to eventually deal with the problem, a solution which might take years if ever.

The neoliberals have a particular abhorrence of unions. Hayek (2011) laid out the case beginning with the observation that an employer will agree to a wage increase "only when he knows that the union has the power to keep out others" (p. 389). Furthermore,

Unions that had no power to coerce outsiders would thus not be strong enough to force up wages above the level at which all seeking work could be employed, that is, the level that would establish itself in a truly free market for labor in general.

(p. 389)

Hayek (2011) revealed a particular dose of venom for unions:

we have now reached a state where they have become uniquely privileged institutions to which the general rules of law do not apply. They have become the only important instance in which governments signally fail in their prime function—the prevention of coercion and violence.

(p. 384)

Lieberman (1990) also cast light on the conflict between teacher unions and advocates of choice and a market-based approach to education upon observing that, "Perhaps the most important basis of teacher opposition is their fear that public school choice would force teachers to give up their monopoly and compete for pupils" (p. 98).

Core Pillar 4: Government's Role Is to Create Markets and Simultaneously Restrict Their Regulation of Them

A watchword for neoliberal ideology is *competition* "between individuals, between firms, between territorial entities (cities, regions, nations, regional groupings) and is held to be a primary virtue … the ground rules for market competition must be properly observed" (Harvey, 2009, p. 65). And if such rules do not exist or are vague, the state must create and impose them. Methods of creating alternatives are de-regulation, privatization, and encouraging competition. This cocktail of methods is posed as the way "to eliminate bureaucratic red tape, increase efficiency and productivity, improve quality, and reduce costs" (p. 65).

The whole neoliberal ideological package came closest to a total erasure of a base of various protections enjoyed by individuals and social classes in Britain and the United States. Neoliberal doctrine included efforts to negate nearly all forms of state power. At the front of the confrontation between old and new social orders were efforts to curb trade union power,

> attacking all forms of social solidarity that hindered competitive flexibility (such as those expressed through municipal governance, and including the power of many professionals and their associations) dismantling or rolling back the commitments of the welfare state, the privatization of public enterprises (including social housing), reducing taxes, encouraging entrepreneurial initiatives, and creating a favourable business climate to induce a strong inflow of foreign investment.
>
> *(Harvey, 2009, p. 23)*

Core Pillar 5: Government Policies and Watchdogs Work against Creativity

When it comes to what governmental policies should be avoided, neoliberals argue that any policy that restricts the consumer from choice should be avoided because, as Friedman (1962) noted,

> Our problem today is not to enforce conformity; it is rather that we are threatened with an excess of conformity. Our problem is to foster diversity, and the alternative would do this far more effectively than a nationalized school system.
>
> *(p. 97)*

The idea that the state is overly bureaucratic and inefficient and needs to just get out of the way of the private sector because it is more innovative owing to fewer rules is a myth challenged by the facts. Mazzucato (2014) offered the evidence for the belief that governments could not be creative:

> most of the radical, revolutionary innovations that have fueled the dynamics of capitalism … from railroads to the Internet, to modern-day nanotechnology and pharmaceuticals … trace the most courageous, early, and capital-intensive "entrepreneurial" investments back to the State … all of the technologies that

make Jobs' iPhone so "smart" were government funded (Internet, GPS, touch-screen display, and the recent Siri voice-activated personal assistant. Such radical investments ... which embedded extreme uncertainty ... did not come about due to the presence of venture capitalists nor of "garage tinkerers." It was the visible hand of the State which made these innovations happen. Innovation that would not have come about had we waited for the 'market' and business to do it alone.

(p. 3)

Core Pillar 6: Destruction of Existing Institutional Services and Relationships Is a Sign of Progress

Neoliberal antagonism towards agencies of the state that create real or partial monopolies are prime targets to attack, dismantle, wither away by successive budget cuts, or become transformed by outright privatization. An array of public services to help the poor and middle class provide for public health and safety, subsidize food distribution, and provide a free public education have been targeted over the past several decades by neoliberal legislation. If government actions worked to create regulations and agencies to ensure fair treatment, or to protect the "common good," and they are subsequently erased, abolished, or minimized, the results are seen as unequivocally "good." The destruction of such regulations is viewed as a step forward, an action that lets market forces act without hindrance.

Neoliberals worry that "the elimination of the market as a steering mechanism would necessitate the replacement of it by a system of administrative directions" (Hayek, 2011, p. 401). In turn, those directions would have to be anchored in a mechanism that controlled the whole economy. Such controls would lead to a centrally planned society. Inevitably the concept of individual freedom would be severely compromised and/or lost. Trammell (2005) indicated, "some analysts hold that reforms based on free-market ideology, whereby schools ultimately become profit-making, entrepreneurial entities, support an agenda to end all government participation in education" (p. 31). The destruction of such government support would be a sign of progress, a sign that systems of schools would be run by market logic and market demand.

Core Pillar 7: Erasure or Diminution of Any Mechanism Seeking to Foster *Social Justice*

Hayek (2011) was particularly antagonistic to the idea of social justice, if by that is meant the notion that the government ensures that all social advantages and assets are provided in equal measure to all persons. For that condition to exist, the power given to the government would be used to control virtually all of a society's wealth. That control would be used to deprive some individuals of their assets and bestow on others those same assets. An extension of this idea means that if a person belonged to a group and their condition also applied to that same group, the entire group would have to be compensated similarly or, on the other hand, penalized equally.

Hamowy (2011) summed up the argument against this concept of *social justice* upon observing, "It is the antithesis of the idea of justice based on a theory of individual rights that holds that only those responsible for a wrong should be held to account" (p. 15). This posture would form a formidable barrier to the efforts of some African Americans who argue that they be compensated for the past sins of slavery by White America. It would mean that all of White America, including those whose ancestors never owned slaves, would be penalized.

Furthermore, any effort to equalize the chances that some individuals and families inherit by way of social position or wealth, called by neoliberals as "accidents," would jeopardize progress:

> the growth of civilization rests largely on the individuals' making the best use of whatever accidents they encounter, of the essentially unpredictable advantages that one kind of knowledge will in new circumstances confer on one individual over others.
>
> However commendable may be the motives of those who fervently desire that, in the interest of justice, all should be made to start with the same chances, theirs is an ideal that is literally impossible to realize.
>
> *(Hayek, 2011, p. 507)*

Frankson (2018) neatly summarized the neoliberal boilerplate privileging of individuals over groups: "In neoliberal thinking, success or failure is completely dependent on the choices and talents of the individual student with no regard to the limitation imposed upon them by our economized and compromised education and political system" (p. 21).

Problems with the "Free Market" Conjecture

Linkage between the economics and politics was supplied by the "free market conjecture." A *conjecture* is defined as "forming an opinion or judgment upon evidence insufficient for definite knowledge" (Webster, 1972, p. 176).

When claiming that regulation was unnecessary by the state because the dynamics of a free market meant in the end that the right balance between economics and politics would be established over time, neoliberals forgot that

> the market is a devilish thing. It is far too devilish to be captured by a single simple theory of behavior, and certainly not by a theory that allowed for nothing but calm rationality as far as the eye could see.
>
> *(Fox, 2009, p. xv)*

The result of leaning on the concept of the free market conjecture would be that inferior markets and services in them would be eliminated as consumers came to prefer the best and most efficient services. Poor services and poor products would be driven out because the best would prevail. Furthermore, "as more stocks, bonds, options, futures, and other financial instruments were created and traded, they would inevitably bring more rationality to economic activity. Financial markets possessed a wisdom that individuals, companies, and governments did not" (Fox, 2009, p. xiii).

Nobel Prize winning economist Joseph Stiglitz (2010) summarized the idea that markets can make good on all of the claims from neoliberals looking back at the Great Recession of 2008:

> In short, America's financial markets had failed to perform their essential societal functions of managing risk, allocating capital, and mobilizing savings while keeping transaction costs low. Instead, they had created risk, misallocated capital, and encouraged excessive indebtedness while imposing high transaction costs. At their peak in 2007, the bloated financial markets absorbed 41 percent of profits in the corporate sector
>
> (p. 7)

Stiglitz (2010) concluded,

> there is a role for government. If it does its job well, there will be fewer accidents and when the accidents occur, they will be less costly ... Every successful economy—every successful society—involves both government and markets. There needs to be a balanced role"
>
> (p. 17)

The Intersection with Managerialism

When neoliberalism is intertwined with the ideology of *managerialism*, a powerful and seductive discourse has been created that captured the reform rhetoric of both the Republican and Democratic political parties. There is little difference between them when it comes to the discourse of educational reform. A discourse consists of both written and spoken language. It has three dimensions: The first is a piece of writing known as *the text*. The second is a consistent interpretation of *actions*. The third is a collection of *social practices*. According to Fairclough (1992), "discourses do not just reflect or represent social entities and relations, they construct or 'constitute' them" (p. 3). Bourdieu (2008) wrote,

> The purpose of the dominant discourse on the social world is not simply to legitimize domination but also to steer action designed to perpetuate it,

giving moral and morale, directions and directive, to those who direct and who put it into effect.

(p. 109)

While neoliberalism is an ideology in which policy and practice are nested, *managerialism* is the technology of its enactment of both in the real world of schooling. Dolan (2020, p. 92) spoke of it by saying "managerialism [is] a version of school leadership that is the solution to formulated problems of inefficiency and ineffectiveness."

Managerialism is defined as:

> associated with managerial techniques that have been imposed on public sector organizations or institutions and which require a focus on efficiency, effectiveness and the measurement of outcomes and performance (staff and the institution). A core feature of a managerial organization is the adoption of "for profit" values and competitive practices to secure the best advantage possible. In a managerial organization, professional autonomy and direction are largely absent.

(Fitzgerald & Hall, 2020, p. 328)

Dolan (2020) finds in the watchwords of *managerialism* a surface discourse that uses such words as quality, efficiency, effectiveness, standards, accountability, competition, market share, customers, choice, excellence, and entrepreneurship to lash the principalship to "formulated problems of inefficiency and ineffectiveness" (p. 92). Dolan (2020) avers that his analysis of managerialism "works to refute its neutral, apolitical, and strategic posturing by revealing it as a political project for governing the conduct of principals" (p. 92). Thomas and Watson (2011), too, observed that, "School leaders now work under the conditions where their governance is legitimated by a rationality defined by the market" (p. 190).

The mantle of managerialism is an approach that certain measures would be employed that indicate what is to be taught, how it will be taught, and when it is to be taught, and as Block (2005) explained, "and how they test student 'knowledge' in the form of standardized test-aligned curricula, teachers' manuals, and standardized tests" (p. 85). "Teachers and schools are held accountable through student performance on these tests and, when necessary, corrected or replaced by individuals and/or remedics assumed to ensure children a quality education" (p. 85).

Managerialism/neoliberalism comprise the master discourse of today's concepts of a well managed school system or school. These two ideologies are behind the GERM (Global Educational Reform Management) discourse that has been embraced by the World Bank. Spring (2004) indicated that "the World Bank supports privatized educational systems, including private schools and charging tuition for government schools" (p. 35). The free market ideology is also part of the World Bank's outlook, summarized as:

> The World Bank assumes that what is called a neoliberal approach to government is pervading the globe. The basic assumption of neoliberalism is that government services, such as schools, water and sewer systems, electric power, and so on, can be better provided by private companies and non-profit organizations. The assumption is based on the unproven idea that corporate bureaucracies are more efficient than government bureaucracies and that the free market is more responsive to public interests than governments. The primary role of government ... is regulating the market to ensure the free flow of goods.
>
> *(Spring, 2004, p. 41)*

The intersection of *neoliberalism* and *managerialism* led more than one public sector organization into an appalling financial vulnerability when COVID-19 occurred. François Furstenberg (2020), a professor of history at the Johns Hopkins University, spelled out in some detail why his university was "Suddenly anticipating losses of over $300 million in the next 15 months" (p. 30). Furstenberg recounted how Johns Hopkins' administrative structure was centralized for over a decade with non-academics proliferating and at handsome salaries. At Johns Hopkins that meant employing two senior vice presidents, 12 vice presidents, an acting vice president, a vice provost, a secretary and three senior advisors. Furstenberg noted that "only the provost has significant classroom and research experience" (p. 30).

The salaries paid out for this administrative structure included the University's president who was paid

> $1.6 million in salary plus $1.1 million in deferred and other compensation for a total of $2.7 million. That tidy sum doesn't include the money he receives for serving on other boards, including the $310,000 he received that year from T. Rowe Price—whose chief executive happens to serve on the Johns Hopkins Board of Trustees.
>
> *(Furstenberg, 2020, p. 31)*

Furstenberg (2020) noted that the senior vice president for finance earned $1.2 million and the vice president for development made $1 million. The vice president for investments earned $950,000. The President's Chief of Staff earned over $670,000. The provost, the only true academic in the upper administration, "did not rank even in the top 10 earners at the university ... the compensation of the 28 key employees reported to the IRS in 2018 amounted to over $29 million" (p. 31). The term that describes some of the deleterious outcomes when the values of the corporate world are grafted onto the university has been called *corporatization*. This word stands for

the ways that public education and, more specifically, educational leadership have been refashioned based on the model of the private business corporation. It encompasses a number of aspects, including the ability of business interests to influence changes in educational policy and curriculum, changes in the ownership and control of schools, changes to the labour force of schools, changes to the culture of schools and the culture of school leadership, and changes to how people are taught to think about schools.
(Saltman & Means, 2020, p. 341)

Furstenberg (2020) commented, "A university exists for values different from those that dominate the for-profit world" (p. 31).

A Case Study of Pushing Back against Neoliberal Reforms

There are very few examples of successful pushback against neoliberal reforms being implemented in U.S. school districts. Pazey (2020) chronicled the fight against neoliberal ideas working to close a so-called "failing school" in an urban Texas high school between spring 2008 and summer 2011. Because of low test scores, the high school was headed for closure. However, homeowners in the area of the school got the Texas commissioner to repurpose the school, fearing that the loss of a community high school would further hasten the fate of a community's decline.

Pazey's (2020) study focused on what kinds of narratives district administrators used to mark a school as failing, and the types of neoliberal reforms being considered in the closing or repurposing of the high school. It was revealed that a compelling deficit narrative was advanced and rejected by the high school's students and parents. Turning the school over to a private company or turning it into a charter school were options considered and rejected by the community, parents, and students. However, the deficit narrative that their school was academically unacceptable proved an obstacle that had to be confronted. The tenets of DisCrit Theory were employed to turn the neoliberal metaphors around and challenge their efficacy. DisCrit Theory "highlights how race and ability are used to marginalize particular groups in society by focusing on the interdependent ways that racism and ableism shape notions of normalcy" (Pazey, 2020, p. 1872). DisCrit Theory also challenges the assumption that race and/or disability were biological facts rather than socially constructed categories. From such challenges a counter narrative could be and was constructed that challenged the district's sanctions imposed by the state.

Many board meetings transpired considering the fate of this high school:

> Students addressed the school board or held signs to denounce the potential threat to convert their [high school] into a charter school. Student speakers (a) described the punitive, *low performing* label branded on their school and failure-ridden descriptors characterizing their school identity, (b) accentuated

their capabilities, achievements, and overall school improvement scores, and (c) refuted the deficit narrative spoken and written about them and their school.

(Pazey, 2020, p. 1876)

Lessons learned from this controversy in Texas included that neoliberal "reforms" imposed a discourse in which the creation of an *achievement gap* was embedded. The neoliberal discourse further arbitrarily categorized schools as "good" or "bad" and equally arbitrarily divided students into those who were successful and those who were failures. The imposition of this deficit-centered lens led to framing students in terms of what they could not do: The "disciplinary forces of the state apply sanctions to schools located in urban, low-income neighborhoods with high African American, Hispanic immigrant student populations, and students with disabilities" (Pazey, 2020, p. 1897).

This application of neoliberal reform of public education teaches that the creation of "haves" and "have nots" by socio-economic "accidents" is given as a "fact" when they are simply one set of social constructions that—in the name of reform—ensure that there won't be any change at all because the assumptions of how school systems really work were never challenged. Such social constructions are passed off as factual and inevitable instead of being challenged as artifices of a specific deficit narrative. Neoliberal reforms remain anchored in the very language, images, metaphors, and assumptions that they were supposed to solve. Instead, they reinforce and continue the failures of the past. The ventriloquism of the discourse of neoliberalism is rarely exposed. Educators and the public must stop listening to debating the dummy's chatter and to expose and take action against the ventriloquist.

References

Applebaum, B. (2020, September 9). Blaming Milton Friedman, *The New York Times*, A22.

Barker, R. (2002), Neo-liberalism. In J. Bothamley (Ed.) *Dictionary of theories* (p. 369). Visible Ink Press.

Block, J. (2005). Children as collateral damage: The innocents of education's war for reform. In R. Boyles (Ed.) *Schools or markets? Commercialism, privatization, and school-business partnerships* (pp. 83–118). Lawrence Erlbaum.

Bourdieu, P. (2008). The royal science and the fatalism of probability. In D. Fernbach, Trans. *Political interventions: Social science and political action* (pp. 103–112). Verso.

Bourdieu, P. (1999). The abdication of the state. In P. Bourdieu et al. (Eds.) *The weight of the world: Social suffering in contemporary society* (pp. 181–188). Stanford University Press.

Cassidy, J. (2009). *How markets fail: The logic of economic calamities*. Farrar, Straus & Giroux.

Diamond, A. J. (2020). Towards a history of neoliberal urbanism in the United States. In S. Dawes and M. Lenormand (Eds.) *Neoliberalism in context: Governance, subjectivity and knowledge* (pp. 105–120). Palgrave Macmillan.

DeLong, J. B. (1990). In defense of Henry Simons' standing as a classical liberal. *Cato Journal* 9(1), 601–618.

Dolan, C. (2020). *Paradox and the school leader: The struggle for the soul of the principal in neoliberal times*. Singapore.

English, F. W., & Papa, R. (2018). A discursive analysis of neoliberal policies and practices in education, in R. Papa, & S.W.J. Armfield (Eds.) *The Wiley handbook of educational policy* (pp. 3–28). Wiley Blackwell.

Fairclough, N. (1992). *Discourse and social change*. Polity Press.

Fitzgerald, R., & Hall, D. (2020). Performativity, managerialism and educational leadership. In S. Courtney, H. Gunter, R. Nische, & T. Trujillo (Eds.) *Understanding educational leadership: Critical perspectives and approaches* (pp. 323–3387). Bloomsbury Academic.

Frankson, J. E. (2018). Admitting privilege. In J. Spring, J. Frankson, C. McCallum, & D. Banks (Eds.), *The business of education: Networks of power and wealth in America* (pp.16–29). Routledge.

Fox, J. (2009). *The myth of the rational market: A history of risk, reward, and delusion on wall Street*. Harper Business.

Friedman, M. (1962). *Capitalism and Freedom*. University of Chicago Press.

Friedman, M., & Friedman, R. (1990). *Free to choose: A personal statement*. Harcourt.

Furstenberg, F. (2020, June 26). University leaders are failing: The pandemic reveals ineptitude at the top. Change is needed. *The Chronicle of Higher Education*, 66(32), 30–31.

Giroux, H. A. (2004). *The terror of neoliberalism*. Paradigm Publishers.

Hamowy, R. (2011). Introductory essay. In R. Hamowy (Ed.) *The constitution of liberty: The definitive edition* (pp. 1–22): *The collected works of F.A. Hayek*. University of Chicago Press.

Harvey, D. (2009). *A brief history of neoliberalism*. Oxford University Press.

Hayek, F. (2011). *The constitution of liberty: The definitive edition: The collected works of F.A. Hayek*. University of Chicago Press.

Lieberman, M. (1990). *Public school choice: Current issues/future prospects*. Technomic.

Madrick, J. (2011). *Age of greed: The triumph of finance and the decline of America, 1970 to the present*. Alfred A. Knopf.

Mason, P. (2015). *Postcapitalism: A guide to our future*. Penguin Books.

Mazzucato, M. (2014). *The entrepreneurial state: Debunking public vs. private sector myths*. Anthem Press.

Mullen, C. A. (2016). Corporate networks and their grip on the public school sector and education policy. In C. H. Tienken and C. A. Mullen (Eds.) *Education policy perils: Tackling the tough issues* (pp. 27–62). Routledge.

Pazey, B. (2020, August) Ya Basta! Countering the effects of neoliberal reform on an urban turnaround high school. *American Educational Research Journal*, 57(4), 1868–1905. doi:https://doi.org/10.3102/0002831219886530.

Popper, K. R. (1959). *The logic of scientific discovery*. Harper & Row.

Ravitch, D. (2010). *The death and life of the great American school system*. New York: Basic Books.

Rosenblatt, H. (2019, August). A liberal history. *History Today*, 69(8), 76–81.

Saltman, K., & Means, A. J. (2020). Corporatization and educational leadership, In S. Courtney, H. Gunter, R. Niesche, & T. Trujillo (Eds.) *Understanding educational leadership: Critical perspectives and approaches* (pp. 339–354). Bloomsbury Academic.

Spring, J. (2004). *How educational ideologies are shaping global society: Intergovernmental organizations, NGOs, and the decline of the nation-state*. Lawrence Erlbaum.

Stiglitz, J. E. (2010). *Freefall: America, free markets, and the sinking of the world economy*. W.W. Norton.

Thomas, S., & Watson, L. (2011). Quality and accountability: Policy tensions for Australian school leaders. In T. Townsend, & J. MacBeath (Eds.) *International handbook of leadership for learning, Part* 1 (pp.189–208). Singapore.

Trammell, L. (2005). Measuring and fixing, filling and drilling: The ExxonMobil agenda for education. In D. R. Boyles (Ed.), *Schools or markets? Commercialism, privatization, and school–business partnerships*. Lawrence Erlbaum.

Trujillo, T., & Douglass Horsford, S. (2020). Critical perspectives and approaches to educational leadership in the United States. In S. Courtney, H. Gunter, R. Niesche, & T. Trujillo (Eds.) *Understanding educational leadership: Critical perspectives and approaches* (pp. 15–28). Bloomsbury Academic.

Webster's Seventh New Collegiate Dictionary (2007). G & C. Merriam Company Publishers.

Weiner, E. J. (2005). *Private learning, public needs: The neoliberal assault on democratic education*. Peter Lang.

Wilkinson, R., & Pickett, K. (2010). *The spirit level: Why greater equality makes societies stronger*. Bloomsbury Press.

3

THREATS TO MEANINGFUL REFORM OF CIVIC EDUCATION

Patricia H. Hinchey and Pamela J. Konkol

> The tyranny of a prince is not so dangerous to the public welfare as the apathy of a citizen in a democracy.
>
> *(Montesquieu, 1748, The Spirit of Laws)*

Since the founding of the United States, education has been considered essential to the country's survival as a representative democracy. Founding Father and U.S. President Thomas Jefferson (1816) repeatedly stressed the need for education to prepare a citizenry schooled in democratic norms and vigilant in safeguarding democratic institutions:

> [E]xperience hath shown, that even under the best forms, those entrusted with power have, in time, and by slow operations, perverted it into tyranny; and it is believed that the most effectual means of preventing this would be, to illuminate, as far as practicable, the minds of the people at large .... If a nation expects to be ignorant & free, in a state of civilisation, it expects what never was & never will be. [T]he functionaries of every government have propensities to command at will the liberty & property of their constituents. [T]here is no safe deposit for these but with the people themselves.
>
> *(1778, 1816)*

Human nature, as Jefferson noted, is human nature: the powerful tend naturally toward accumulating more power and wealth at the expense of the less powerful. The Constitution's checks and balances attempt to rein in these tendencies, but the population must provide governmental oversight. Education is one intended tool to cultivate a population capable of holding government to account.

DOI: 10.4324/9781003108511-3

Necessary Safeguards

There is widespread agreement, however, that public education policy has been failing to promote and protect the civic education necessary to safeguard democratic institutions and the welfare of the people. It is all too easy to find evidence of pervasive civic ignorance and apathy along with charges that graduates emerge from schools with little or nothing in the way of civic knowledge, understanding or dispositions.

The Annenberg Civics Knowledge Survey (2019) found that only about a third of Americans can name all three branches of government, a quarter can name one, and a fifth of the population cannot name any. Shapiro and Brown (2018) noted less than a quarter of eighth-graders met the standard of proficient or above on the National Education Progress civics exam. A 2019 American Bar survey found additional, troubling gaps in basic government literacy. A third of survey respondents believed that the Declaration of Independence gave women the right to vote, and 20% did not think the First Amendment protected freedom of the press or the right to peaceful assembly; a third of respondents between the ages of 18 to 44 had heard of the commander in chief—but could not correctly identify the president in that role. So severe is the shortage of civics instruction in schools that in 2018 public school students and parents filed a federal lawsuit against Rhode Island charging that its schools failed in teaching students to "'function productively as civic participants' capable of voting, serving on a jury and understanding the nation's political and economic life" (Goldstein, 2018, para. 4).

Etzioni (2020) observed that because citizens lack understanding of their democratic rights and responsibilities, they now "treat each other as if we lived in different nations and not in one union" (para. 1). Dangerously, a largely disengaged and divided citizenry failed to hold government to meaningful account, resulting in a divided and dysfunctional executive branch and Congress content to stand by and watch as a global pandemic inflicted hundreds of thousands of needless deaths upon the population, and destroyed both the daily and economic life of the nation. Massive protests reminiscent of the Civil Rights era spotlighted both inequities and disenfranchisements almost daily. And, obvious authoritarian trends among political leaders as well as increasing and shocking chasms between "haves" and "have-nots" illustrated that some countries reached the danger zone Jefferson foresaw. Educators have no choice but to make reform of civic education policy a priority if public education is to nurture citizens capable of safeguarding their own welfare and that of the democracy.

Tipping Point

The United States did not reach the moment when civic education has emerged as a critical issue for policymakers because no one noticed, cared, or tried to intervene. For decades, scholars and researchers warned of troubling trends and sought educational interventions to undermine them. Nearly a decade ago, the Campaign for the Civic Mission of Schools (2011) summarized in its *Guardian of Democracy report*,

> It is the current crisis of America that great civic exertions are required of a divided people. Our bonds are strained, our civility has worn thin, and our sense of common purpose has weakened, just as the need for cooperation on large challenges grows urgent.
>
> *(p. 9)*

The United States seems dangerously close to a point of no return in maintaining the republic that Benjamin Franklin, one of the Founding Fathers of the nation, reportedly said is ours—if we can keep it.

Earlier movement toward educational improvement seemed modest, but recently some efforts intensified. Shapiro and Brown (2018) reported that 31 states required only a half-year of civics or U.S. government education whereas ten states had no civics requirement at all. However, they also noted an emerging trend as 17 states implemented graduation policies requiring students to pass the U.S. citizenship exam—the same required for foreign applicants for citizenship. Arizona and North Dakota were the first to pass the requirement, in 2015 (Zubrzycki, 2016). While an exit exam is a relatively painless addition to the curriculum since students can be told to study independently, Kahne (2015) and others asserted that knowledge about government is a necessary but glaringly insufficient element of effective and engaged citizenship.

As divisiveness and government callousness regarding social needs have increased since the 2016 presidential election, some states have begun to show greater interest in more serious reform. Policymakers in particular have been busy proposing change. According to Sawchuk (2019), "More than 80 pieces of civic education legislation were introduced across 30-odd states in the 2018–19 legislative session .... And [since 2018], the National Conference of State Legislatures counted nearly 115 civic education-related bills" (para. 4).

Although a great chasm often exists between proposal and passage of legislation, clearly much continues to happen in the policy arena. Stakeholders pursuing policy change will find numerous organizations and reports eager to offer ideas on best policy and practices. However, when policy is translated to practice, results too often produce outcomes far removed from intentions (Hinchey & Konkol, 2018). Regarding citizenship education, the authors believe the stakes are too high not to do everything possible to ensure new policies actually steer classroom practice in desirable, intended directions.

Our purpose for this chapter is to explicate major factors we believe are likely to cause disconnects between the intentions of policy and the outcomes of practice in order to help policymakers and other stakeholders safeguard against them. First, we survey practices being widely promoted as tools to promote informed and engaged citizenship. Then, we identify threats to effective implementation of multiple strategies. If these threats can be forestalled, the success of well-crafted policy can not only help to restore eroded democratic norms and dispositions, but also help American society move closer to its historically aspirational goals.

Core Elements and Best Practices in Citizenship Education

Effective civic education has three interrelated strands:

1. knowledge: having information about the political system, the government, citizen rights and responsibilities, and so on;
2. skills: the ability to discriminate between facts and propaganda (or "fake news") and the ability to engage in civil discourse about contentious issues, and so on; and,
3. dispositions: the inclination to translate information and skills into real world, engaged action like volunteering, voting, or running for public office.

Each strand prompted multiple ideas and reports from think tanks, policymakers, scholars, and the education community about how to improve educational outcomes, including specific suggestions for practice.

Some suggestions for improvement largely reflect six "best practices" outlined in the widely collaborative and highly influential *Guardian of Democracy* (2011) report. These are classroom instruction in related subjects (government, history, law, etc.); classroom discussion of current events and controversial issues; service learning; extracurricular activities; student participation in school governance; and simulations of democratic processes and procedures. Researchers at the Brown Center (Hansen et al., 2018) suggested additions to this list, including news media literacy; action civics; social–emotional learning; and school climate reform. The authors noted that the most popular strategies currently employed include traditional coursework and discussion of current events—very much "business as usual" for schools, as is student government as rehearsal for such practices as voting and holding office. Increased policy and practice interest has focused on activities in or involving the community beyond the schoolhouse, especially service learning. Action civics programs that involve students in youth participatory action research (YPAR) receive increased attention in policy circles and within the schoolhouse walls. Action civics programs provide students opportunities to research an issue of local concern and devise practical strategies for improvement.

Threats to Improvement

We argue that several of these pedagogical strategies are failing in practice and that others are threatened by largely unacknowledged factors. To maximize the success of policy to influence practice, we believe that both the policymaking and education practitioner and preparation communities would be wise to take every step imaginable to ameliorate the following four threats to effective reform.

Threat #1: Failure to Respect and Value Young People

Citizenship education intends to work to help students develop the dispositions necessary to proactively contribute to the health and welfare of their communities and to be actors inclined to invest in personal efforts they understand to be valuable to a democracy. In a summary of the characteristics to be nurtured in civic education, the Center for Educational Equity (2019) noted the importance of *efficacy* or *agency*: the belief that one has the power to make a difference. This belief correlates strongly with civic action. Educating students to become engaged citizens, then, includes helping them to see themselves as agents with the power to make a difference in the world.

However, as John Dewey (1916/2018) noted long ago when discussing the relationship between educating for citizenship and health of the democracy, "The required beliefs cannot be hammered in; the needed attitudes cannot be plastered on …. We never educate directly, but indirectly by means of the environment" (pp. 14, 22). Simply *telling* students they have agency is useless if they are powerless in their environment. And, unfortunately, the school environment often strips students of any power at all. Herding young people in large numbers into classrooms means that school leaders can legitimately claim to need policies emphasizing keeping order, allowing them to routinely hide behind that claim as an excuse for draconian control. Students' constitutional rights, which they do not leave at the schoolhouse door, are nevertheless routinely trampled when student newspapers are censored. Although issues like potential libel and dangerous bullying may call for some intervention, school officials routinely simply prohibit discussions of topics they fear might hurt the school's "brand" or upset adult stakeholders. Schools have additionally worked to punish students who miss school to participate in protests, even when the protests are passionate cries for gun control in a time when school shootings are increasingly common.

Students of color and students in under-resourced contexts are typically expected to be compliant, and even white students or those in relatively privileged or abundantly resourced contexts are expected to be "nice," to "toe the line," and to "not make waves" by showing any signs of independent agency. Thus, rather than encourage students to understand themselves as citizens with rights who have a stake in their communities and government, some policymakers and educators treat students as subjects who are not to question the status quo or do anything to upset the proverbial apple cart. And this is precisely the situation Dewey (1916/2018) warned about: lessons in classrooms about constitutional rights cannot be "plastered on." In autocratic schools, the environment teaches unquestioning obedience and passivity, lessons diametrically opposed to creating an active and engaged citizenry.

It should not be this way. Teen power in particular is a vastly underappreciated resource. The BBC highlighted the accomplishments of "[f]ive teens who changed the world" (Day, 2019). These include Greta Thunberg, climate change activist; Malala Yousafzai, the youngest person ever to win the Nobel Peace Prize; Emma González, whose efforts promoted eventual Florida legislation increasing gun regulation; Jack Andraka, whose pancreatic cancer detection invention is awaiting FDA approval and marketing (Perez-Hernandez, 2018); and Amika George, whose efforts resulted in the UK government providing free feminine sanitary products in all English schools and colleges, effective 2020 (Adams, 2020). Nor is it only teens who can make a difference. William Winslow has worked on ending childhood hunger since he learned about it in first grade in 2013 and persuaded his mother to take him to a grocery store, then persuaded shoppers to buy food to send home with students during spring break (Nargi, 2020). In addition to organizing *Food Drive Kids*, Winslow has collected more than 55,000 pounds of food and raised $63,000 in the years since.

Despite such accomplishments, young people are routinely subjected to adult ridicule when they are perceived as taking on more than adults think they can, as evidenced when former U.S. President Donald Trump advised Greta Thunberg, who had been named *Time* magazine's Person of the Year, to learn to manage her anger, go to a movie, and "Chill Greta, Chill!" (Taylor, 2019, para. 4). Too often, big ideas from young people are met by amusement, or even scorn, by adults who warn them against being "too big for their britches."

Lessons on having a voice and the ability to make a difference will fall flat in such policy and school climates. If educators expect engaged and optimistic citizens to emerge from environments that denigrate authentic civic engagement, they are spitting in the wind. To nurture the citizens necessary to nurture a representative democracy, as Dewey said, the school must become a microcosm of the society we hope to create.

Threat #2: Failure to Provide Meaningful Experiences

Failure to take student agency seriously often leads to not engaging students in the genuinely meaningful and authentic work such as service learning and action research. Ensuring high quality education experiences is particularly challenging in an environment that gives civic education short shrift by lack of curricular emphasis, or by less visible elective status, or by complete exclusion. But even when potentially engaging pedagogies are adopted, they often fail to effectively cultivate the hoped-for sense of agency and commitment to democratic values in students. Rather than provide real world experiences, their superficiality or implicit exclusivity render them meaningless. That is, even the most well-intended attempts to implement "best" pedagogical strategies can produce experiences that are diluted and inauthentic, or in some cases, socially and culturally tone-deaf, or even outright racist.

Connor and Erickson (2017) explained that when service-learning requirements were linked to the curriculum, they provided students with the opportunity to develop their creativity, personal responsibility, understanding of social problems, familiarity with cultural perspectives, and the systemic marginalization of some populations. However, executed poorly, such experiences are counterproductive. For some students in some education contexts, service learning or community service requirements amount to little more than volunteerism; for others, they mean only a desperate, albeit relatively benign, attempt to log enough random but mandated "service" hours. Like many other elements of sterile "seat time" curriculum, the service requirement can become one more meaningless box to check off. Worse, when volunteerism amounts to perceived charity, as in cases in which relatively privileged students step out of their comfort zones to aid "the great unwashed" it can actually cause harm. Students' service requirements can reinforce deficit perspectives and negative stereotypes about the people or populations supposedly being served (Jones, 2002).

Mitchell and colleagues (2012) analyzed how unintended problems with service requirements arise. Although their worked focused on the context of higher education, the analysis can apply to public school settings. They noted that service learning is most often implemented by white faculty with white students in predominantly white institutions; that the language of service learning, such as "underprivileged," reinforces stereotypes; that experiences often frame problems like drug addiction or homelessness as individual problems rather than the result of social and political forces; and that racial identity development, including their own, is rarely discussed. In such circumstances, students' actual experiences undermine or even contradict the democratic understandings that the requirement may have been intended to promote. In contrast, to effectively promote true democratic engagement requires that service learning and volunteer experiences be explicitly connected to relevant curriculum and thoughtfully discussed with teachers and peers.

Other pedagogies can similarly be perverted in practice so that they undermine genuinely democratic impulses. McFarland and Starmanns (2009) found that student government, which theoretically provides practice for serving in leadership roles and participating in such civic rituals as voting, is by design inauthentic. Few public schools actually cede any real power to such bodies or any voice in administrative and faculty decision making, especially in schools with a majority of low-income students and/or students of color, while elections can sometimes devolve into popularity contests. Similarly, in-school elections mirroring state and national elections are also inauthentic because the votes are not real and do not count, whereas if students worked on campaigns for their preferred candidates they would actually be engaging in authentic activity. Action research projects that theoretically help students develop strategies for real world change are rendered meaningless when they result in posters rather than live presentations to, or meetings with, appropriate real world leaders.

Intended civics lessons can lose their meaning when some student populations do not see their experience reflected in those lessons. Despite what we presume are their best intentions, teachers sometimes fail to recognize course assignments or experiences that privilege some students' experiences, cultural contexts, social and intellectual capital, and funds of knowledge while failing to recognize, include, or actively reflect those of others. Too often, assignments reflect a culturally White and socially dominant perspective, heedless of the reality that White students no longer comprise the majority of the U.S. student population (NCES, 2020).

For example, a recent public Facebook post illustrated an incident that involved a history assignment requiring family immigration stories, to which a student responded by rewriting the assignment to reflect the fact that her family arrived as enslaved people (Reneau, 2020). The embedded assumption was that of the dominant cultural narrative, evident in much of the prevailing U.S. history curriculum and state mandated content standards, that the ancestors of every student in the class journeyed to the country by choice and that America was the land of opportunity for all who arrived. Nowhere in that narrative are places for the descendants of the enslaved, the Indigenous, or the undocumented. In this case, which spread through social media like wildfire, fortunately the teacher recognized the assignment's implicit bias and vowed to do better. Although the eventual outcome was positive, far too many such assignments go unnoticed, except by the dutiful students who complete them while gritting their teeth.

Students are also taught that schoolhouse lessons are meaningless when school authorities insist on keeping the world outside at bay, even when critical elements of their lived experience are involved. For example, at a time when protests seemed to occur daily involving critical issues such as school shootings and police brutality, some educators actually punished students who take part in public demonstrations (Williams, 2018). Teachers, for their part, sometimes purposefully avoid topics with the faintest whiff of controversy, and state curriculum standards rarely mandate that students engage with controversial topics in authentic ways; and this despite the fact that a key element of civic education is learning how to engage in respectful discourse with others holding opposing viewpoints. Facilitating difficult discussions requires a great deal of sensitivity and skill on the part of the teacher and also support from school leaders.

Threat #3: Failure to Honor Teacher Professionalism

The history of education reform is littered with good policies promoting effective classroom strategies. Ultimately, however, many reforms failed because teachers charged with implementing new pedagogies were given little or no support. Contemporary ideas for reform are likely to fail as well if appropriate professional development isn't a key part of new policy.

Engaging students meaningfully with the world outside the classroom inevitably means bringing controversies inside that are likely to excite opposing passions in students and that must be handled carefully. Zimmerman and Robertson (2017) noted, teachers are not prepared for such important work:

> [t]hanks to poor preparation, some teachers have not acquired the background knowledge or the pedagogical skills—or both—to lead in-depth discussions of hot-button political questions. Most of all, though, teachers have often lacked the professional autonomy and freedom to do so.
>
> *(para. 6)*

Some principals and parents prefer that schools operate quietly, maintaining the fiction that public education is a value free, apolitical undertaking. Like "good" students, teachers are enjoined from "rocking the boat." Steady efforts to control and deskill teachers mean that they remain largely unprepared to effectively implement many reform strategies being promoted; notably, such efforts include narrowing of both teacher education and PK-12 curriculum.

Perhaps not surprisingly, Will (2017) cited an *Education Week* Research Center survey that found that in an intensely divisive and bitter political context, only 44% of respondents said they had been adequately prepared to facilitate civil discussions of controversial topics, while 23% reported receiving no training at all. Neither, said most teachers, had administrators offered any such guidance. Although many teachers reported that they tackle controversy in the classroom despite the lack of preparation, they are largely lone agents bucking strong currents against a curriculum more inclusive than that reflected in highly circumscribed, traditional texts. For example, although it was not eventually passed, a 2019 bill in Arizona would have required a "classroom code of conduct" that would have

> [prohibited] teachers and teaching assistants in public schools from a whole host of activities. These range from endorsing or opposing candidates and legislation, to introducing any "partial political issue that is not germane to the topic of the course or academic subject being taught."
>
> *(Fischer, 2019, paras. 3–4)*

Ultimately, teachers might be fired for introducing any topic in any classroom that might speciously be called "political." Decades of efforts to keep evolution out of the science curriculum illustrate how permeable the boundary between political and non-political can be. A teacher introducing any topic or text someone doesn't like is always subject to charges of "advocacy," no matter the factual background or actual teacher neutrality on a topic. Westheimer (2006) reported that teachers suffered suspension or other disciplinary action for classroom discussions on such topics as the Iraq war and the Patriot Act. Controversy is easily sparked, ubiquitously unwelcome, and sometimes harshly punished in U.S. public schools, and teachers know it.

With education's legacy as "women's work" and even often considered primarily a child care service that allows parents to work outside the home, disrespect for teaching as a profession and subsequent efforts to control both teachers and curriculum have a long history. Teachers have struggled against such trends at least since activist Margaret Haley pioneered organizing of the Chicago Federation of Teachers in 1898, and they remained evident throughout the 20th century.

In the post-recession austerity era beginning in 2009, school curriculum had been so severely narrowed that teachers are told what to teach, how to teach it, and, to add insult to injury, themselves evaluated on how well students perform on standardized tests (Nuñez, 2015). Moving vital professional decisions about what is taught, by whom, to whom, and in what ways demotes teachers from professionals to technicians.

Even a partial list of factors advancing this trend makes clear the scope of efforts that have combined to forcefully attack teacher autonomy and professionalism: the forced use of scripted curricula and pedagogic processes such as Open Court, Reading First, and Success for All (Fitz & Nikoladis, 2019); high-stakes testing associated with standards-based reform (David, 2011); the influx of Teach for America-style part-time training programs and the prevalence of under or altogether unlicensed teachers in classrooms (Nuñez et al., 2015); the rampant and ill-conceived "Value Added Model" of teacher evaluation that links student standardized assessment scores to teacher evaluation (Michie, 2019); the diversion of resources into charter and private enterprise education schemes and concurrent divestment in public education (Magner & Bacon, 2019); and the removal of educational foundations coursework from teacher and administrator preparation programs and the dismantling of Social Foundations of Education departments in colleges of education (Tozer, 2017).

The importance of teachers and school leaders who do not have adequate initial preparation or continued professional development to do the kinds of citizenship education that so many reports and theorists say is important cannot be overstated. Disagreements about the nature and content of teacher preparation and professional support are not new, but how teacher preparation and professional support have been reconceptualized, particularly since 2009 when Linda Darling-Hammond and her colleagues at SCALE first developed the EdTPA to assess preservice teaching candidates, is troubling (Will, 2019). The EdTPA alone caused a narrowing of the initial teacher preparation curriculum, which critics say forces colleges of education to "teach to the test" instead of providing students with the kinds of coursework and practical experiences that will benefit them far more in actual classrooms (Cronenberg et al., 2016). Consequently, colleges of education have been forced to make difficult decisions about which courses and experiences will best help teacher candidates pass the high stakes assessment versus which help them craft creative or critical lessons and activities.

Not surprisingly, the increased focus on ensuring PK-12 students do well on requisite standardized assessments has resulted in coursework for teacher candidates emphasizing core subjects like reading and math as well as how to prepare their future students for intensified focus on those assessments. This means that, even if classroom teachers did miraculously suddenly gain the curricular or pedagogic freedom to make good on the promises of the proven civic education reform practices now being promoted, new teachers in particular lack the skill to successfully launch such localized and difficult pedagogies.

Threat #4: Failure to Acknowledge and Accommodate the Political Context of American Education

When specific practices in citizenship education are promoted as "best," rarely is there discussion of the question "Best for what purpose?" The facile answer would be "to ensure schools nurture good citizens." However, different people have very different ideas about what the characteristics of a "good citizen" are, and many theorists have proposed frameworks for considering differences (Hinchey & Konkol, 2018). And yet, despite acknowledged differences on such issues as whether a good citizen simply gives money or more ambitiously gives time and effort to the community, there is near universal agreement that citizens must be *patriotic*. However, *patriotism* is itself a contested term integral to vastly different political worldviews, so that the issue of how to enact civic education is at heart a political one. To ignore the ideologies underlying specific reform strategies risks having specific pedagogical strategies co-opted or fiercely resisted.

For our purposes, Westheimer's (2006) distinction between *authoritarian patriotism* and *democratic patriotism* is particularly useful. Whereas *authoritarian patriotism* requires individuals to display fealty to the leader and obedience to the government, *democratic patriotism* is reflected through individual commitment to "the nation, its symbols, and its political leaders, but also to each of its citizens and their welfare" (p. 3). Essentially, the authoritarian approach is a conservative "love-it-or-leave-it" approach, and the democratic approach is a liberal/progressive "citizen as loyal critic" approach. One obvious example of how each conception influences curriculum is the longstanding dispute over whether lessons in American history should continue to focus on triumphs (say, the outcome of World War II) as authoritarian proponents argue, or should acknowledge shames (say, the internment of Japanese American citizens during that war) in the hope of guarding against mistakes of the past, as democratic proponents argue. We believe that in the area of citizenship education, the most obvious and dangerous disconnect is likely to be that between policy intended to replace an authoritarian approach with a democratic one and the perversion of related pedagogies.

For decades, the authoritarian approach has governed public education, so that much of the current demand for reform comes from proponents of the democratic approach. Many of the reforms seek to connect students with their communities in order to cultivate concern for citizens unlike themselves and spark efforts to improve issues ranging from local recycling availability to demands for shifts in government policy on gun control. Such reforms are supported by multiple organizations using multiple approaches to what is known as *action civics*:

> an experiential, youth-centered approach to civic education—to create a world that invites young people to take collective action inside and outside the classroom—transforming their schools, neighborhoods and cities.
> *(National Action Civics Collaborative, 2020, para. 1)*

Many organizations supporting this democratic approach through a variety of projects belong to the National Action Civics Collaborative (NACC). Its website allows those with interest to explore efforts to move civic education from the traditional, text-based approach glorifying the status quo to one promoting active engagement with history, issues, and leaders in the interest of positive change.

It is essential for supporters of such efforts to understand that stakeholders embracing an authoritarian concept of patriotism will tolerate such reforms only so long as they are rendered ineffective in practice by being divorced from real world outcomes. Among others, Hess (2020), a prominent conservative, warned that implicit ideological differences between civic education advocates threaten the process of translating policy to practice by sparking controversy over specific pedagogical strategies. He notes that the real challenge lies in how this advocacy manifests in practice, as "translating this [heightened interest in civics education] into real schools and classrooms," as that is the place where "submerged disagreements suddenly reemerge, provoking cultural clashes that swamp nuanced discussions of curricula and instruction" (para. 2).

Hess is unlikely to support movement toward a democratic approach, but his point is well-taken. When "the rubber hits the road" of actual classroom activity, clashes are quick to emerge.

More specifically, when efforts to affect the world outside the classroom become too real, reaction is swift. When the democratic project Generation Citizen reached widespread acceptance in Oklahoma, critics quickly argued for shutting it down:

> Generation Citizen is a social justice organization using civics education as a Trojan Horse to take over Oklahoma's K-12 school system. It can, should, and must be banished from Oklahoma's schools—and so should all "civic engagement," "experiential learning," and "social justice education."
> *(Randall, 2019, para. 15)*

Heading off any threat to the status quo is a common goal by those that oppose progressive civic education; no youth meddling in issues, no hint that the fabric of American society might be inequitable. Adults who see "patriotic" Americans as compliant have a menu of charges to level against young critics, claiming "that students don't understand the issue, that young people are angry and rude, that they're un-American, and that they are parroting what other adults have told them" (Prothero, 2019, para. 27).

The political divide permeates all of the threats articulated above. Students disrespected in schools and made nearly powerless are conditioned to accept their role as a "deliberate and complicit populace" unlikely to provoke or participate in dissent, especially if they hear little about successful protest movements of the past. Students can engage in research of a local issue or run for student government —as long as they aren't given any reason to think that they actually have any power. Teachers with less and less power and ability to control their classrooms are more and more constrained from introducing discussion of topics and issues that actually matter in the lived world.

Policymakers who wish to support democratic reform need to recognize the deeply embedded political issue and defend against perversion of their intent when new policies are translated to classroom action. For example, service learning as a means of cultivating empathy and active interest in equity is perverted when students simply hang around a soup kitchen for an artificial number of hours rather than explore why many local residents go hungry. Youth participatory action research is sterilized when it ends not in meetings with powerbrokers but with a poster competition rewarded with a blue ribbon rather than real change. And when students do take their work into the public sphere on their own, it is cheapened by rampant disrespect of youth permeating typical school climate. As Prothero (2019) illustrates, youth are often encouraged to take an active role in political and community issues at the same time as they are derided for their efforts. As one youth activist noted,

> "I'm often viewed as, 'Oh, how cute, you're a 16-year-old kid,'" said [one teen] gun-control advocate. "I don't want to be seen that way. I know my facts. I want to do the same things the adults want to do: I want to advocate for legislation."
>
> *(para. 4)*

Disrespect for youth is part and parcel of a political worldview that interprets youth activism, like any activism, as a threat to the status quo and to the conservative *love-it-or-leave-it* ideology. If disrespect in the school isn't strong enough to undermine students' sense of agency, then it must be intensified in the world outside.

Exactly as we were drafting this section on politics, the embedded partisan divide we were describing suddenly became explicit in national discourse when a series of interrelated events led then President Donald Trump to announce he was creating a commission to promote "patriotic education" and a grant to develop a "pro-American curriculum" (Wise, 2020, para. 1). In response to rampant social justice activism, the President sided with conservatives in protecting Confederate monuments, branding Black Lives Matter a hate group, outlawing diversity training in federal agencies, and denouncing the *New York Times*

1619 curriculum. His rhetoric in doing so is classic language of the conservative authoritarian right, which insists on American exceptionalism and denying that the United States treated any of its citizens inequitably, its immigrants unjustly, or its Indigenous population inhumanely. He portrayed efforts toward a more inclusive curriculum as an effort to paint the country as "wicked and racist," launched by "Marxist" activists promoting "left-wing rioting and mayhem" through "left-wing indoctrination in our schools" (Crowley, 2020, paras. 8–9). Trump's call for patriotic education is an example of how attempts to create authentic civic education experiences can be met with powerful opposition. The former president may not have the power to impose a national curriculum, but he advanced awareness of the curricular struggle, and multiplied and energized opponents to democratic reforms as well.

Taking Action

Stakeholders interested in substantive reform must take care to build a clearly coherent and effective program as a safeguard against the many ways opponents who would reify the status quo will find to undermine their efforts. Opposition to meaningful change toward authentic civics education is real, vocal, and powerful. Any proponent of the conception of civic education that Westheimer terms *democratic*, a conception that promotes the goal of educating engaged citizens prepared to hold leaders to account for overreach, must anticipate and be prepared to deliver a well-articulated defense against the politically motivated opposition they may encounter.

The most critical factor in civic education policies is not lack of well-researched, potentially effective pedagogies: it is that the policy arena continues to be contested and divided terrain. Designing and implementing coherent school policy and practice is exceedingly difficult in a social and political climate fraught with discord and discontent. However, school leaders have little choice but to guide local decisions and policies if civic education is to improve—as it must, if citizens are to safeguard the democracy as intended. We suggest the following starting points, along with the observation that the more stakeholders who participate in designing a new program, the more defenders the program will have.

First, it is imperative to engage the school community in a process to determine *which* approach to civic education will guide its efforts. Without a clearly defined goal, programs are likely to remain the same hodge-podge of contradictory practices that have historically accomplished little—lip service for diverse perspectives undermined by an authoritarian history text, for example. Asking whether a specific strategy or text will address or undermine specific goals before adoption is the only way to ensure a coherent program. To avoid this central political question is not to be neutral: it is to abandon the responsibility to provide an effective, rather than an illusory, civic education program.

The word *program* is equally important. School leaders need to make space for a multi-pronged approach, not just a single required course in social studies. Civic knowledge and principles need to be embedded throughout the curriculum, over multiple years. When opportunities for service work are included, school leaders must ensure that opportunities connect to the curriculum and school culture. If they appear instead as a gift to "others" perceived to be "less than," they will likely do more harm than good.

School climate is no less essential: all school personnel must model the traits they espouse as essential to later citizenship. Such modeling includes genuine respect for all community members. Students and their concerns must be recognized, respected, and given space for meaningful, rather than token, action within and outside of the school. It also includes school leaders respecting teachers' professionalism, offering them real voice in shaping the school community and its programs as well as genuine classroom autonomy. All members of the school community must be free to dialogue about difficult issues in a respectful atmosphere without fearing retribution or demonization. Adults must model compromise and the ability not to confuse speakers' opposing perspective with their worth as human beings. In short, to avoid the counterproductive "Do as I say, not as I do" phenomenon, all adults in the school must routinely model the habits and attitudes they hope to inculcate in students.

A daunting task. But the journey of a thousand miles ….

References

Adams, R. (2020, January 17). Free period products to be available in schools and colleges in England. *The Guardian*. www.theguardian.com/education/2020/jan/18/free-p eriod-products-to-be-available-in-schools-and-colleges-in-england.

American Bar Association. (2019). *Executive summary. ABA Survey of Civic Literacy*. www. americanbar.org/content/dam/aba/administrative/public_education/ABASurveyOfCivi cLiteracy-summary.pdf.

Annenberg Public Policy Center. (2019). *Annenberg Civic Knowledge Survey*. www.annen bergpublicpolicycenter.org/political-communication/civics-knowledge-survey/.

Campaign for the Civic Mission of Schools. (2011). *Guardian of democracy: The civic mission of schools*. http://cdn.annenbergpublicpolicycenter.org/wp-content/uploads/Guardia nofDemocracy_report_final-12.pdf.

Center for Educational Equity. (2019). *Research summary: Values, dispositions and attitudes*. Teachers College, Columbia University. www.civxnow.org/sites/default/files/basic_page/ Research%20Summary-Values%20Dispositions%20 and%20Attitudes%2012-2013-18.pdf.

Conner, J., & Erickson, J. (2017). When does service-learning work? Contact theory and service-learning courses in higher education. *Michigan Journal of Community Service Learning*, 23(2), 53–65.

Cronenberg, S., Harrison, D., Korson, S., Jones, A., Murray-Everett, N. C., Parrish, M., & Johnston-Parsons, M. (2016). Trouble with the edTPA: Lessons learned from a narrative self-study. *Journal of Inquiry & Action in Education*, 8(1), 109–134.

Crowley, M. (2020, September 17). Trump calls for 'Patriotic Education' to defend American history from the left. *New York Times*. www.nytimes.com/2020/09/17/politics/trump-patriotic-education.html.

David, J. L. (2011). Research says ... high stakes testing narrows the curriculum. *Educational Leadership*, 68(6), 78–80.

Day, H. (2019). Five teens who changed the world. BBC. www.bbc.co.uk/bbcthree/article/0e9e80de-62cb-4782-a26f1cd480d28f26.

Dewey, J. (1916/2018). *Democracy and education*. (P.H. Hinchey, Ed.). Myers Education Press.

Etzioni, A. (2020). America and the dark days of social divisiveness. *The National Interest*. https://nationalinterest.org/feature/america-and-dark-days-social-divisiveness-164677.

Fischer, H. (2019). New initiative drive would block Arizona teachers from classroom political advocacy. Tucson.com. https://tucson.com/news/local/new-initiative-drive-would-block-arizona-teachers-from-classroom-political-advocacy/article_b0f62820-62711-52ca-9297-9293d0fc92ff717.html.

Fitz, J. A., & Nikolaidis, A. C. (2019). A democratic critique of scripted curriculum. *Journal of Curriculum Studies*, 52(2), 195–213.

Goldstein, D. (2018, November 28). Are civics lessons a constitutional right? This student is suing for them. *New York Times*. www.nytimes.com/2018/11/28/us/civics-rhode-island-schools.html.

Hansen, M., Levesque, E., Valant, J., & Quintero, D. (2018). *The 2018 Brown Center report on American education: How well are American students learning?* www.brookings.edu/wp-content/uploads/2018/06/2018-Brown-Center-Report-on-American-Education_FINAL1.pdf.

Hess, F. M. (2020, March 25). Where Left and Right agree on civics education, and where they don't: An introductory note. Education Next. www.educationnext.org/where-left-right-agree-civics-education-where-they-dont/.

Hinchey, P. H. H., & Konkol, P. J. (2018). *Getting to where we meant to be*. Myers Education Press.

Jefferson, T. (1778). *Bill for the more general profusion of knowledge*. National Archives: Founders Online. https://founders.archives.gov/documents/Jefferson/01-02-02-0132-0004-0079.

Jefferson, T. (1816, January 6). *Letter to Charles Yancey*. National Archives: Founders Online. https://founders.archives.gov/documents/jefferson/03-09-0209.

Jones, S. R. (2002). The underside of service learning. *About Campus*, 7(4), 10–15.

Kahne, J. (2015, April 4). Why are we teaching democracy like a game show? *Education Week*. www.edweek.org/ew/articles/2015/04/22/why-are-we-teaching-democracy-like-a.html.

Magner, M., & Bacon, E. (2019, July 8). The secretary of school choice. *CQ Magazine*, 17–27.

McFarland, D., & Starmanns, C.E. (2009). Inside student government: The variable quality of high school student councils. *Teachers College Record*, 111(1), 27–54.

Mitchell, T. D., Donahue, D. M., & Young-Law, C. (2012). Service learning as a pedagogy of whiteness. *Equity and Excellence in Education*, 45(4), 612–629.

Michie, G. (2019). *Same as it never was: Notes on teacher's return to the classroom*. Teachers College Press.

Nargi, L. (2020, April 14). Food drive organizer is "passionate" about helping hungry kids. *The Washington Post*: G5.

National Action Civics Collaborative (2020). https://actioncivicscollaborative.org/about-us/.

National Center for Education Statistics (NCES). (2020). *Racial/ethnic enrollment in public schools*. https://nces.ed.gov/programs/coe/indicator_cge.asp.

Nuñez, I. (2015). Teacher bashing and teacher deskilling. In M. F. He, B. D. Schultz, & W. H. Schubert (Eds.) *The SAGE guide to curriculum in education* (pp. 174–182). SAGE.

Nuñez, I., Michie, G., & Konkol, P. (2015). *Worth striking for: Why education policy is every teacher's concern (Lessons from Chicago)*. Teachers College Press.

Perez-Hernandez, D. (2018). Mission CISD students hear from nationally recognized scientist Jack Andraka. *The Monitor*. www.themonitor.com/2018/01/21mission-cisd-students-hear-from-nationally-recognized-scientist-jack-andraka/.

Prothero, A. (2019, October 4). Participate, but know your place: Young civic activists get mixed messages. *Education Week*, 39(08), 1, 14.

Randall, D. (2019). Oklahoma education agency promotes progressive activism masquerading as civics. Oklahoma Council of Public Affairs. www.ocpathink.org/post/oklahoma-education-agency-promotes-progressive-activism-masquerading-as-civics.

Reneau, A. (2020, September 2). Student's response to a school assignment bravely challenges its cultural assumptions. Upworthy. www.upworthy.com/students-response-to-ancestry-assignment.

Shapiro, S., & Brown, C. (2018). *A look at civics education in the United States*. American Federation of Teachers. www.aft.org/ae/summer2018/shapiro_brown.

Sawchuk, S. (2019, June 26). How 3 states are digging in on civics education. *Education Week*. www.edweek.org/ew/section/multimedia/how-3-states-are-digging-in-on.html.

Taylor, D. B. (2019, December 12). Trump mocks Greta Thunberg on Twitter, and she jabs back. *The New York Times*. www.nytimes.com/2019/12/12/us/politics/greta-thunberg-trump.html.

Tozer, S. (2017). Social Foundations of Education as an unwelcome counter-narrative and as praxis. *Educational Studies*, 54(1), 89–98.

Westheimer, J. (2006). Politics and patriotism in education. *Phi Delta Kappan*, 87(8), 608–620.

Will, M. (2017, April 4). Survey: Teachers talk politics to students, despite divisive atmosphere. *Education Week*. www.edweek.org/ew/articles/2017/04/05/survey-national-politics-causing-classroom-divisions.html.

Will, M. (2019, December 10). Researchers: Stop using EdTPA scores in teacher-certification decisions. *Education Week*. https://blogs.edweek.org/teachers/teaching_now/2019/12/edtpa_scores_teacher_certification_decisions.html.

Williams, D. (2018, February 21). Schools threaten to punish students who join walkouts over gun control. CNN. www.cnn.com/2018/02/21/us/student-walkout-punishment-trnd/index.html.

Wise, A. (2020, September 19). Trump announces 'patriotic education' commission, a largely political move. National Public Radio. www.npr.org/2020/09/17/914127266/trump-announces-patriotic-education-commission-a-largely-political-move?fbclid=IwAR1nD2kiEiRk-0nbsAzcdREbIwvmMmO0RBThX0g238Dj MEeZJn8In53Akmw.

Zimmerman, J., & Robertson, E. (2017, April 26). The case for contentious curricula. *The Atlantic*. www.theatlantic.com/education/archive/2017/04/the-case-for-contentious-classrooms/524268/?gclid=EAIaIQobChMIl_rnsLL_6wIVD43ICh0luAy5EAAYASAAEgKmdfD_BwE.

Zubrzycki, J. (2016, June 7). Thirteen states now require grads to pass citizenship test. Curriculum Matters (blog), *Education Week*. http://blogs.edweek.org/edweek/curriculum/2016/06/fourteen_states_now_require_gr.html.

4
BROWN VERSUS BOARD DID NOT WORK

Finding a New Pathway to Educational Justice

Ryan W. Coughlan

Most schoolchildren in the United States learn about the Supreme Court's 1954 declaration in *Brown v. Board of Education* that "in the field of public education, the doctrine of 'separate but equal' has no place." Despite this court decision ending legalized segregation, few public school students in this country experience integrated schooling. In fact, research shows that school segregation is on the rise across the country (Frankenberg et al., 2019).

For the purposes of this chapter, I use *desegregate* and *integrate* in distinct ways. *Desegregate* specifically refers to ending segregation and bringing people of different races together in the same town, district, or school. *Integration* goes beyond desegregation and requires the meaningful, equitable, and just treatment of people of different races within the same town, district, or school. It is worth noting that I use *segregate* to reference the inverse of *desegregate*.

When advocating for desegregation, many scholars and organizers emphasize that it is one of the most effective tools for closing the racial achievement gap (Mickelson, 2016). More often than not, the current conversation around persistent school segregation focuses on the negative impact on Black and Latinx students who are frequently isolated in under-resourced districts, schools, and classrooms. What policymakers have failed to acknowledge is that persistent school segregation's effect on US society is even more insidious—in addition to trammeling the educational prospects of many children, segregation also contributes to the perpetuation of a culture of White supremacy that upholds systemic racism in the nation. School segregation creates a barrier between children of different races that fuels the development of harmful stereotypes. It validates curricula that elevate the voices and achievements of White people while muting those of others, demonstrating to children that society directly and indirectly supports a racial caste system.

Purpose

In this chapter, I argue that it is time to change the narrative around school segregation and adopt new strategies to achieve educational justice. I begin by outlining the current state of school segregation to underscore the scope of the issue. Then I review the most compelling research about the benefits and drawbacks of integration. While a robust and ever-expanding body of scholarship demonstrates the value of school integration, a number of critical voices demand that educational leaders carefully consider the ways in which many desegregation efforts have endangered the well-being of students of color. Following this review of the potential value and disvalue of desegregation, I turn to a discussion about the mechanisms used to resist school integration, then offer insights into the policy mechanisms that some communities have used to successfully advance school integration. Before concluding, I present a perspective on advancing integration in a way that centers educational justice rather than diversity and that explicitly aims to dismantle White supremacy culture in schools.

The State of School Integration

In a report marking the 50th anniversary of *Brown v. Board of Education*, the University of California, Los Angeles (UCLA) Civil Rights Project declared that "schools across the nation are becoming increasingly segregated" (Orfield & Lee, 2004). Fifteen years later, the UCLA Civil Rights Project reported that "As we mark the 65th anniversary of *Brown* ... intense levels of segregation—which had decreased markedly after 1954 for black students—are on the rise once again" (Frankenberg et al., 2019, p. 4). Countless studies echo these findings and underscore the reality that despite public awareness of persisting—and in some places, worsening—school segregation, our society has failed to address this issue. Court-monitored desegregation efforts in the 1970s and 1980s led to marked levels of school desegregation, particularly in the South. During the 1990s, most judicial oversight of desegregation plans ended, and school segregation returned to many school districts that had previously made progress towards desegregation (Reardon et al., 2012). Even though isolated policy efforts spurred piecemeal school desegregation programs and the occasional lawsuit has led to changes within individual districts and regions, the overall trend is towards stagnating or deepening segregation.

Although US society viewed school segregation as a Black and White racial issue at the time the Supreme Court heard arguments in *Brown v. Board of Education*, the contours of school segregation are markedly different today. The student population in American public schools is rapidly diversifying. As of the

2014–15 school year, the nation's public schools no longer enrolled a White majority. In the 2020–21 school year, 46.2% of public school students in pre-K through Grade 12 identified as White, 27.6% as Hispanic, 15.0% as Black, 5.5% as Asian, 4.5% with two or more races, 1.0% as American Indian or Native Alaskan, and 4% as Pacific Islander (U.S. Department of Education, 2020a, 2020b). In addition to the fact that racial and ethnic diversity has grown dramatically since *Brown*, public schools have increasingly diverse students by way of religious background, disability status, language, gender identity, sexual identity, and more.

The growing diversity at the national level has not translated into diversity at the school level. Over three-quarters of White public school students in the United States currently attend a school where less than 10% of the student population identifies as Black. And 17.6% of White students attend a school in near total racial isolation, where 90% or more of their peers are also White. The dissimilarity index shows that 67.2% of Black or White students would need to transfer schools to ensure proportional representation of both groups in all public schools across the country.[1] In addition to Black and White students, the nation's American Indian, Asian, Hispanic, and Pacific Islander students experience similar levels of school segregation.

Even though public schools in the United States are characterized by high levels of racial segregation, many neighborhoods are becoming more diverse. In a recent study, I (Coughlan, 2018) highlighted the divergent trend across urban areas in the country of increasing racial diversity at the neighborhood-level, even though schools in corresponding areas have grown more segregated. Despite the positive trend of neighborhood diversification, many institutions—including schools, workplaces, and religious institutions—remain deeply segregated. As I noted at the start of this section, scholars have been pointing to the persistence of segregation for decades. The fact is that US society has upheld a system of racial segregation, and the nation's education system is unlikely to change this reality without a sustained, intentional, and massive effort to do so.

One key challenge educational leaders and policymakers face is establishing metrics that distinguish between segregated and desegregated schools. Given the reality that student demographics are dramatically different in areas across the US, it is impossible to distinguish a single profile of desegregated schools. However, policymakers should consider using a proportionality measure that compares the demographics of a school to its host district, county, and state (Tractenberg & Coughlan, 2018). If a school's racial demographics are proportional to the student population in a district, county, and state, then school leaders would know the institution is desegregated in relationship to these surroundings. Since it is usually feasible to transport children within a county, policymakers should be able to ensure that a school's demographics are proportional to the student population in both its host district and county. If a school's student population is proportional to its host district and county but not its state, then state policymakers should develop policies that remedy the specific contours of racial isolation in the state. Similarly, states with little racial diversity need to adopt measures that diversify their populations before they can harness the full benefits of integrated schooling.

Benefits of School Integration

A growing body of scholarship places value on integration for individual students as well as US society at-large (Mickelson, 2016; The Century Foundation, 2019). Most notably, research demonstrates school integration's immediate educational benefits, long-term personal benefits, lasting societal benefits, and compelling economic efficiency. Here, I review some of the scholarship relating to each of these findings.

Educational Benefits

Across demographic groups, children who attend racially integrated schools tend to achieve at equal or higher levels (as measured by standardized tests, graduation rates, and college matriculation rates) than their peers at segregated schools. School integration's benefits look different for every child and demographic group; however, there is no significant evidence that integrated schooling harms any group of students (Frankenberg et al., 2016). Mickelson and Bottia (2010) consistently found that students who attend racially integrated K-12 schools achieve at higher levels on both English Language Arts standardized tests (also, Mickelson et al., 2020) and standardized tests in mathematics. Data from the National Assessment for Educational Progress also indicate that desegregation helped reduce racial achievement gaps. The Black–White achievement gap on the National Assessment of Educational Progress tests steadily decreased in the decades following *Brown* but began expanding again in conjunction with the school resegregation trends of the 1990s (Sadovnik et al., 2018).

Perhaps more important than school integration's effects on test scores are the harder-to-measure ways in which a child benefits from attending a diverse school. When school integration is done well, children have meaningful interactions with diverse peers and are challenged to think more critically about how other people experience the world (Wells et al., 2016). Furthermore, children in truly integrated schools encounter a broader curriculum that highlights a history and collection of achievements that extend beyond the traditional canon of White America. Research on diverse workplaces, though not the same as K-12 schools, also shows that diverse groups inspire creativity, stronger collaboration, and innovative progress (Page, 2007). All of these documented benefits of integration and diversity are just part of a burgeoning field of scholarship that points to the conclusion that integration improves education.

Personal Benefits

There are a growing number of documented ways in which attending an integrated school benefits individuals beyond academic achievement. Most immediately, school integration is tied to a reduction in school dropout (Mickelson, 2008). Data demonstrate that Black and Latinx students attending integrated schools are far less likely to drop out than their peers in racially isolated schools (Balfanz & Legters, 2004). Integrated schooling is also tied to higher graduation and college matriculation rates (Palardy, 2013). Clearly, students who stay in school are more likely to graduate from high school, and graduates are more likely to enroll in college. Increased rates of persistence through high school and college lead more people to find high-wage jobs. Johnson (2018) demonstrated that school desegregation is tied to increased adult wages, lower poverty, lower rates of incarceration, and better health for Black Americans. Scholars will continue to identify new ways that school integration benefits the life prospects for members of our society.

Societal Benefits

Panning out from the ways in which school integration benefits individuals, data suggest that society as a whole functions better when children attend integrated schools. Literature illustrates that meaningful intergroup interaction is essential for developing healthy attitudes towards people with different identities (McGlothlin & Killen, 2010; Pettigrew & Tropp, 2006). Bias and stereotypes thrive when people remain isolated. Racial bias, in particular, is fomented in the minds of young people when they attend racially isolated schools embedded in a societal culture of White supremacy and anti-Black racism (Boisjoly et al., 2006; Rutland et al., 2005). Research and logic highlight the reality that children in integrated schools that foster healthy intergroup relationships will develop into adults who value diversity and operate with fewer racial biases. In fact, children who build meaningful interracial friendships generally continue to value these relationships as they mature and inherently support the advancement of a more just and equitable society (Tropp & Saxena, 2018). Evidence supports these claims and shows that people who attend integrated schools as children are more likely to seek out diverse communities as adults (Wells, 2009).

Economic Efficiency

Finally, there is compelling evidence that school integration is the most economically efficient tool for improving education. In an in-depth analysis of the return on investment of school integration, scholars estimate that decreasing segregation by half leads to a net gain of $26,500 per student. This estimate deducts an estimated $6,500 per pupil cost of implementing school integration reforms from the $20,000 in projected societal benefits and the $13,000 in projected private benefits resulting from such reforms (Basile, 2012). Using this measure, a state like New Jersey, with 1.37 million students in some of the nation's most segregated schools (Tractenberg & Coughlan, 2018), could see a return on investment exceeding 36 billion dollars for the students currently enrolled if it effectively integrated its public schools. Although this estimated return on investment is only theoretical, a wide range of data support the claim.

Beyond the research highlighting the return on investment associated with school integration, scholarly literature also demonstrates that integration leads to a more equitable distribution of educational resources that meets the needs of more students (Chiu & Khoo, 2005; Raudenbush, 1998). As researchers learn more about school integration, they provide the increasingly evident conclusion that integration is just and leads to a wide range of social and economic benefits.

Drawbacks of School Desegregation

Despite the considerable benefits of school integration, policymakers cannot ignore the drawbacks of desegregation. More often than not, White Americans have responded to desegregation by developing countless mechanisms to perpetuate racialized systems of power and privilege. While many Americans believe that the violent struggles over school integration are behind us, White people continue to physically, verbally, and psychologically attack Black children in desegregated schools. Furthermore, schools across the United States maintain a curriculum that celebrates the contributions and achievements of White people while generally ignoring other races and ethnicities. Not only do Black children and other children of color rarely see themselves in the curriculum, they are often surrounded by White school personnel and miss out on having people of color as role models in their schools. Commonly, White teachers track Black students into lower level courses, impose harsh disciplinary measures on Black students, and funnel educational opportunities to White students (Carter & Welner, 2013). The reality for many children of color is that school desegregation does not equate to justice or equity.

Prior to *Brown v. Board of Education*, many Black children attended segregated schools with Black school leaders and Black teachers. Governments systematically under-resourced segregated Black schools, but children in these schools received an education that celebrated the achievements of Black people and taught an accurate history of race in America (Anderson, 1988). Additionally, Black children in segregated schools had Black teachers as mentors and role models, and these students were free from the anti-Black bias, hate, and violence common in desegregated schools (Walker, 2018). Following *Brown v. Board of Education*, most Black children lost the opportunity to learn from Black teachers and experience a curriculum that honestly represented the struggles and greatness of Black people. As White-dominated school boards worked to meet the most basic requirements of *Brown v. Board of Education*, they often fired Black school personnel and placed Black children in classes with a whitewashed curriculum.

In the years since *Brown v. Board of Education*, a number of Black leaders and scholars highlighted the drawbacks of school desegregation and noted the harm Black students face in White-dominated schools. There is a growing recognition among critical theorists that policymakers, educators, and society at large must adopt a deep understanding of anti-Blackness to "capture the depths of suffering of Black children and educators in predominantly White schools, and connect this contemporary trauma to the longue durée of slavery from bondage to its afterlife in desegregating (and now resegregating) schools" (Dumas, 2016, p. 16).

Recognizing that systemic anti-Black racism inflicts harm on Black children in White-dominated schools, some Black leaders have fought for community control of schools. Most of these efforts have met tremendous resistance from White-dominated school boards. As a result, most children in American society attend schools that privilege White students as a result of longstanding and deeply embedded White supremacy ideals. Compelling arguments about the failures of, and drawbacks to, school desegregation demand that society takes a new approach to school integration.

Mechanisms for Resisting School Integration

In order to develop and implement effective school integration policies, educational leaders must understand the mechanisms people have employed to resist school desegregation and integration. Many White Americans motivated by self-interest, fear, racism, and White supremacy culture, have used whatever means they could to preserve the system of segregated schooling. Primary tools for maintaining segregated schools in the United States include government policies, individual biases, and school structures. As policies, laws, and public opinion concerning segregation and racism have shifted throughout time, people have drawn upon these instruments to maintain a complex system that helps perpetuate racial inequality.

Government Policies

Recent scholarship has sharpened society's understanding of the ways in which government policy built and maintains segregation. Traditional storylines about school segregation emphasized that *de jure* segregation (resulting from policies) ended with *Brown v. Board of Education* while *de facto* segregation (resulting from individual choices) persisted. However, more recent work demonstrates discriminatory housing policy, which created racialized zoning and mortgage provisions, and established patterns of residential segregation (Rothstein, 2017). Even though US courts and legislative bodies have since outlawed redlining practices and other overtly discriminatory housing practices, the government has done little to rectify the persistent segregating effects of these policies. Today, White families have greater generational wealth tied to their history of home ownership, and they often live in the same racially isolated communities that the government helped establish through its former housing policies. Because housing patterns largely determine school assignment, persistent residential segregation resulting from past housing policy contributes to contemporary school segregation.

Individual Biases

Although policymakers and courts outlawed *de jure* segregation, people's underlying biases endure. Racially biased individuals make decisions and take a wide range of actions that continue school segregation and thwart desegregation efforts. Some of these actions are illegal, and others are fully accepted. One common way that individual bias illegally perpetuates segregation is through the actions of real estate agents. Investigative journalism demonstrates that real estate agents mimic the discriminatory housing practices of the past and steer White buyers to predominantly White communities while offering people of color lower-quality service and steering them towards properties in communities of color. A large-scale investigation of housing discrimination on Long Island, New York found that Asian customers faced discriminatory treatment 19% of the time, Hispanic customers endured it 39% of the time, and Black customers were discriminated against 49% of the time (Carrozzo, 2019). The overall effect of these kinds of real estate practices across the country is immeasurable. What is clear is that there is a complex machinery operated by biased individuals who help preserve a system of segregation that the government established.

Real estate agents' actions like those on Long Island are illegal, though difficult to identify and prosecute. However, it is important to acknowledge that they would not act this way if buyers did not display, or passively buy into, racial biases that supported this system. Families with the economic means to buy homes often make their choice as where to make a purchase based on their perception of the quality of the zoned school (Lareau & Goyette, 2014). In large part, parents judge school quality on how others in their social networks view the schools. White parents, in particular, use race as a primary indicator of whether neighborhoods and schools are "good" (Doane & Bonilla-Silva, 2013). In one case study, a Black real estate agent in an award-winning, racially diverse school district noted that he often had to contend with buyers new to the area who said their companies steered them away from the diverse district and towards predominantly White communities (Tractenberg et al., 2020).

Bias, particularly anti-Black racism, runs deep in the United States. While the federal government has specifically outlawed segregation, people continue to actively resist it. Until this country addresses the underlying bias that allows an unjust system to persist in privileging White Americans, the segregation that many Americans profess to detest will continue.

School Structures

Even in places where residential and school desegregation occurs, people find ways to separate children by race. Most notably, policies in schools with diverse populations often facilitate racialized tracking systems to divide students. In many places educational tracking begins as early as kindergarten. Under the auspices of "gifted and talented" programs, policies in school districts like New York City use standardized tests to admit children into specialized education programs. Even though its public school population is nearly 70% Black and Latinx, only 27% of children in the district's gifted and talented program are Black and Latinx (Veiga, 2018). While proponents of gifted and talented programs emphasize their purportedly meritocratic entrance requirements, evidence shows that well-resourced families use their wealth and connections to prepare their children for tests in a way that ends up correlating educational advantage and race (Roda, 2015).

School boards and educators use policy tools to divide students throughout their education. For example, a policy in one New Jersey district often lauded for its diversity, the South Orange-Maplewood School District, begins formal tracking students into different math courses in sixth grade. In the 2017–18 school year, approximately 30% of sixth, seventh, and eighth graders in the district were Black; yet a highly disproportionate 52% of sixth graders, 63% of seventh graders, and 64% of eighth graders in the lowest level math classes were Black (Coughlan, 2020). Racialized tracking often intensifies in high school. When describing the extreme nature of racialized tracking in one desegregated Midwestern high school, Lewis and Diamond (2015) wrote, "Once black, Latina/o, and White students pass through Riverview's entrance, they mostly pass by each other on the way to different classrooms" (p. 83). In addition to the fact that tracking in diverse schools almost always leads to high levels of within-school segregation, decades of research have failed to show whether homogenous ability grouping even produces different educational outcomes than heterogeneous grouping (Loveless, 1999; Oakes, 2017).

Government policies, individual biases, and school structures all contribute to persistent segregation between and within schools. People's actions demonstrate an intense desire and willingness to maintain school segregation, even when they rhetorically claim to value diversity. As a result, we have a society in the US that lauds the victory of *Brown v. Board of Education* while consistently upholding the very problem that the Supreme Court sought to resolve back in 1954. If reformers hope to end segregation and advance educational justice, they must consider the root causes of segregation, understand the opposition to desegregation, and devise strategic plans that engage all stakeholders in this work.

Tools for Advancing School Integration

History demonstrates that people interested in maintaining the status quo will find ways to thwart new approaches to ending school segregation and advancing educational justice. However, history also shows that justice-minded reformers can bring about meaningful changes in policy and practice in schools. In the decades that have passed since the Supreme Court's ruling in *Brown v. Board of Education*, much has been learned about how to effectively desegregate schools, how to prevent the desegregation process from further harming students of color, and how to ensure that desegregation leads to meaningful integration and educational justice within schools. Reformers must draw from the wealth of knowledge we have gained over time and strategically use effective tools to create meaningful and lasting change.

Residential segregation fuels school segregation. Therefore, any effort to desegregate schools must confront residential segregation. In *The Color of Law*, Rothstein (2017) outlines a range of policy initiatives that federal, state, and local governments could enact to spur residential integration. Among other recommendations, Rothstein suggests (a) banning zoning ordinances that limit multifamily housing, (b) providing subsidies for middle-class African American families to purchase homes in predominantly White areas, and (c) enacting a federal housing purchase program for African Americans that simulates the advantages White Americans received through past Federal Housing Administration programs. Such policies would help reverse the government-sanctioned residential segregation that took place in the middle of the 20th century, but they are only a portion of the widespread effort needed to advance meaningful levels of school integration.

A growing number of policies help desegregate schools where residential segregation persists. In some places, like New Jersey's Morris School District, the government has merged or regionalized geographically proximate districts to bring diverse communities together in schools (Tractenberg et al., 2020). Other areas, like the Harford, Connecticut region, use a system of magnet schools and busing to transport children across municipal boundaries to create diverse student bodies. Countless districts across the US have used a range of school choice mechanisms, like the one in Connecticut, to encourage voluntary interdistrict (Eaton, 2020) and intradistrict (Grant, 2009) transfers that aim to stimulate school desegregation. Most of these school desegregation efforts share a common challenge—they require the continuous attention and fierce commitment of unswerving leaders or the efforts falter since they do not address the structural problem of residential segregation.

In addition to enacting policies that diversify schools through residential and school desegregation, governments must adopt policies that advance educational justice. As noted earlier in the chapter, desegregation neither guarantees integration nor ensures that schools nurture children of all backgrounds. District and school leaders must institute policies that facilitate integration across all aspects of education; diverse students within a school should attend class together, participate in extracurricular activities together, and socialize together. One key step in ensuring that this kind of integration takes place within schools is developing data systems that help monitor local patterns of integration.

During the US Obama Administration, the Department of Education's Office of Civil Rights collected data from all schools that illuminated the degree to which tracking systems isolate students of color in low-level courses and White students in advanced courses. This kind of data system sheds light on racialized tracking systems and provides educational leaders, advocacy groups, and communities with the information needed to fight for school equity. With these data in hand, schools must adopt tools to eliminate tracking to the greatest extent possible and address the biases of school personnel that often exacerbate racialized course placement (Burris & Garrity, 2008).

Policies that compel residential desegregation, school desegregation, and classroom diversification alone do not ensure integration. True integration requires education systems to implement policies that ensure equity and inclusion. Public school leaders need to rethink curriculum, programming, discipline, staffing, and other structural elements of education that shape the day-to-day experiences of children. In order to serve all students well, school personnel must root out structures that privilege Whiteness and middle-class norms. Policymakers should mandate and enforce the implementation of curriculum and pedagogical practices that uplift people of all backgrounds and provide honest and critical representations of the role of race, racism, and other forms of bias in American society. New York State's Culturally Responsive-Sustaining Education Framework, New Jersey's Amistad Law, and the 1619 Project Curriculum are excellent examples of the kind of work leaders must advance to make schools more equitable and inclusive.

Alongside reshaping curriculum and pedagogy, school leaders must also implement policies that cultivate growth and treat all children fairly. Not dissimilar from the country's justice system, some school personnel discipline students of color with greater frequency and harshness than White students (Bradshaw et al., 2010). The Office of Civil Rights data collection, noted earlier, also captured this racial discipline gap. Governments should reinstate this kind of data system and enact policies to address the problems these data surface. School personnel have found great success replacing traditional discipline systems with restorative justice practices that focus on growth instead of punishment (Payne & Welch, 2015). Although restorative justice practices have proven to be effective, they do not necessarily address the underlying bias that contributes to the racial discipline gap. If policymakers and school leaders want to make true integration a reality they must develop and enact policies that end racism and other biases. Education leaders should make sure that all school personnel have regular professional development that includes anti-bias training, and schools of education should ensure teacher candidates interrogate their own biases and learn how to implement culturally responsive pedagogy.

Perhaps most importantly, education systems must adopt hiring practices that lead to the diversification of school personnel. Research demonstrates that institutions are more effective when they are staffed by diverse teams (Page, 2007). Beyond the fact that diverse school staff are better equipped to develop creative and effective solutions to the challenges they face, they also provide students with a model of how diverse groups can collaborate. There is also evidence that students of color are more likely to succeed when they receive instruction from teachers of color (Yarnell, 2017). Given the shared experience of living as a person of color in American society, teachers of color are often better equipped to serve as role models for students of color and provide them with the mentorship and form of relational teaching that matters (Nelson, 2016).

Each of these tools for advancing school integration has proven effective in schools and districts across the United States, but most of the education systems remain segregated and unjust. As a society, policymakers and school leaders need to do far more work to enact the policies we know work to integrate our schools. We also need to continue developing new policies that further support efforts to end school segregation.

Conclusion

Past experiences provide policymakers and school leaders with a useful roadmap for advancing school integration. However, they must remain clear-eyed about the ways in which the realities of race and racism in America sustain segregation. White privilege and White supremacy are baked into institutions and power structures—from school boards to the US presidency. While some people actively uphold racist systems, even more people passively support the status quo by accepting unjust privileges. Building an anti-racist society is the only lasting solution to the problem of school segregation. In order to integrate schools and advance educational justice, school leaders need to bring attention to the racist structures that pervade American education systems and enact policies that replace these structures with equitable ones.

Unfortunately, the public has seen that when the country makes progress towards integrating schools, people find new ways to maintain segregation. Because of this, achieving integration requires that school leaders remain persistent and find ways to bring more people into the struggle for educational justice.

Note

1 The author completed these calculations using data from the federal government (U.S. Department of Education, 2020a).

References

Anderson, J. D. (1988). *The education of Blacks in the South, 1860–1935*. University of North Carolina Press.
Balfanz, R., & Legters, N. (2004). Locating the dropout crisis. Which high schools produce the nation's dropouts? Where are they located? Who attends them? Report 70. Center for Research on the Education of Students Placed at Risk CRESPAR.

Basile, M. (2012). The cost-effectiveness of socioeconomic school integration. In *The future of school integration: Socioeconomic diversity as an education reform strategy* (p. 25). Century Foundation Press.

Boisjoly, J., Duncan, G. J., Kremer, M., & Levy, D. M. (2006). Empathy or antipathy? The impact of diversity. *The American Economic Review*, 96(5), 1890.

Bradshaw, C. P., Mitchell, M. M., O'Brennan, L. M., & Leaf, P. J. (2010). Multilevel exploration of factors contributing to the overrepresentation of Black students in office disciplinary referrals. *Journal of Educational Psychology*, 102(2), 508–520.

Burris, C. C., & Garrity, D. T. (2008). *Detracking for Excellence and Equity*. ASCD Press.

Carrozzo, A. (2019, November 17). Undercover investigation reveals evidence of unequal treatment by real estate agents. *Newsday*. https://projects.newsday.com/long-island/real-estate-agents-investigation/.

Carter, P. L., & Welner, K. G. (2013). *Closing the opportunity gap: What America must do to give every child an even chance*. Oxford University Press.

Chiu, M. M., & Khoo, L. (2005). Effects of resources, inequality, and privilege bias on achievement: Country, school, and student level analyses. *American Educational Research Journal*, 42(4), 575–603.

Coughlan, R. (2020). South Orange-Maplewood School (In)Equity Report (p. 29). Black Parents Workshop. https://img1.wsimg.com/blobby/go/0eecdc25-95dd-4c0d-b7be-497d46996bd1/downloads/South%20Orange%20Maplewood%20School%20Inequity%20Report_.pdf?ver=1599844099099.

Coughlan, R. W. (2018). Divergent trends in neighborhood and school segregation in the age of school choice. *Peabody Journal of Education*, 93(4), 349–366.

Doane, A. W., & Bonilla-Silva, E. (2013). *White out: The continuing significance of racism*. Routledge.

Dumas, M. J. (2016). Against the dark: Antiblackness in education policy and discourse. *Theory Into Practice*, 55(1), 11–19.

Eaton, S. E. (2020). *The other Boston busing story: What's won and lost across the boundary line*. Brandeis University Press.

Frankenberg, E., Ee, J., Ayscue, J. B., & Orfield, G. (2019). *Harming our common future: 44*. www.civilrightsproject.ucla.edu/research/k-12-education/integration-and-diversity/harming-our-common-future-americas-segregated-schools-65-years-after-brown/Brown-65-050919v4-final.pdf.

Frankenberg, E., Garces, L., & Hopkins, M. (2016). *School integration matters: Research-based strategies to advance equity*. Teachers College Press.

Grant, G. (2009). *Hope and despair in the American city: Why there are no bad schools in Raleigh*. Harvard University Press.

Johnson, R. C. (2019). *Children of the dream: Why school integration works*. Basic Books.

Lareau, A., & Goyette, K. (2014). *Choosing homes, choosing schools*. Russell Sage Foundation Press.

Lewis, A. E., & Diamond, J. B. (2015). *Despite the Best Intentions*. Oxford University Press.

Loveless, T. (1999). *The tracking wars: State reform meets school policy*. Brookings Institution Press.

McGlothlin, H., & Killen, M. (2010). How social experience is related to children's intergroup attitudes. *European Journal of Social Psychology*, 40(4), 625–634.

Mickelson, R. A. (2008). Twenty-first century social science on school racial diversity and educational outcomes. *Ohio State Law Journal*, 69(6), 1173.

Mickelson, R. A. (2016). School integration and K-12 outcomes: An updated quick synthesis of the social science evidence (No. 5, p. 4). National Coalition on School Diversity. www.school-diversity.org/pdf/DiversityResearchBriefNo5.pdf.

Mickelson, R. A., & Bottia, M. (2010). Integrated education and mathematics outcomes: A synthesis of social science research. *North Carolina Law Review*, 88(3), 993–993.

Mickelson, R. A., Bottia, M., & Larimore, S. (2020). A metaregression analysis of the effects of school racial and ethnic composition on K-12 Reading, Language Arts, and English outcomes. *Sociology of Race and Ethnicity*. https://doi-org /10.1177/2332649220942265.

Nelson, J. D. (2016). Relational teaching with Black boys: Strategies for learning at a single-sex middle school for boys of color. *Teachers College Record (1970)*, 118(6), 1–30.

Oakes, J. (2017). 2016 AERA presidential address: Public scholarship: Education research for a diverse democracy. *Educational Researcher*, 47(2), 91–104.

Orfield, G., & Lee, C. (2004). Brown at 50: King's dream or Plessy's nightmare? UCLA Civil Rights Project. www.civilrightsproject.ucla.edu/research/k-12-education/integration-and-diversity/brown-at-50-king2019s-dream-or-plessy2019s-nightmare/orfield-brown-50-2004.pdf.

Page, S. E. (2007). *The difference: How the power of diversity creates better groups, firms, schools, and societies*. Princeton University Press.

Palardy, G. J. (2013). High school socioeconomic segregation and student attainment. *American Educational Research Journal*, 50(4), 714–754.

Payne, A. A., & Welch, K. (2015). Restorative justice in schools: The influence of race on restorative discipline. *Youth & Society*, 47(4), 539–564.

Pettigrew, T. F., & Tropp, L. R. (2006). A meta-analytic test of intergroup contact theory. *Journal of Personality and Social Psychology*, 90(5), 751–783.

Raudenbush, S. W. (1998). Inequality of access to educational resources: A national report card for eighth-grade math. *Educational Evaluation and Policy Analysis*, 20(4), 253–267.

Reardon, S. F., Grewal, E., Kalogrides, D., & Greenberg, E. (2012). "Brown" fades: The end of court-ordered school desegregation and the resegregation of American public schools. *Journal of Policy Analysis and Management*, 31(4), 876–904. https://doi.org/10.1002/pam.21649.

Roda, A. (2015). *Inequality in gifted and talented programs: Parental choices about status, school opportunity, and second-generation segregation*. Springer.

Rothstein, R. (2017). *The color of law: A forgotten history of how our government segregated America*. Liveright Publishing.

Rutland, A., Cameron, L., Bennett, L., & Ferrell, J. (2005). Interracial contact and racial constancy: A multi-site study of racial intergroup bias in 3–5 year old Anglo-British children. *Journal of Applied Developmental Psychology*, 26(6), 699–713.

Sadovnik, A., Cookson, P., Semel, S., & Coughlan, R. (2018). *Exploring education: An introduction to the foundations of education* (5th ed.). Routledge.

The Century Foundation. (2019, April 29). *The benefits of socioeconomically and racially integrated schools and classrooms*. The Century Foundation. https://tcf.org/content/facts/the-benefits-of-socioeconomically-and-racially-integrated-schools-and-classrooms/.

Tractenberg, P., & Coughlan, R. (2018). 2018 The new promise of school integration and the old problem of extreme segregation. Center for Diversity and Equality in Education. https://drive.google.com/file/d/0B3wV7a_ghtLReDF0ajcxX1Ytd0tjSlo3ZXJVazZaNWpZVEFz/view?usp=sharing&usp=embed_facebook.

Tractenberg, P., Roda, A., Coughlan, R., & Dougherty, D. (2020). *Making school integration work: Lessons from Morris*. Teachers College Press.

Tropp, L. R., & Saxena, S. (2018). Re-weaving the social fabric through integrated schools: How intergroup contact prepares youth to thrive in a multiracial society. In *National Coalition on School Diversity*. National Coalition on School Diversity. https://eric.ed.gov/?id=ED603699.

U.S. Department of Education, National Center for Education Statistics. (2020a). *Elementary/Secondary Information System.* https://nces.ed.gov/ccd/elsi/.

U.S. Department of Education, National Center for Education Statistics. (2020b). *The NCES fast facts tool.* U.S. Department of Education, National Center for Education Statistics. https://nces.ed.gov/fastfacts/display.asp?id=372#PK12_enrollment.

Veiga, C. (2018, June 1). New York City gifted programs show progress towards modest student diversity goals. Chalkbeat New York. https://ny.chalkbeat.org/2018/6/1/21105038/new-york-city-gifted-programs-show-progress-towards-modest-student-diversity-goals.

Walker, V. S. (2018). *The lost education of Horace Tate: Uncovering the hidden heroes who fought for justice in schools.* New Press.

Wells, A. (2009). *Both Sides Now.* University of California Press.

Wells, A. S., Fox, L., & Cordova-Cobo, D. (2016). *How racially diverse schools and classrooms can benefit all students.* The Century Foundation. https://tcf.org/content/report/how-racially-diverse-schools-and-classrooms-can-benefit-all-students/.

Yarnell, L. M. (2017). Student–teacher racial match and its association with Black student achievement: An exploration using multilevel structural equation modeling. *American Educational Research Journal*, 55(2), 287–324.

5
CHARTER SCHOOLS' IMPACT ON PUBLIC EDUCATION
Theory versus Reality

Julia Sass Rubin and Mark Weber

Abstract: The impact of charter schools on public education has been debated since the first one opened in Minnesota, USA, in 1992. Charter schools currently operate in 43 US states and the District of Columbia, educating 6% of all publicly funded K-12 students. Proponents argue that charter schools improve public education by creating competition that encourages local public schools to up their game to retain and attract students and the funding associated with them. This theory, however, is built on problematic assumptions about charter schools; the kind of competition they create; the students who attend charter and traditional public schools; and how to measure their performance. This chapter examines the validity of those assumptions, drawing on extensive research to assess the impact of charter schools on students, district public schools, and communities.

Introduction

The impact of charter schools on public education has been debated since the first one opened in Minnesota, USA, in 1992. Charter schools currently operate in 43 US states and the District of Columbia, educating 6% of all publicly funded K-12 students. The purpose of this chapter is to examine the validity of assumptions made about charter schools; the kind of competition they create; the students who attend charter and local public schools; and how to measure their performance. We draw on extensive research to assess the impact of charter schools on students, on district public schools, and on communities. Proponents argue that charter schools improve public education by creating competition that encourages local public schools to up their game to retain and attract students and the funding attached to them. This theory, however, is built on many problematic assumptions.

DOI: 10.4324/9781003108511-5

Charter schools are privately managed and publicly funded and can be for-profit or nonprofit in form. While charter school laws vary by state, almost all states impose fewer regulations on charter schools than traditional school districts and enable charter schools to operate independent of district oversight. Charter schools are prohibited from charging tuition and must use a lottery to admit students if demand for spots exceeds supply. Students in charter schools must take standardized tests required by the state for federal accountability purposes.

Expectations of some early supporters were that charter schools would be collaborative independent entities, governed by teachers and parents. That vision was soon pushed aside by the reality of multi-school and, increasingly, multi-state charter networks overseen by for-profit and nonprofit management organizations (Henig, 2018).

Why Charter Schools Are a Peril to Education

Charter schools are funded with dollars diverted from traditional public school budgets, leaving public schools without the resources needed to provide students with a high quality education. Segregated by race, ethnicity, income, disability status, and English language proficiency (Rothberg, 2018), charter schools contribute to segregation in traditional public schools (Monarrez et al., 2019, 2020). As charter schools expand, they increase inequities among charter schools, between charter and district schools, and between high-poverty and more affluent school districts (Baker et al., 2015; Rothberg & Glazer, 2018).

These are not the impacts charter school supporters predicted; in fact, these supporters presumed that charter schools would improve all forms of public education without the need for substantial additional resources. This theoretical virtuous cycle would begin with charter schools producing superior academic results through innovation, made possible by their less regulated environment. The superior performance would be reinforced by the ability of charter families to "vote with their feet" and go elsewhere if a given charter school failed to live up to its potential. Competition from high quality charter schools would push traditional public schools to become more effective and efficient. Public schools that could not improve would be forced to close, enabling the higher performing public and charter schools to expand their share of the market, thereby creating better educational opportunities for all publicly funded students (Chubb & Moe, 1990; Hoxby, 2003).

The fact that charter schools have not produced these results exposes problematic assumptions: charter schools will provide a superior education to traditional public schools; parents will select schools with the strongest academic performance; charter and district public schools will compete on an even playing field; and schools offering the highest quality will prevail and improve education for all. To understand how these assumptions measure up to reality, we first examine how the quality of education charter schools provide compares to district public schools.

Educational Quality

Studies comparing the educational quality of different schools are methodologically challenging. They are usually based on the standardized test scores of students attending those schools, a metric that may benefit schools that devote considerable resources to test preparation and teaching to the test. While these practices may produce higher test results, they do not necessarily lead to improved longer-term educational outcomes (Koretz, 2017). Scholars disagree about the best way to select students for such comparisons, with no methodology fully addressing all concerns.

Studies that compare charter schools and traditional public schools have a range of outcomes, with some charter schools producing better standardized test results, others producing worse results, and most performing essentially the same (Center for Research on Education Outcomes (CREDO), 2009, 2013, 2015). In studies that showed stronger performance for charter schools, differences have generally been small. For example, a 2015 review of charter versus districts schools in 41 urban areas found an average effect size of 0.055 standard deviations (SD) in math instruction: this is the equivalent of moving a student from the 50th to the 52nd percentile in the score distribution. The effect for reading was even lower: 0.039 SD, again from the 50th to the 52nd percentile (CREDO, 2015). For comparison sake, the achievement gap between students from high-income and low-income families is much larger at 1.25 SD (Reardon, 2013).

A subset of charter schools, however, have outperformed traditional public schools by a wider margin, although still not enough to overcome the gap found between affluent and disadvantaged students. These charter schools primarily use a "no excuses" model that combines a strong emphasis on strict disciplinary practices and controlled behavior with highly structured teaching methods and extensive testing. No excuses charter schools are found almost entirely in high-poverty urban communities of color. Such schools have been criticized for their harsh discipline and high suspension and expulsion rates, small percentages of students with disabilities and English Language Learners (ELLs), and high attrition, particularly of boys of color (Golann & Torres, 2020). These factors contribute to the challenges of comparing students in no excuses charter schools to district public schools, which must educate all students, including those who leave no excuses charter schools.

Chabrier, Cohodes, and Oreopoulos (2016) examined factors that contribute to the higher standardized test scores of some no excuses charter schools. They found that intensive tutoring was the only practice that helped explain those higher scores at a statistically significant level. This points to the challenges of reproducing charter school models at scale or adopting them in the traditional public school system, particularly without the significant revenues necessary to provide needed individualized instruction.

District public schools are generally unable to attract the large philanthropic contributions that some charter management organizations receive and can spend on instruction and/or facilities (Baker & Miron, 2015). And they cannot adopt the staffing models that some no excuses charter schools use to extend learning time without additional costs. For example, students attending TEAM-KIPP and Uncommon/Northstar—two no excuses charter schools in Newark, New Jersey—have a longer school day (up to two-and-a-half hours) than Newark Public Schools. These charter schools can pay their teachers more by employing a non-unionized staff with much less experience, since teachers, like most other workers, earn higher salaries as they gain more experience. Even if we ignore the concerns this may raise about the treatment of teachers, the national teaching shortage and the protections of tenure and unionization make such a staffing strategy impractical for school districts, especially larger ones like Newark (Weber, 2019a).

No excuses charter schools are certainly not unique in using extended learning time to improve students' outcomes. District community schools, which combine extended learning time with wraparound services and a more participatory management structure, have produced impressive academic results without causing extensive teacher turnover, using harsh discipline, or weeding out students who are more challenging to educate (Oakes et al., 2017). Implementing community school models does require additional resources, but it does not involve the wholesale restructuring of public education called for by charter advocates.

Comparisons of the academic performance of charter and district public schools highlight fallacies behind the belief that all or most charter schools outperform traditional public schools. We next turn to the second assumption behind the theory of charter schools—that parents select schools based on those schools' academic performance.

Parental School Selection

Parents and guardians approach school choices in different ways: more affluent families, for example, tend to rely on familiar and trusted social networks (Altenhofen et al., 2016), while less affluent families often lack access to the same levels of cultural and social capital (Bell, 2008). Inevitably, these differences lead to class and racial segregation in charter schools, even if, on the surface, families have equal access to enrollment systems.

Regardless of how parents investigate school quality, studies find that they base their school choices on factors other than a school's academic performance. For example, Schneider and Buckley's (2002) research of the Internet behaviors of school choice information consumers in Washington, DC found that they accessed a school's demographic composition more than other characteristics. Other studies found that charter schools can serve as instruments of "White flight" where White students enroll in schools that are more segregated than the public schools in their resident district (Renzulli & Evans, 2005). For White, Black, and Hispanic families, race is a strong predictor of the charter school their children attend: families entering charters tend to choose schools with more students matching their own race or ethnicity. Their actions often contradict their stated preference for schools with higher test scores; in other words, students will transfer to schools with worse outcomes that have more students of their own race/ethnicity (Weiher & Tedin, 2002).

Location is another factor in families' school choice, with parents and guardians expressing strong preferences for schools closer to home (Glazerman & Dotter, 2017; Schneider & Buckley, 2002). But parents do not view proximity equally: relatively disadvantaged parents often place greater value on having their child's school be close to home than more advantaged parents, due to issues of inconvenience and practicality (Harris & Larsen, 2015).

Transportation to school is a major hurdle for parents without the resources to move their children to more distant schools within a choice system (Andre-Bechely, 2007). Historically, school "choice" was used in the years following *Brown v. Board of Education* as a tool for maintaining racial segregation in schools. Publicly funded vouchers to pay for private schools allowed white parents to enroll their children in all-white schools and flouted laws requiring racial integration under the guise of exercising their right to choose a school (Carl, 2011; Kruse, 2013). More recently, parents have become less willing to overtly express the desire to withdraw their children from integrated public schools and send them to schools that are less diverse (Altenhofen et al., 2016). Yet, the patterns of segregation found in charter enrollments suggest there is still a desire among at least some parents to enroll their children in less integrated schools. As we see in the next section, charter schools are able, in many instances, to accommodate those parents' wishes.

How Charter Schools Compete

The final set of assumptions is that competition between charter and district public schools will take place on a level playing field and that schools will respond to competition by improving the quality of their academic offerings. In truth, many district and charter schools compete by devoting substantial resources to marketing. Charter schools also compete by attracting and retaining the more advantaged and easier to educate students, by lobbying for a preferential regulatory environment, and by procuring funding from private-sector donors to support both charter schools and charter advocacy organizations.

Devoting substantial resources to marketing. Multiple studies have found that schools respond to competition by investing in marketing (Cucchiara, 2013; Jabbar, 2015). Researching how leaders of 30 primarily charter schools in New Orleans respond to competition, Jabbar (2015) found that marketing existing programs and services was "by far the most common response," adopted by 25 of the schools (p. 648). And schools doubled down on this strategy as competition to attract and retain children increased, pursuing "more sophisticated branding strategies" hiring consultants, and otherwise "investing in branding and marketing" (p. 649).

Marketing is particularly important for charter schools as, unlike most traditional public schools, they do not have a catchment area that automatically assigns students to their schools. Without students, charter schools do not receive public funding. Therefore, there is a strong incentive for them to recruit students. Plenty of resources are available to help charter schools market themselves. For example, the Colorado League of Charter Schools' (2015) school marketing guide suggests using parents, teachers, students, and staff as ambassadors who can "significantly extend [a charter school's] marketing reach and impact" (p. 9).

Attracting and retaining students who are easier to educate. Schools also respond to competition by reducing the number of challenging and expensive-to-educate students. Jabbar's (2015) study of competition among schools found that about a third of them engaged in some kind of selection process to weed out the more challenging students.

Student selection is particularly likely among charter schools because their ability to attract students requires them to be perceived as successful, which generally means having high standardized test scores. This creates strong incentives for charter schools to select and retain students with high test scores, English fluency, no expensive special needs, and whose behavior aligns with the school's philosophy (Mommandi & Welner, 2018).

Mommandi and Welner (2018) identified 14 pre-, during, and post-enrollment approaches that charter schools use to manage who attends. Pre-enrollment measures include creating a specialized curriculum, selecting a location, or using marketing tactics that send a message as to whom the school is trying to serve (making it less attractive or accessible to other populations). Measures taken during enrollment include discouraging students with special needs or ELLs from applying; limiting availability of special needs services; requiring a minimum grade point average (GPA) or standardized test scores, language proficiency, essays, or interviews for admission; forcing applicants to provide birth certificates or social security numbers before enrollment; and requiring parents to volunteer a certain number of hours at the school. Measures taken post-enrollment include encouraging students to leave by holding them back a year, disciplining them, or counseling them out; charging families dues and fees to attend; and not backfilling spots when students leave mid-year.

Lobbying for a preferential regulatory environment. Another way that charter schools respond to competition is by lobbying government for assistance in the form of policies that provide them with additional funding or otherwise advantage them relative to district public schools (Henig et al., 2003). A prominent example of this is Success Academy, a New York-based charter network that at times closed all its schools and bussed students and staff to the state capital to hold rallies and pressure the legislature for preferential treatment (Carpenter, 2014;

Shapiro, 2015). Success Academy also hired DC-based lobbyists to promote its agenda at the national level (Resmovits, 2014).

Most charter schools do not have the resources to hire their own lobbyists, so they rely on state and national charter advocacy organizations. When the Washington, DC City Council was considering legislation requiring that the city's charter schools be subjected to the same freedom of information laws as local public schools, the DC Association of Chartered Public Schools and Friends of Choice in Urban Schools, two organizations supported in part with donations from individual DC charter schools, lobbied to block the bill's passage (Cohen, 2019). In 2019, a third of the National Alliance for Public Charter Schools' (NAPCS, 2019) $16 million annual budget was for state and federal advocacy.

In addition to keeping regulations of charter schools at bay, national organizations like NAPCS also lobby for additional funding. In 2020, for example, lobbying at the national level ensured that charter schools could receive funding from the Economic Injury Disaster Loan (EIDL) program, which provides loans to cover operating expenses and revenue losses to businesses affected by the pandemic, and from the Coronavirus Aid, Relief, and Economic Security (CARES) Act. Thanks to the national lobbying, charter schools were eligible for CARES funding as nonprofit entities through the Small Business Administration's Paycheck Protection Program (PPP), which was intended to help struggling small businesses and nonprofit organizations survive the pandemic-induced economic downturn. In addition, charter schools secured funds as Local Education Agencies through the Elementary and Secondary School Emergency Relief Fund. By contrast, traditional public schools were not eligible for EIDL or PPP loans. Charter schools received "six times more per facility than public schools" through these programs, even though charter schools have lower enrollments on average (Chang, 2020).

Procuring additional funding from private sector donors. Charter schools also compete by raising substantial private donations to augment resources supplied by state and federal governments. Donors who made their fortunes in business—like Bill and Melinda Gates, Jeff Bezos, and Michael Bloomberg—value charter schools' private-sector orientation and competitive ethos.

High profile charter networks such as Success Academy, Rocketship, Summit, and KIPP are favorites of business philanthropists. In 2016, hedge fund billionaire Julian Robertson made a $25 million gift to Success Academy, announced at a gala that generated an additional $10 million for the charter network (Taylor, 2016). Earlier, a coalition of high-tech investors, including Reed Hastings of Netflix and Sheryl Sandberg of Facebook, gave $3 million to Rocketship Education, a network of K-5 charter schools that combines in-person and online instruction (Eslinger, 2011; Kamanetz, 2016). Meg Whitman, former CEO of eBay, donated $2.5 million to the Summit charter network even though it has $43 million in assets and an endowment. Whitman pledged to give another $2.5 million as matching funds for other "Silicon Valley colleagues" (Eslinger, 2011).

Donald and Doris Fisher, founders of the Gap clothing chain, have given over $50 million to the KIPP charter network (Green & Cramer, 2009).

In addition to donating directly to charter schools, philanthropists have increasingly supported a set of "jurisdictional challengers"—charter advocacy organizations and other entities working to "compete with or offer alternatives to public sector institutions" (Reckhow & Snyder, 2014, p. 186). An Associated Press analysis found that, between 2006 and 2018, philanthropists and their private foundations gave almost half a billion dollars to 42 state level charter support organizations. Just one donor, the Walton Family Foundation, run by heirs to the Walmart fortune, gave $144 million to 27 such groups (Ho, 2018).

Impacts of Charter Schools

As we have demonstrated, the theory that charter schools would improve public education for everyone has been refuted by more than 20 years of research. This section examines the effects charter schools have had on public education, specifically their impact on traditional public schools' academic performance, finances, and demographics.

Academic Performance. Multiple state-level studies have examined the impact of charter schools on nearby traditional public schools. These studies, which are based on comparisons of standardized test scores in the two school types, have produced inconclusive results. Some found that the presence of charter schools resulted in lower standardized test scores for traditional public school students (Imberman, 2011; Ni, 2009). In other studies, charter schools appeared to lead to higher standardized test scores (Cordes, 2018; Ridley & Terrier, 2018). In still others, the effects were mixed (Bifulco & Ladd, 2006), or the presence of charter schools had little to no impact on the test scores of traditional public school students (Zimmer & Buddin, 2009).

To try and reconcile these discrepancies, Han and Keefe (2020) used national data to examine how the prevalence of charter schools impacted the academic performance of students attending traditional public schools in the same district. They used a range of measures of charter penetration, including levels of charter enrollment, numbers of charter schools, and district payments to charter schools. Regardless of the measure used, they found a small negative relationship between the presence of charter schools and both math and English Language Arts standardized test scores for students in the local district schools. They were not able to determine whether the lower scores reflected "cream-skimming" of the top students by the charter schools, which would concentrate lower scoring students in traditional public schools, or if it reflected the impact of cuts in educational programs by traditional public schools, as their resources were shrunk by payments to charter schools.

Finances. One of the most frequently raised concerns about charter school proliferation is its negative financial impact on district public schools, whose funding is diverted to pay for charter school expansion. Rothberg (2018) captures these dynamics, explaining how Philadelphia public schools have been impacted by the growth of charter schools.

> The district loses the per-pupil expenditure for each student who attends a charter school, but the expenses of the traditional schools are not reduced by a commensurate amount. A class of 25 instead of 30 students, for example, still needs a teacher, and the district still needs to operate the school and to fund central services that apply to all students, whether in traditional or charter schools .... [T]raditional schools [also] have proportionately more students who require additional resources for their education. The problems are compounded by student enrollment rates that are fluid and unpredictable. Charter schools open and close, sometimes mid-year .... Students leave charter schools and return to traditional schools at various times during the school year. It is virtually impossible to estimate enrollment counts for any given school and make realistic resource allocation projections.
>
> (p. 48)

Consistent with this account, studies examining the impact of charter schools on local public schools have generally found that charter school expansion has harmed the finances of districts. In Chester, Pennsylvania, for example, pernicious aspects of the state's charter funding law (particularly related to special education funding) have left the local school district in financial distress for years (Mezzacappa & Hangley, 2016). Similarly, studies of California (Bruno, 2017), upstate New York (Bifulco & Reback, 2014), North Carolina (Ladd & Singleton, 2017), Michigan (Arsen & Ni, 2012), and Ohio (Cook, 2018) found that charter school expansion has had negative fiscal impacts on hosting districts.

However, using national data, Weber (2019b) found that growing charter enrollments lead, in many states, to increased per pupil spending and revenues, at least in the short term. This is consistent with Ridley and Terrier's (2018) research on Massachusetts charter schools, which found that increased charter attendance raised the per-pupil expenditures of traditional public schools. Research on the New Jersey charter sector identified a more complex relationship between charter growth and public school district finances: per pupil spending rises and falls as charter enrollments proliferate within a hosting district (Weber, 2019a).

One likely explanation for these diverse findings is that state policy environments for charter schools vary greatly, with different authorizing, oversight, and funding systems in different states (Wixom, 2018). It may well be that the effects found in these studies differ significantly as policy contexts change. Charter school proliferation also has different financial impacts within individual states, exacerbating inequities between high-poverty and more affluent school districts (Rothberg, 2018).

There are two additional considerations to keep in mind when evaluating the financial impact of charter schools on nearby school districts. First, there is a difference between district spending or revenue and district costs. Spending is merely what a district lays out for its expenses. Cost, on the other hand, is the amount necessary for students to meet some desired outcome. Changes in student populations can lead to additional costs for school districts as charters expand, regardless of how much they spend.

For example, traditional public schools enroll more students with disabilities than charter schools (Lancet et al., 2020). These students cost more to educate; therefore, if growing charter enrollments concentrate students with disabilities into hosting public school districts, per pupil costs tend to rise. Evidence from New York State shows this happened for districts that saw an increase in charter enrollments: per pupil costs rose as student populations changed, becoming more expensive to educate. In the longer-term, district efficiency increased. However, it is unclear whether efficiency gains came from better delivery of instruction or changes in the district's focus on those outcomes being measured at the expense of other goals (Buerger & Bifulco, 2019).

An additional consideration is that charter expansion has financial impacts beyond nearby district public schools. Because charter schools operate separately from district public schools, their growth creates more small, independent school districts (Baker, 2016). Research on school size and economies of scale suggests that schools with smaller enrollments are inefficient (Andrews et al., 2002). If charter school expansion leads to the creation of more inefficiently small schools, it creates an additional burden on taxpayers.

Demographics. Except for a subset of charter schools designed to increase integration, charter schools tend to be segregated by race, income, disability status, and English language proficiency (Baker, 2016). In many cases, the segregation in charter schools exceeds that of nearby district public schools (Frankenberg & Lee, 2003; Weber & Rubin, 2014, 2018).

In a national study examining the effects of charter schools on school system demographics, Monarrez et al. (2019) found that charter schools increased the levels of segregation of Black, Hispanic, and White students within traditional public schools, particularly in urban districts with high percentages and suburban districts with low percentages of Black and Hispanic students. Their subsequent analysis (Monarrez et al., 2020) found that charter schools worsened segregation for Asian students as well and that segregation would fall 6% if charter schools were eliminated from the average district.

Greater segregation in charter schools reflects the communities where charter schools are located and the mechanisms that some charter schools use to control who attends (Mommandi & Welner, 2018). Segregation also reflects the preferences of families selecting charter schools, at least in part, to avoid more diverse traditional public schools (Mickelson et al., 2018). Charter schools contribute to the greater segregation of traditional public schools by providing an alternative for those families, by reducing the number of students available to integrate traditional public schools, and by syphoning off critically needed resources, which negatively impacts the perceived and real quality of education provided by traditional public schools.

In a study of North Carolina's Charlotte-Mecklenburg school district, Mickelson and colleagues (2018) found that charter schools also constrained the policy options available to create more diverse public schools. The authors note that the threat of charter school enrolling White students is "an ever-present cloud [for] Mecklenburg County's policy actors" that "becomes part of the calculus of any reform strategy designed to reduce segregation in public schools and likely 'puts the brakes' on considerations of bolder solutions" (p. 128).

Conclusion

The United States' nearly three-decade experience with charter schools highlights the fallacies of simple market-based solutions to public education challenges. Claims that charter schools will improve educational opportunities for all children have been undermined by the reality of increasing segregation and inequality, and fewer educational resources for the neediest students attending traditional public schools.

Charter schools do not have to hurt public education or worsen inequalities, and the relationship between charter and traditional public schools does not have to be adversarial. These outcomes reflect the current legal parameters and distorted incentives, particularly at the state level where charter schools are regulated. Charter school laws must be tightened to address segregation, prevent additional abuses, and create a more level playing field with traditional public schools (Baker, 2016; Weber, 2019a).

Given the current regulatory environment, charter school policies are likely to take on an increasingly partisan tenor, reflecting the sector's shifting politics. Support for charter schools by former US President Trump and Secretary of Education DeVos, and the constant stream of charter school scandals, have made Democrats—particularly progressives—increasingly skeptical, if not outright hostile, to charter expansion (Keierleber, 2019; Schneider, 2019). Most 2020 Democratic presidential candidates opposed for-profit charter schools. US President Biden pledged to support measures to increase accountability for all charter schools. Charter schools will likely continue to have the backing of more conservative Democratic politicians, most Republicans, and many philanthropists.

More broadly, the American public wants additional funding for public schools and less emphasis on standardized testing (Phi Delta Kappan, 2020). More than half of all Americans and nearly 70% of Blacks and Hispanics believe that school segregation is a serious problem, and 53% of Americans believe that the federal government should take steps to reduce it (McCarthy, 2019). This confluence of political preferences makes possible policies that increase financial equity and integration in public education while moving away from reliance on high-stakes standardized testing—changes that would substantially impact charter schools. Lessons of the last three decades can help determine whether we pursue these opportunities for greater equity or continue down the path of market-based competition and growing inequality.

References

Altenhofen, S., Berends, M., & White, T. G. (2016). School choice decision making among suburban, high-income parents. *AERA open*, 2(1), 1–14.

Andre-Bechely, L. (2007). Finding space and managing distance: Public school choice in an urban California district. *Urban Studies*, 44(7), 1355–1376.

Andrews, M., Duncombe, W., & Yinger, J. (2002). Revisiting economies of size in American education: Are we any closer to a consensus? *Economics of Education Review*, 21(3), 245–262.

Arsen, D., & Ni, Y. (2012). Is administration leaner in charter schools? Resource allocation in charter and traditional public schools. *Education Policy Analysis Archives*, 20(31).

Baker, B. D. (2016). *Exploring the consequences of charter school expansion in U.S. cities*. Washington, DC: Economic Policy Institute. www.epi.org/publication/exploring-the-consequences-of-charter-school-expansion-in-u-s-cities/.

Baker, B. D., Libby, K., & Wiley, K. (2015). Charter school expansion and within-district equity: Confluence or conflict? *Education Finance and Policy*, 10(3), 423–465.

Baker, B. D., & Miron, G. (2015). *The business of charter schooling: Understanding the policies that charter operators use for financial benefit*. National Education Policy Center, December 10. https://nepc.colorado.edu/publication/charter-revenue.

Bell, C. A. (2008). Social class differences in school choice. In W. Feinberg & C. Lubienski (Eds.), *School choice policies and outcomes: Empirical and philosophical perspectives* (pp. 121–148). Albany, NY: State University of New York Press. http://ebookcentral.proquest.com/lib/rutgers-ebooks/detail.action?docID=3407332.

Bifulco, R., & Ladd, H. F. (2006). The impacts of charter schools on student achievement: Evidence from North Carolina. *Education Finance and Policy*, 1(1), 50–90.

Bifulco, R., & Reback, R. (2014). Fiscal impacts of charter schools: Lessons from New York. *Education Finance and Policy*, 9(1), 86–107.

Bruno, P. (2017). *Charter competition and district finances: Evidence from California*. Working paper. https://edpolicyinca.org/publications/charter-competition-and-district-finances.

Buerger, C., & Bifulco, R. (2019). The effect of charter schools on districts' student composition, costs, and efficiency: The case of New York state. *Economics of Education Review*, 69, 61–72.

Carl, J. (2011). *Freedom of choice: Vouchers in American education*. Praeger.

Carpenter, Z. (2014, March 14). Were charter teachers and students pressured to rally for charter schools in Albany? *The Nation*. www.thenation.com/article/archive/were-charter-teachers-and-students-pressured-rally-charter-schools-albany/.

Chabrier, J., Cohodes, S., & Oreopoulos, P. (2016). What can we learn from charter school lotteries? *Journal of Economic Perspectives*, 30(3), 57–84.

Chang, M. (2020, August 27). Private and charter schools receive approximately $5.7 billion in PPP loans, raising questions about equity in education. COVID Stimulus Watch. https://covidstimuluswatch.org/blog/2020-08/private-and-charter-schools-receive-approximately-57-billion-ppp-loans-raising.

Chubb, J. E., & Moe, T. M. (1990). *Politics, markets and America's schools*. The Brookings Institution.

Cohen, R. M. (2019, September 5). How charter schools won D.C. politics. *The Washington City Paper*. https://washingtoncitypaper.com/article/178670/how-charter-schools-won-dc-politics/.

Colorado League of Charter Schools (2015). *Stand out: A guide to school marketing*. https://charterschoolcenter.ed.gov/sites/default/files/files/field_publication_attachment/StandOut-Marketing-Tookit-2015.pdf.

Cook, J. B. (2018). The effect of charter competition on unionized district revenues and resource allocation. *Journal of Public Economics*, 158, 48–62.

Cordes, S. A. (2018). In pursuit of the common good: The spillover effects of charter schools on public school students in New York City. *Education Finance and Policy*, 13(4), 484–512.

Center for Research on Education Outcomes. (CREDO, 2009). *Multiple choice: Charter school performance in 16 states*. https://credo.stanford.edu/sites/g/files/sbiybj6481/f/multiple_choice_credo.pdf.

CREDO. (2013). *National charter school study 2013*. https://credo.stanford.edu/sites/g/files/sbiybj6481/f/ncss_2013_final_draft.pdf.

CREDO. (2015). *Urban charter school study report on 41 regions*. http://urbancharters.stanford.edu/download/Urban%20Charter%20School%20Study%20Report%20on%2041%20Regions.pdf.

Cucchiara, M. (2013). *Marketing schools, marketing cities: Who wins and who loses when schools become urban amenities*. University of Chicago Press.

Eslinger, B. (2011, September 20). Meg Whitman says she'll donate at least $2.5 million for Redwood City-based Summit charter schools. *San Mateo County Times*. www.mercurynews.com/2011/09/20/meg-whitman-says-shell-donate-at-least-2-5-million-for-redwood-city-based-summit-charter-schools/.

Frankenberg, E., & Lee, C. (2003). Charter schools and race: A lost opportunity for integrated education. *Education Policy Analysis Archives*, 11(32).

Glazerman, S., & Dotter, D. (2017). Market signals: Evidence on the determinants and consequences of school choice from a citywide lottery. *Educational Evaluation and Policy Analysis*, 39(4).

Golann, J. W., & Torres, C. A. (2020). Do no-excuses disciplinary practices promote success? *Journal of Urban Affairs*, 42(4), 617–633.

Green, E., & Cramer, P. (2009, February 17). KIPP charter school funders are major Republican Party donors. *Chalkbeat*. https://ny.chalkbeat.org/2009/2/17/21084999/kipp-charter-school-funders-are-major-republican-party-donors.

Han, E. S., & Keefe, J. (2020). The impact of charter school competition on student achievement of traditional public schools after 25 years: Evidence from national district-level panel data, *Journal of School Choice*, 14(3), 429–467.

Harris, D. N., & Larsen, M. F. (2015, January 15). *What schools do families want (and why)? New Orleans families and their school choices before and after Katrina*. https://educationresearchalliancenola.org/files/publications/Technical-Report-Final Combined.pdf.

Henig, J. R. (2018). Charter schools in a changing political landscape. In I. C. Rothberg & J. L. Glazer (Eds.), *Choosing charters: Better schools or more segregation* (pp. 6–23). Teachers College Press.

Henig, J. R., Holyoke, T. T., Lacireno-Paquet, N., & Moser, M. (2003). Privatization, politics, and urban services: The political behavior of charter schools. *Journal of Urban Affairs*, 25(1), 37–54.

Ho, S. (2018, July 16). Billionaires fuel US charter schools movement, AP. https://apnews.com/92dc914dd97c487a9b9aa4b006909a8c/AP-Exclusive:-Billionaires-fuel-US-charter-schools-movement.

Hoxby, C., (2003). School choice and school productivity: Could school choice be a tide that lifts all boats? in C. Hoxby (Ed.), *The economics of school choice* (pp. 287–342). University of Chicago Press.

Imberman, S. A. (2011). The effect of charter schools on achievement and behavior of public school students. *Journal of Public Economics*, 95(7–8), 850–863.

Jabbar, H. (2015). "Every kid is money": Market-like competition and school leader strategies in New Orleans. *Education Evaluation and Policy Analysis*, 37(4), 638–659.

Kamanetz, A. (2016, June 24). High test scores at a nationally lauded charter network, but at what cost? NPR. www.npr.org/sections/ed/2016/06/24/477345746/high-test-scores-at-a-nationally-lauded-charter-network-but-at-what-cost.

Keierleber, M. (2019, August 20). America divided: Public support for charter schools is growing—but so is opposition, new poll finds. *The 74*. www.the74million.org/america-divided-public-support-for-charter-schools-is-growing-but-so-is-opposition-new-poll-finds/.

Koretz, D. (2017). *The testing charade: Pretending to make schools better*. University of Chicago Press.

Kruse, K. M. (2013). *White flight: Atlanta and the making of modern conservatism*. Princeton University Press.

Ladd, H., & Singleton, J. (2017). The fiscal externalities of charter schools: Evidence from North Carolina. https://papers.ssrn.com/sol3/papers.cfm?abstract_id=3082968.

Lancet, S., Morando Rhim, L., & O'Neill, P. (2020). Enrollment of students with disabilities in charter schools and traditional public schools. National Center for Special Education in Charter Schools, June. www.ncsecs.org/wp-content/uploads/Enrollment-of-Students-with-Disabilities-in-Charter-Schools-and-Traditional-Public-Schools.pdf.

McCarthy, J. (2019, September 17). Most Americans say segregation in schools a serious problem. https://news.gallup.com/poll/266756/americans-say-segregation-schools-serious-problem.aspx.

Mezzacappa, D., & Hangley Jr., B. (2016). Chester Upland: Exhibit A for broken charter law. *The Notebook*. https://thenotebook.org/articles/2016/06/03/chester-upland-exhibit-a-for-broken-charter-law/.

Mickelson, R. A., Giersch, J., Nelson, A. H., & Bottia, M. C. (2018). Do charter schools undermine efforts to create racially and socioeconomically diverse public schools? In I. C. Rothberg & J. L. Glazer (Eds.). *Choosing charters: Better schools or more segregation* (pp. 116–132). Teachers College Press.

Mommandi, W., & Welner, K. (2018) Shaping charter enrollment and access practices, responses, and ramifications. In I. C. Rothberg & J. L. Glazer (Eds.). *Choosing charters: Better schools or more segregation* (pp. 61–81). Teachers College Press.

Monarrez, T., Kisida, B., & Chingos, M. (2019). Charter school effects on school segregation. The Urban Institute. www.urban.org/sites/default/files/publication/100689/charter_school_effects_on_school_segregation_0.pdf.

Monarrez, T., Kisida, B., & Chingos, M. M. (2020). The effect of charter schools on school segregation. EdWorkingPaper: pp. 20–308. Annenberg Institute at Brown University.

National Alliance for Public Charter Schools. (NAPCS, 2019). *2019 annual report*. www.publiccharters.org/sites/default/files/documents/2020-03/2019-Annual-report-web_0.pdf.

Ni, Y. (2009). The impact of charter schools on the efficiency of traditional public schools: Evidence from Michigan. *Economics of Education Review*, 28(5), 571–584.

Oakes, J., Maier, A., & Daniel, J. (2017, June 5). Community schools: An evidence-based strategy for equitable school improvement. Learning Policy Institute. https://learningpolicyinstitute.org/product/community-schools-equitable-improvement-brief.

Phi Delta Kappan. (PDK, 2020). *PDK poll of the public's attitudes toward the public schools.* https://pdkpoll.org/wp-content/uploads/2020/08/Poll52-2020_PollSupplement.pdf.

Reardon, S. F. (2013). The widening income achievement gap. *Educational Leadership*, 70(8), 10–16. www.ascd.org/publications/educational-leadership/may13/vol70/num08/The-Widening-Income-Achievement-Gap.aspx.

Reckhow, S., & Snyder, J. W. (2014). The expanding role of philanthropy in education politics. *Educational Researcher*, 43(4), 186–195.

Renzulli, L. A., & Evans, L. (2005). School choice, charter schools, and white flight. *Social Problems*, 52(3), 398–418.

Resmovits, J. (2014, October 9). Success Academy charter schools has lobbyists in DC, records show. *Huffington Post*. www.huffpost.com/entry/success-academy-lobbyists_n_5955180.

Ridley, M., & Terrier, C. (2018). Fiscal and education spillovers from charter school expansion. https://seii.mit.edu/wp-content/uploads/2018/07/SEII-Discussion-Paper-2018.02-Ridley-Terrier.pdf.

Rothberg, I. C. (2018). A school system increasingly separated. In I. C. Rothberg & J. L. Glazer (Eds.), *Choosing charters: Better schools or more segregation* (pp. 41–60). Teachers College Press.

Rothberg, I. C., & Glazer, J. L. (2018). Concluding thoughts on choice and segregation. In I. C. Rothberg & J. L. Glazer (Eds.), *Choosing charters: Better schools or more segregation* (pp. 221–232). Teachers College Press.

Schneider, J. (2019, May 30). Charters were supposed to save public education. Why did people turn on them? *Washington Post*. www.washingtonpost.com/news/posteverything/wp/2019/05/30/feature/charter-schools/.

Schneider, M., & Buckley, J. (2002). What do parents want from schools? Evidence from the internet. *Educational Evaluation and Policy Analysis*, 24(2), 133–144.

Shapiro, E. (2015, February 23). Success Academy to close schools, again, for Albany rally. *Politico*. www.politico.com/states/new-york/city-hall/story/2015/02/success-academy-to-close-schools-again-for-albany-rally-019906.

Taylor, K. (2016, April 12). Success Academy charter school network receives $25 million gift. *The New York Times*. www.nytimes.com/2016/04/13/nyregion/success-academy-charter-school-network-receives-25-million-gift.html.

Weber, M. A. (2019a). Ten important facts about New Jersey charter schools... and five ways to improve the New Jersey charter sector. New Jersey Education Policy Forum. https://njedpolicy.wordpress.com/2019/04/26/ten-important-facts-about-new-jersey-charter-schools-and-five-ways-to-improve-the-new-jersey-charter-sector/.

Weber, M. A. (2019b). The effects of charter proliferation on public school district finances. Working paper. Rutgers Scholarly Open Access.

Weber, M. A., & Rubin, J. S. (2014). New Jersey charter schools: A data-driven view, Part I. http://www.saveourschoolsnj.org/nj-charter-school-data/.

Weber, M. A., & Rubin, J. S. (2018). New Jersey charter schools: A data-driven view— 2018 Update, Part I. https://rucore.libraries.rutgers.edu/rutgers-lib/56004/.

Weiher, G. R., & Tedin, K. L. (2002). Does choice lead to racially distinctive schools? Charter schools and household preferences. *Journal of Policy Analysis and Management*, 21(1), 79.

Wixom, M. A. (2018). 50-State Comparison: Charter school policies. Education Commission of the States. www.ecs.org/charter-school-policies.

Zimmer, R., & Buddin, R. (2009). Is charter school competition in California improving the performance of traditional public schools? *Public Administration Review*, 69(5), 831–845.

6
OECD, PISA, AND GLOBALIZATION

The Influence of the International Assessment Regime

Svein Sjøberg

Beginning in the mid-1990s, the Organisation for Economic Co-operation and Development (OECD) started creating the Programme for International Student Assessment, now well known as PISA. Since the first administration of the assessment in 2000, and subsequent publication of PISA rankings in December 2001, the results have, according to the OECD, become a global "gold standard" for educational quality. Although the political and educational importance of PISA varies from one country to another, the results often set the scene for public debates on the quality of education for the majority of countries that participate in the test. PISA performance league tables are widely published in mass media and also used by politicians and education policymakers. In many countries, educational reforms are launched as direct responses to PISA results.

The PISA testing takes place every three years and as of 2021, there are data from seven rounds of testing. The intentions of PISA are, of course, related to the overall political aims of OECD and the underlying commitment to a neoliberal, global free-market economy. PISA was initially constructed and intended for the 35 most industrialized and wealthy OECD countries. Gradually, PISA participation has grown, and the OECD has welcomed and encouraged "associates" and "partner countries" to take part in PISA. Some 90 "countries and economies" are involved in PISA, and it is an objective of the OECD to "broaden the global coverage of PISA" as noted in the call for the tender of PISA 2024 (OECD, 2020b). (Data collection to be delayed to 2025 due to the Covid-19 pandemic.)

When PISA results are presented, the importance is stated by claiming that participating countries and economies "make up nine tenths of the world economy" (OECD, 2010b, p. 3). The focus on economy might also account for the extreme importance that is now attributed to PISA rankings worldwide. It is now accepted, without question, by laypeople that high scores on PISA are predictors

DOI: 10.4324/9781003108511-6

for the country's future economic competitiveness. Bad rankings on PISA are thought to be ominous signals for the economic future of a country, although results from multiple studies suggest otherwise. We will return to this crucial point of interpreting rankings toward the end of this chapter.

The PISA undertaking is a well-funded multinational "techno-scientific" machinery; undoubtedly the world's largest assessment of schools and education. Key elements of developing and reporting PISA are sub-contracted to external providers, like Pearson, McGraw Hill, Educational Testing Service (ETS). The PISA studies are inevitably expensive to conduct, but data on these costs are not readily available. A detailed review and explanation of the costs incurred only by the US is provided by Engel and Rutkowski (2018, 2019). They estimate the direct annual costs to be approximately 6.7 million USD, with additional costs being incurred by individual States and in paying teachers and school coordinators to participate.

Given its size and importance, PISA has to be understood not just as a study of student learning, but also as a "social phenomenon" in a wider political, economic, social, and cultural context. (Lundgren, 2011). PISA rankings create panic and discomfort among policymakers in practically all countries, including the high-scoring ones (Alexander, 2012).The discomfort produces an urge for politicians and bureaucrats to do "something" to rectify the situation that they believe the results describe. However, because PISA does not, by its design, tell anything about cause and effect, creative educational reforms that are not at all empirically founded are introduced, often overnight.

Purpose

This chapter will raise questions about the PISA project, focused on two critical arguments with implications for education policymaking. The first argument relates to the PISA project itself. That is, basic structural problems inherent in the PISA undertaking and, hence, cannot be "fixed." I argue that it is impossible to construct a test that can be used across countries and cultures to assess the quality of learning in "real life" situations with "authentic texts." Problems arise when the intentions of the PISA framework are translated into concrete test items to be used in a great variety of languages, cultures, and countries. The requirement of "fair testing" implies by necessity that local, current, and topical issues must be excluded if items are to transfer "objectively" across cultures, languages, and customs. This runs against most current thinking in science education, where "science in context" and "localized curricula" are ideals promoted by UNESCO and many educators, as well as in national curricula.

The second critical argument relates to some of the rather intriguing results that emerge from analyses of PISA data. It seems that pupils in high-scoring countries also develop the most negative attitudes toward the subjects on which they are tested. It also seems that PISA scores are unrelated to educational resources, funding, class size, school leadership, and similar factors. PISA scores are also negatively related to the use of active teaching methods, inquiry-based instruction, and computer technology.

What Does PISA Claim to Measure?

The emerging picture of what PISA tests measure is in many ways confusing. In some places, the PISA authors claim that the tests do *not* measure school knowledge or competencies acquired at schools; but in other places, they state that the tests actually do measure the quality of the nations' school systems. Let us consider some details. The overall aims of PISA had already been stated in 1999, as follows, before the first PISA testing took place in 2000:

> How well are young adults prepared to meet the challenges of the future? Are they able to analyze, reason and communicate their ideas effectively? Do they have the capacity to continue learning throughout life? Parents, students, the public and those who run education systems need to know.
>
> *(OECD, 1999, p. 11)*

Those exact words have been repeated in PISA reports from OECD during the more than 20 years since then. Another clear statement also reoccurs in most recent PISA reports:

> Over the past two decades, PISA has become the world's premier yardstick for evaluating the quality, equity and efficiency of school systems, and an influential force for education reform. It has helped policy makers lower the cost of political action by backing difficult decisions with evidence—but it has also raised the political cost of inaction by exposing areas where policy and practice are unsatisfactory. Today, PISA brings together more than 90 countries, representing 80% of the world economy, in a global conversation about education.
>
> *(OECD, 2019a, p. 5)*

PISA is explicit that they do *not* measure quality according to national school curricula, but based on the definitions and frameworks made by the OECD-appointed PISA experts, as also noted in the call for tender for PISA 2024 (postponed to 2025).

> The PISA Frameworks are not curriculum-based and go beyond assessing the reproduction of subject-matter knowledge with the aim of assessing students' capacities to extrapolate from what they know and apply their knowledge in real-life contexts.
>
> *(OECD, 2020a, p. 20)*

In essence, the PISA creators are blatantly claiming that they have identified the critical skills necessary for future life, for all humans on the planet. Hence, PISA results are interpreted and presented by OECD officials and policymakers around the globe as valid measures of the quality of national schools systems, and the PISA reports are chock full of policy recommendations regarding schools (Loveless, 2009).

The politics and normative nature of the PISA Project

The OECD is the umbrella organization for the industrialized and economically developed nations. The mandate of the organization lies in the name: Organisation for Economic Co-operation and Development. The home site (www.oecd.org) is explicit about the mission of OECD. Its aim is, above all, to promote policies and set standards for economic development in a competitive, global, free-market economy. One should remember that the E in OECD stands for Economy, not Education. But education is certainly a driving force in economic development and national competitiveness, and has therefore over the years become an important element of the OECD's concerns and policy advice.

The very mandate of the OECD also explains why the PISA domains are reading, mathematics, and science. This selection also carries an implicit message about what is considered to be important in schools and in the development of young people. One should note the domains that are *not* included when PISA measures the quality of schools and education systems: the humanities, social sciences, ethics, foreign languages, history, geography, and physical education. One should also note that PISA does not address aspects and values that are essential in participating countries' official purposes of education, such as equity, empathy, solidarity, curiosity and engagement, and care for the environment. In national public and political debates, these statements about the agreed (and legally binding) purposes of the nation's school system are often forgotten or ignored when the quality of the school is reduced to PISA scores and rankings. PISA scores seem to function like a kind of IQ test on the world's education systems. A most complex issue is reduced to simple numbers that may be ranked with high accuracy. But, as for IQ scores, there are serious concerns about the validity of the PISA scores.

It is interesting to note that in the PISA 2012 testing, an optional component was added to the three core domains: "financial literacy" (OECD, 2013), as a consequence of the economic mandate and priorities of the OECD. OECD makes it very clear about the economical purposes of PISA and the competitive, international nature of the PISA rankings:

> In a global economy, the yardstick for success is no longer improvement by national standards alone, but how education systems perform internationally. The OECD has taken up that challenge by developing PISA, which

evaluates the quality, equity and efficiency of school systems in some 70 countries that, together, make up nine-tenths of the world economy.

(OECD, 2010b, p. 3)

Andreas Schleicher, leader of PISA, is direct and honest when it comes to the normative aspects of PISA. In a TED-talk, seen by 800,000 visitors and with text translated to 29 languages, his very first words are these: "PISA is really a story of how international comparisons have globalized the field of education that we usually treat as an affair of domestic policy" (Schleicher, 2013). In a book with the ambitious and normative title *World Class: How to build a 21st-century school system*, the PISA leader unashamedly stated that "In essence, PISA counts what counts" (Schleicher, 2018, p. 18).

PISA/OECD and political advice: an example

The OECD makes regular economic reports to many countries, with advice on future policy. My own country, Norway, is an example. In the Economic Survey report to Norway in 2008, OECD experts gave the following general advice: Norway should increase differences in salaries, reduce public spending, increase the rate of unemployment, and reduce the level of sick leave salaries and reduce pensions for disabilities (OECD, 2008).

This particular OECD report to Norway had the education system as the focus. With PISA data as input for calculations, the OECD gave advice on how to make Norwegian schools better. The operational definition of a "better school" was a school that is "cost-effective," that is, could give more PISA points per dollar spent on education. The very definition of a good school is thereby ignoring the national priorities set for our school system. The OECD educational advice was that Norwegian schools can become better by closing smaller schools, increasing class size, introducing more testing, publishing results at school (and teacher) level, and basing teacher payments on achieved test results. The report ended with a clear warning: "Higher spending on schools will have no effect" (OECD, 2008).

The essence of this "expert advice" is that Norway should become a different kind of country—hardly objective, neutral, "scientific" advice. In fact, Norway is not the only country to receive this kind of advice. PISA creates country-specific reports for all participating OECD countries.

The impact of PISA on national curriculum policies

The attention given to PISA results in national media varies from country to country but in most cases, it is substantial and has increased with each round of PISA testing (Breakspear, 2012, 2014). In some countries, the media coverage has been highly dramatic. In Norway, for example, the PISA 2000 and 2003 results provoked headlines like "Norway is a school loser" across two pages of a national newspaper (*Dagbladet*, December 5th, 2001). (Norway was actually in the middle of the OECD countries.) For the Conservative Minister of Education, the PISA 2000 outcome was "like coming home from the Winter Olympics [in which Norway normally excels] without a medal."

Historians and educators have examined in detail how successive Norwegian governments have used the country's PISA results to "legitimize school reforms" (Helsvig, 2017; Sjøberg, 2019). The essence of these reforms are characterized as New Public Management (Møller & Skedsmo, 2013). Curiously, some of the reforms introduced to enhance the PISA results of students in Norway, Denmark, and Sweden are at odds with what characterize schools in high-scoring neighboring Finland.

Norway is by no means alone in giving PISA results an unwarranted significance. In the USA the 2018 results headlines claimed "It isn't just working: PISA test Scores Cast Doubt on U.S. Education Efforts" (*New York Times*, 3rd December 2019). The decline in PISA scores in 37 countries, including those in high performing countries like Finland, Japan, and Korea, was blamed on students: "Sleepless, distracted and glued to devices: no wonder students' results are in decline" (*Sydney Morning Herald*, December 5th, 2019).

Interestingly, the United States ranks 28th on the PISA listing based on the scoring of "informing policy-making process," with its influence classified as "moderate" (Breakspear, 2012, p. 14). Rutkowski (2014) argued that this rather limited impact of PISA on American schools may be the main reason why the federal government and OECD are eager to introduce the "PISA for Schools" testing in the United States. That move could get PISA closer to the decision makers in the U.S. education system and thereby increase its normative power. The OECD has partnered with the Australian-owned technology provider Janison to offer an online version of the OECD Test for Schools in the United States. By November 2020, more than 500 schools in the US had bought this test, which "aims to unlock the power of PISA to provide schools with an international benchmark of their students' learning outcomes" according to the statement by PISA-leader Andreas Schleicher on Janison's website (https://www.janison.com/about/partners/oecd/). By 2020, schools in some 14 countries were taking part in this commercially available PISA for schools.

PISA, Free-market Thinking, and Globalization

The Finnish educator Pasi Sahlberg (2015) describes the current PISA-driven educational reforms by the acronym GERM: Global Educational Reform Movement, characterized by privatization, free school choice, competition, and test-driven accountability. The term New Public Management is used to describe these reforms, which are supposed to make the public sector more efficient. Public services such as schools and higher education, culture, and healthcare all are being invaded by market terms. Words like *quality, efficiency, transparency, accountability*, and *value for money* are among those used to describe these policy reforms.

Other public sectors are experiencing the same trend. Services such as police, security, postal delivery, transportation, water supply, household garbage handling, and sewage and waste water all come under attack in the name of efficiency and value. Traditional public services are increasingly subjected to competitive bids from private actors. Outsourcing of key public services, a process that is eased by new regulations on international trade, is increasingly going to multinational companies. Most major international trade agreements now include provisions for privatizing public sectors. This trend toward marketization and privatization characterizes the development in several countries. And the education sector is in the forefront, with OECD and its PISA project as an efficient tool (Meyer & Benavot, 2013). For a comprehensive analysis of neoliberal school reforms with a focus on the US, see Münch (2020).

The political/economical perspective that pervades PISA is that of neoliberal globalization. Large multinational corporations are important actors, and the workforce has to be flexible and moveable. National and multinational corporations compete in a common market. Hence, the thinking goes, there is a need for common standards in education, common systems for exams, degrees, and qualifications. Such tendencies to standardize education processes operate within units such as the European Union, where an example is introduction of a common degree system and course descriptions in higher education in Europe. In key areas, OECD is playing an increasingly important role by developing and monitoring common standards, indicators, and measures (Grek, 2009). A driving force behind these reforms is often the use of indicators—quantifiable and measurable standards that can be used for calculations (Popkewitz, 2011).

Universally Valid "Real Life" Indicators?

An underlying, fundamental premise for the PISA project is that it is possible to "measure" the quality of a country's education by a simple, universal, and unidimensional indicator; common to all countries and unconstrained from differences in national values and purposes of schools, social structure, traditions, culture, natural conditions, ways of living, and access to free public education.

Although life in many countries does have some similar traits, one can hardly assume that the 15-year-olds in the United States, Japan, Turkey, Mexico, and Norway are preparing for the same challenges, careers, and economies, or that they need identical life skills and competencies. It is also important to remind ourselves that the PISA assessment framework and its test are mainly meant for young people in the relatively rich and modernized OECD countries. When this instrument is also used as a "benchmark" for the now more than 40 non-OECD member countries that take part in PISA, the mismatch between the PISA test and the needs of the youth in those nations becomes even more obvious.

It is important to remember that the target population of the PISA testing is the age cohort of 15-year-olds. This is, in most countries, towards the end of obligatory school. The great majority of these young people have to face realities that are local and national; only a minority of these young people will operate in the global, international marketplace.

All countries have their own school and education systems based on national priorities and concerns, at least ideally negotiated and developed by democratically elected governments and institutions over time. National deliberations have resulted in foundational legal frames and statements about the overall purposes of the school, the level or levels of government with jurisdiction and influence over public schooling, and more concrete details such as time allocations for school subjects, aims, objectives and curricula, and exam structure. These traditions are often at the heart of the nations' identity, and the set of such laws and regulations is the mandate that society has given to the schools and its teachers.

As mentioned, the PISA framework does not relate to any national school system or curriculum. The framework is supposed to be a universal, presumably culture-free, curriculum, decided by the OECD and its selected experts. An explicit goal of the OECD for its PISA project is to be an agent of change in the education system in the participating countries. In this respect, one may say that PISA is a success story (Sjøberg, 2019). The international test movement, in particular PISA, often in cooperation with commercial providers of tests and teaching material, leads to policy convergence across nations., as also noted in a UNESCO working paper titled "Is it worth it? Rationales for (non)participation in international large-scale learning assessments" (Addey & Sellar, 2019).

Steps toward the PISA Test

The first step from intention to test is the selection of the knowledge domains (or school subjects) that should be included. OECD chose three domains (or "literacies") for the PISA testing: reading (in the mother tongue), mathematics, and science.

Of course, one single test, even a test like PISA, cannot assess all possible school subjects. But by selecting some and ignoring others, PISA sends a message to the public as well as politicians about what is important for schools and future life. The actual choice of reading, science, and mathematics also reflects the basic concern of the OECD: economic competitiveness in a global market economy. As mentioned, when PISA in 2012 extended its repertoire, the added domain was "financial literacy."

The PISA Framework

An important step in the process of developing the actual PISA test is to create a testing framework, in reality a "PISA curriculum." The persons selected for this purpose are well-known international experts in their fields, often among the most respected and merited in the world. But, of course, they work within the frames decided by PISA as a project, and they must all be fluent in English, which is the dominating language in all deliberations and working documents. In addition to the subject-matter specialists, psychometricians also play a key role in the whole process.

Most educators will probably find the PISA frameworks developed by these expert groups to be of high quality, with ideas, perspectives, and subject-matter detail that is of very high quality (see, e.g. OECD, 2019b). These documents could be used as sources for inspiration and to stimulate the debate over educational priorities. The problem is, however, that this framework now serves as a normative universal curriculum and a framework for an international testing regime.

Item Selection and Test Construction

The next step is to "operationalize" the framework—that is, to use the framework for the development and selection of test items, and for the construction of the PISA tests as a whole. For more detail on the technicalities in this complicated process, readers are encouraged to access the voluminous technical reports for each PISA round (e.g., OECD, 2009) (the technical report for PISA 2018 was by the end of 2020 only partly completed (OECD, 2021).

Each PISA country (OECD countries only) is invited to propose test items that fit the framework and are based on "authentic texts" and "real life situations." Through an elaborate process with initial screening and selection, national and international piloting, pre-field trials, main field trial round, and psychometric analysis that involve many actors and subcommittees and many meeting for negotiations and debate, the final series of test items is decided. The complication of this single stage in the process is apparent from the following extract from the technical report:

> These analyses … included the standard ConQuest® item analysis (item fit, item discrimination, item difficulty, distracter analysis, mean ability and point-biserial correlations by coding category, item omission rates, and so on), as well as analyses of gender-by-item interactions and item-by-country interactions. On the basis of these critical measurement statistics, about 40 new items were removed from the pool of items that would be considered for the main study.
>
> *(OECD, 2009, p. 41)*

A logical consequence of wanting to make a fair international test is that an item cannot be used if it "behaves" in an "unfair" fashion. While this is an important argument from a statistical, psychometric point of view, it also means that items too close to real-life contexts of some countries, but not of others, have to be removed. The principles for exclusions are described as follows:

The main reasons for assessing units as unsuitable were lack of context, inappropriate context, cultural bias, curriculum dependence, just school science and including content that was deemed to be too advanced.
(OECD, 2009, p. 34)

This section of the technical manual clearly states that units (items) that relate to issues considered "inappropriate" (controversial in a particular country), have a "cultural bias" (positive or negative), or are close to the school curriculum (in some countries but not in others) were excluded. The statement also explicitly states that "just school science" should be excluded. This is, again, a clear statement that PISA does not measure school knowledge or issues related to school curricula. Based on these criteria, it seems somewhat strange that such a test is used to judge the quality of science taught at school in each country.

For example, in the final science literacy test, Norwegian students will find nothing about the key elements of the Norwegian economy. They will not find questions on topics such as oil and gas in arctic conditions on the continental shelf, aqua-culture and fish farming, and hydroelectric power plants. Neither will they find anything about current topical issues and conflicts regarding conservation of nature, current political conflicts between nature conservation (e.g., wild wolves) and sheep farming, snow, skiing or skating, the Northern lights, or the challenges of an arctic climate. Students in other countries, of course, are not likely to find questions relating to their own culture, nature, history, or current national challenges.

In reality, the test items on the science test are decontextualized, or the context is contrived or historical. This cleansing of culture and context does not occur because of nefarious intentions built into the testing framework, but of statistical necessity and concern for "fairness." The decontextualized and contrived nature of the assessments runs contrary to recommendations by educators as well as by many national curricula of promoting a curriculum that is relevant, interesting, and context-based.

It should also be noted that the final PISA test consists of about ten hours testing time, while each student only answers a fifth of these during their two hours testing time. This complicates the calculation of the PISA test score, a point we return to further down.

Item Text, Language, and Translations

A further set of complications relates to item text, language, and translation. Most PISA items are based on rather lengthy texts that constitute the stem, called the "stimulus." The intention is to present real, authentic texts and real-life situations. This intentionally realistic format—in particular, the length and complication of the stimulus text, make the PISA items different from most tests that are commonly used in mathematics and science, also in TIMSS (Trends In Mathematics and Science Study), the other large-scale study of science and mathematics achievement. This test format is, of course, a deliberate choice by PISA specialists, and it reaffirms that PISA does not really test subject-matter school knowledge.

It may be claimed that many PISA items are testing reading skills rather than science and mathematics competencies. The fact that the correlations between individuals' PISA scores on reading, mathematics, and science across all countries tested are 0.77–0.89 (OECD, 2005) lends some support to the view that testing in the different domains measures more or less the same underlying construct.

The "authentic texts" that constitute the stimulus in each item originate in a certain situation in one of the OECD countries and in the language of that country. This text is then translated into the two official PISA languages, English and French, before being submitted to PISA organizers for consideration. If accepted, the item is then translated into the language of each of the participating PISA countries. This translation process follows very strict rules and detailed instructions (see, e.g., OECD, 2009).

This translation process raises many questions. Unfortunately, PISA items are well kept secrets; not available even in their original form. The reason for the secrecy is, of course, that some items will be reused in coming PISA studies as links to provide measures of trends over time. Since PISA is high-stakes testing for national governments, there is a fear that publication of items may lead to cheating in some countries.

Thorough analysis of some PISA reading test items has been done by Arffman (2010). She provided a detailed text-analytical study of the translation from English to Finnish of three PISA items as an example of how meaning and context change in the translation. From a linguistic, translation theoretical perspective, her study reveals in detail many critical dimensions in this process. One of her conclusions is that one can never arrive at what may be called "equivalence of translation." Something is always lost or meaning is modified in translation. Arffman (2010) also noted that bad translations also may cause readers to lose interest and motivation to become engaged with the text, and that this may have a severely negative effect on the tests results. This effect may be greater in countries where students are critical, independent, and unwilling to obey the authority of schools and teachers.

There seems to be a lack of empirical studies to look into this important aspect of PISA testing. The key role played by text in PISA makes such a scrutiny very important. A thorough cross-national check of translation requires cooperation of researchers from many countries with considerable linguistic skills as well as subject-matter knowledge. The secrecy of PISA items makes such inquiries difficult.

Some languages, however, lend themselves to rather easy comparisons, even for non-linguists. The three Scandinavian languages provide good examples. Swedish, Danish, and Norwegian are very similar languages—in fact, more like dialects, in part with a common literary tradition.

The following is a simple example from a released PISA item to be answered digitally. The item called "Running in hot weather" (OECD, 2018) addressed the issue of possible *overheating* and *dehydration* when running in hot weather under different humidity conditions. The key term "dehydration" is (correctly) translated to "dehydrering" in Norwegian and Danish, but is translated with the much simpler, everyday term "uttorkad" (literally "dried up") in Swedish. This, of course, makes the stem much simpler for a reader.

PISA reports assert that it has top quality in translation processes as well as in all other aspects of its work. In the light of this, it is rather surprising that big blunders can be discovered by just a cursory look at published items.

PISA-test as "Real Life Situation"?

As noted before, the PISA ambition to test students' preparedness for "real life situations" is the key component in official presentations of PISA, already from its inception (OECD, 1999, p. 11). More than 25 years later, in the call for tender for the PISA 2025 contractors, the short presentation of PISA is the following: "PISA assesses how well students can apply what they learn in school to real-life situations" (PISA, 2020b, p. 6).

A standardized global "real life" test assumes that the future challenges are common across all cultures, and that they are already known by the PISA experts. Moreover, this "real life" assertion is contradicted by the test situation: The PISA test is, like other school tests, a traditional pen-and-paper test, where students sit for 2.5 hours to answer written questions, in solitude and without access to sources of information. (For most countries, the PISA test has been computer-based (without internet access) from PISA 2015 onwards.)

How "real life" is that test situation? How does it relate to the challenges that young people may face in their future life as citizens, as participants in tomorrow's democracy, and as skilled workforce? Put in this form, the questions are rhetorical: The PISA test situation does not resemble any real life, problem-based situations. The only place where you sit in solitude with a written test is in fact in exams at schools and universities. The only places where students are not allowed to communicate, collaborate, or use modern information technologies are similar artificial test situations.

Real life, in private, at leisure, as well as at the workplace, is more or less the opposite of the PISA test situation. While one should expect that an organization like OECD should emphasize the competencies needed by the big international actors on a competitive global market, the PISA test situation is different. Therefore, PISA does not even live up to serving the political/economic goals of the OECD.

It should be noted, however, that each PISA round includes an optional assessment of an "innovative domain." These range from Learning Strategies (2000) and Complex Problem Solving (2003) to Collaborative Problem Solving (2015), and Global Competencies (2018). Creative Thinking is meant to be the domain included in PISA 2022 (postponed from 2021 due to the Covid-19 pandemic), and Learning in a Digital World is planned for PISA 2025 (OECD, 2020c, p. 7). All these "innovative domains" have only been used once, with limited participation, and most of them have been rather problematic.

Problematic Statistics and Lack of Transparency

The PISA project is a large undertaking that has many of the characteristics of "big science" and "techno-science." Hundreds of experts from several fields of expertise are involved. Contracts with international and national, mostly commercial, sub-contractors are given by bids. Thousands of schools and teachers participate, with half a million students spending 2.5 hours answering the test and the questionnaire.

The final test consists of items that are selected according to a process previously described, but the actual test booklets and questions that are answered by the students are not identical. A system of "rotation" of items means that the students answer several different booklets. In this way, PISA can include a larger number of items in its test. Each student has only two of a total ten hours' testing time. After the time-consuming and tedious coding and data-entry process, the data undergo complicated statistical analysis. The statistical processes that lead from actual responses to these numbers are based on Item Response Theory (IRT) and Rasch modeling. Moreover, the final overall scores are normalized to provide an international mean score of 500 with a standard deviation of 100 for the OECD as a whole.

The statistical procedures that link individual test scores to the published parameters such as PISA mean scores have been seriously challenged. Soon after the publication of the results of PISA 2006, the Danish statistician Svend Kreiner presented a critique of the scaling methods used to calculate the PISA scores. By re-analyzing the publicly available PISA data files, Kreiner demonstrated that the procedures used by PISA could result in placing countries very differently in the PISA rankings: the PISA scaling methods could put Denmark on anything from PISA rank 2 to 42, depending on how it was used. This critique was basically ignored by PISA. In later publications, Kreiner and his colleague Christensen developed and concretized their critique in several articles in highly respected journals. In 2014 they addressed "some of the flaws of PISA's scaling model" and questioned the robustness of PISA's country rankings (Kreiner & Christensen, 2014). This critique was then taken seriously and was influential in changing PISA's procedures with respect to the PISA 2015 data. This change of scaling model caused the resulting PISA scores of some countries to jump dramatically, much more than was deemed educationally possible for a three year period.

Children as "Human Capital"

The importance of education for the modern economy is the foundation upon which the PISA project rests. This foundation is known as Human Capital Theory. The development of human resources of a workforce in a modern economy is considered to be even more important than other forms of capital such as machines, buildings, and infrastructure. The efficient development of a productive workforce thus becomes the key to economic development. From this perspective, expenditure on education is principally seen as an investment in future economic growth and competitiveness. Other purposes of education than the economic are often forgotten and pushed aside.

An important corollary of this perspective which has become something of "a given" is that high scores on science and mathematics tests at school come to be regarded as key indicators of such growth and competitiveness. Disappointing PISA results and rankings on PISA are therefore to be avoided and appropriate corrective action needs to be taken. Tienken (2008) looked into this assertion, using the World Economic Forum's Growth Competitiveness Index and looked at how these correlate with scores on international tests of TIMSS (using data since the early 1960s) and PISA (since 2000). He found that for nations with strong economies, such as the United States, the relationship is nonsignificant.

The current focus on education for Human Capital and economic prosperity owes much to the work of Eric Hanushek, professor at the Hoover Institution, a well-known conservative US think tank, and often considered to be the father of the field of "school effectiveness." Hanushek advocates the highly controversial Value Added Model for calculating the "value added" effect that a school or a teacher has on student learning. Results from these calculations are then used in accountability systems. In the USA, for example, the model is used to rank schools and individual teachers, to determine salaries and to dismiss teachers or principals if they don't "deliver" satisfactory results. Hanushek's work is widely used by the World Bank and the OECD in their analysis of the relationship between economic investment and educational quality.

In collaboration with the German professor Rudger Woessman, Hanushek authored an OECD report on "The long run Economic Impact of Improving PISA Outcomes" (OECD, 2010a). This report includes calculations that predict how much an individual country would gain by improvements in its PISA score. As an example, the authors assert that an increase in 25 PISA points (a quarter of a standard deviation) over time (until 2090) would increase the Gross Domestic Product (GDP) of the USA with a staggering 40,647 billion USD (OECD, 2010a, p. 23). Using another scenario, they also predict that if the USA raised its PISA score to the level of Finland, the PISA-winner in 2000, the country would see a USD 103,073 billion, nearly seven times the current GDP. They note that "All of these calculations are in real, or inflation-adjusted, terms" (OECD, 2010a, p. 25).

These and other findings based on Hanushek's economic modeling have been strongly rejected by scholars from different academic fields. In 2017, Komatsu and Rappleye offered a direct challenge in an article with the title "A new global policy regime founded on invalid statistics? Hanushek, Woessman, PISA, and economic growth" (Komatsu & Rappleye, 2017). Using precisely the same data, they came to a totally different conclusion. Referring to the "highly influential comparative studies [that] have made strong statistical claims that improvements on global learning assessments such as PISA will lead to higher GDP growth rates," they identified the consequence of the continued utilization and citation of such claims as "a growing aura of scientific truth and concrete policy reforms." For Komatsu and Rappleye "the new global policy is founded on flawed statistics" and they urged "a more rigorous global discussion of education policy" (Komatsu & Rappleye, 2017, p. 1).

Problematic Aspects and Intriguing Results

The political/economic aspects and the fundamental weaknesses of the PISA undertaking project, as discussed above, should be the focus in the critique of PISA. But other serious concerns also should be addressed, especially by those who believe that PISA provides valid data on student achievement and school quality. The following is an overview of some of these concerns.

Resources and Finance Have No Influence?

PISA claims to measure nothing less than "the quality, equity and efficiency of school systems." While the alleged measure for *quality* is the PISA score, the operational definition for *efficiency* is simple: PISA point per dollar. Hence, from the beginning of the PISA project, the reports have produced indicators and graphs that show the relationship between countries' mean PISA points and spending on schools (OECD, 2001). The data suggest small or negligible correlations between a country's PISA scores and it's spending on education. This has led to the OECD advice that more spending on education will *not* improve the quality. And many politicians use this claim in creative ways.

When comparing the five Nordic countries, the relationship between public spending and PISA scores is actually strongly negative. Finland, a country that ranks high in all areas of PISA, has one of the lowest levels of spending per student; while Denmark, Sweden, Norway, and Iceland have higher spending and lower PISA score. This inverse relationship between public spending on schools and PISA points is used by political actors in the ongoing debates about return on public investment. Finnish teachers have difficulties asking for higher salaries and more funding because the Finnish scores already rank so high and, hence, no changes need to be made. Norway, on the other hand, is lower in the PISA rankings, but with higher public spending on schools. Based on PISA, Norwegian politicians have argued that it has "scientifically" been demonstrated that more spending would not increase the quality of schools. As noted earlier, the OECD (2008) economic report to Norway actually advised Norway not to increase spending on schools, warning that "this will not improve the quality."

PISA Scores Associated with Lower Interest and Negative Attitudes

PISA tests include a student questionnaire that has many questions designed to probe young people's attitudes towards science. This was an important element of the PISA 2006 study, when science was the core subject for the first time. The definition of science literacy in PISA 2006 included "willingness to engage in science-related issues, and with the ideas of science, as a reflective citizen" (OECD, 2006). A special issue of International Journal of Science Education (2011, 33 (1)) presents several interesting results from analysis based on these data.

One finding is that many countries with the highest mean PISA science score were at the very bottom of the ranking of students' interest in science (Bybee & McRae, 2011). Finland and Japan are prime examples; being at the top of PISA science scores, and at the very bottom on constructs such as "interest in science," "future-oriented motivation to learn science," as well as on "future science job" is an inclination to see themselves as scientists in future studies and careers. In fact, the PISA science score correlates negatively with future science orientation ($r = -0.83$) and with future science job ($r = -0.53$) (Kjærnsli & Lie, 2011).

It should be noted that these negative relationships occur when countries are the units of analysis. When individual students within each country are the units of analysis, some of the correlations are positive.

Although applying the statistical inference from differences between groups to individual differences is an ecological fallacy, the findings remain disturbing. If students in PISA top-ranking countries leave compulsory school with negative orientations towards science, it is important to identify the reasons and the possible consequences. Correlation is of course not to be identified with causation but there is a clear pointer to the need for caution in countries that score highly in PISA science tests as role models for reform elsewhere.

In an analysis of the PISA 2015 data, Zhao (2017) pointed out that students in the so-called PISA-winners in East-Asia (Japan, Korea, Hong Kong, Singapore) seemed to suffer from what he called the "side-effects" of the struggle to get good marks and high test scores. Zhao draws upon PISA data to show that students in these countries get high scores but have very low self-confidence and self-efficacy related to science and mathematics. He points out that:

> There is a significant negative correlation between students' self-efficacy in science and their scores in the subject across education systems in the 2015 PISA results. Additionally, PISA scores have been found to have a significant negative correlation with entrepreneurial confidence and intentions.
>
> *(Zhao, 2017).*

Educators might reasonably conclude that there is a need for a deeper understanding of the relationship between PISA science scores and measures of student attitudes and interest. Attitudes are difficult to measure reliably and it may be that the perception that students have of science as a result of their school studies differs from their perception of science beyond the world of school.

PISA and Gender Differences

Many of the countries whose students who score highly in PISA science tests have the largest gender differences in performance. Finland is a prime example. Finnish girls strongly outperform boys on all three PISA subjects. In reading literacy, the difference in means is about half of a standard deviation. A robust finding of PISA and other reading tests such as Progress in International Reading Literacy Study (PIRLS) is that girls outperform boys in all countries. However, PISA test scores in science and mathematics follow a gender pattern that is different from, for example, the results of TIMSS testing. These findings contrast with the more familiar pattern of national examinations where boys normally outperform girls in science and mathematics. Is it possible that these differences stem, at least in part, from the nature of PISA testing which places heavy demands on reading?

PISA and Inquiry-based Teaching

The concept of science as inquiry has a long history and recent years have seen resurgence in interest among policymakers. Inquiry-based science education (IBSE) is now widely advocated, also by an influential policy report from the European Commission (2007). IBSE also plays a major role in the recommendations in the International Council for Science reports to the Science Academies and Unions world-wide (ICSU, 2011) and the international science education initiatives of The European Federation of National Academies of Sciences and Humanities, ALLEA (All European Academies) (https://allea.org/science-education/).

In PISA 2015, where science was for the second time the core subject, nine statements in the student questionnaire constituted an *Index of inquiry-based teaching*. These statements included: "Students spend time in the laboratory doing practical experiments"; "Students are required to argue about science questions"; "Students are asked to draw conclusions from an experiment they have conducted"; "Students are allowed to design their own experiments"; and "Students are asked to do an investigation to test ideas" (OECD, 2016, p. 69). Among the interesting findings is that in most of the "PISA-winners" (Japan, Korea, Taiwan, Shanghai, Finland) students report very little use of inquiry-based teaching.

In terms of the variation within a given country, PISA concludes that "in no education system do students who reported that they are frequently exposed to enquiry based instruction [….] score higher in science" (OECD 2016, p. 36). Although the relationship between IBSE and PISA test score is negative, it is a different story with respect to interest in science, epistemic beliefs, and motivation for science-oriented future careers:

Across OECD countries, more frequent enquiry-based teaching is positively related to students holding stronger epistemic beliefs and being more likely to expect to work in a science-related occupation when they are 30.
(OECD, 2016, p. 36).

One of the questions in the Inquiry Index is of particular interest. Experiments play a crucial role in science and play an important role in science teaching at all levels. But when it comes to PISA results, "activities related to experiments and laboratory work show the strongest negative relationship with science performance" (OECD 2016, p. 71).

Key concepts and acronyms in current thinking in science education are well known: science in context, inquiry-based science education (IBSE), hands on-science, active learning, nature of science (NOS), socio-scientific issues (SSI), argumentation, Science, Technology and Society (STS). There seems to be no evidence from PISA to lend support to any of these pedagogical strategies. Indeed, PISA findings seem to suggest that they hinder attainment. Sjøberg (2018) explores these issues and fears that the current strife to increase PISA scores may result in neglecting experimental and inquiry-based teaching in schools. The conflict between the recommendations and priorities of scientists as well as science educators on the one hand, and PISA results on the other hand is highly problematic and requires investigation.

PISA and ICT

The student background questionnaire in PISA includes several questions regarding the use of Information and Communication Technology (ICT) in schools, and has two constructs based on these questions. One construct or index is related to the use of the internet at school, the other to the use of software and educational programs.

In a detailed study of the five Nordic countries, Kjærnsli et al. (2007) documented a clear negative relationship between the use of ICT and PISA score. It is also interesting to note that a PISA "winner," Finland, is not only by far the Nordic country with the least use of ICT but usage is also below the OECD average. In contrast, whereas Norway makes the most use of ICT in schools in all the OECD countries, it has only an average PISA score.

In a comprehensive special OECD/PISA report on the use of computers in teaching and learning, the highlighted conclusions are strikingly clear:

What the data tell us.
Resources invested in ICT for education are not linked to improved student achievement in reading, mathematics or science. […] Limited use of computers at school may be better than no use at all, but levels of computer use above the current OECD average are associated with significantly poorer results.
(OECD, 2015, p. 146)

In spite of these clear findings, many countries strongly promote more ICT in schools, in order to climb the PISA rankings.

Critique from Academics

Parallel to the increasing global influence of PISA on educational debate and policy, there has been a growing critique in the academic world of the PISA project. Several anthologies have raised serious questions about the meaningfulness of the results (Hopmann et al., 2007; Meyer & Benavot, 2013). The authors raising important questions represent a cross section of thinkers and research that come from many countries and academic fields, and include well-known philosophers, sociologists, economists, and educators. In a recent synthesis of "two decades of havoc" caused by PISA critique, Zhao (2020) concludes:

> It is clear from the criticism raised against PISA that the entire enterprise is problematic and does not deserve the attention it enjoys from all over the world. Its flawed view of education, flawed implementation, and flawed reasoning are sufficient to discredit its findings and recommendations. Its negative impact on global education is emerging.
>
> *(Zhao, 2020).*

It seems fair to say that the criticism of the uses and misuses of PISA is now common among academics concerned about schooling and education. Critique is also directly addressing how PISA itself is using its data in normative and misleading ways. Leading researchers in comparative education provide examples and "call for a more measured approach to reporting and interpreting PISA results" (Rutkowski & Rutkowski, 2016).

Expanding and Extending PISA

By providing rankings, data, and indicators based on its data, the OECD sets the scene for discussions about quality of schooling and entire school systems. And in most countries, politicians and policymakers follow suit. Given this success; it is easy to understand that the OECD is also broadening its scope and influence on the education sector with other "PISA-like" studies, ranging from kindergarten to adult life, from the national level to school level, and from highly developed OECD countries to developing countries. A brief description follows:

"Starting Strong," also called "Baby PISA" is one of several OECD-programs to address preschool/kindergarten level, also by comparing attainments and competencies and the return of investments in early child care (OECD, 2017).

"PISA-based Test for Schools" is a "PISA-like" test that may be used to test how well a school or school district compares with each other or with the PISA-winners. It may thereby bring the power of influence closer to school districts, local authorities and even particular schools and their teachers. The product is commercially available in the USA, the UK, and Spain. (OECD, 2020b).

"PIAAC, Survey of Adult Skills" (often called "PISA for adults") is measuring skills and competencies of the adult workforce (16–65 years), on a scale similar to the PISA scale for "PISA-like" competences. The survey measures adults' proficiency in key information-processing skills—literacy, numeracy, and problem solving in technology-rich environments—and gathers information and data on how adults use their skills at home, at work and in the wider community. In each country, a representative sample of about 5,000 are interviewed in face-to-face settings.

Some 40 countries took part in the first testing round, a second round is planned for 2022–24.

"PISA for Development" (PISA-D) is a version of PISA that is meant to be used by low- and middle-income countries. It will do this using "enhanced PISA survey instruments that are more relevant for the contexts found in middle- and low-income countries but which produce scores that are on the same scales as the main PISA assessment." In this project, the OECD also defines supposedly globally valid competencies that are needed for young people in all developing countries. Results are likely to be used as benchmarks for development assistance from the World Bank and other donors. PISA for Development publishes regular policy briefs with progress reports and findings.

"Education at a glance: OECD Indicators" is an annual publication that brings indicators and statistics from the above and other sources, and is widely used by policymakers and researchers worldwide. It is presented as "the authoritative source for information on the state of education around the world" and is published in English, German, and French. It contains data from the best available sources, where the OECD's own data constitutes the core. These data are also available in different formats (like Excel) to be downloaded for analysis. It provides key information on the output of educational institutions; the impact of learning across countries; the financial and human resources invested in education; access, participation, and progression in education; and the learning environment and organization of schools.

Given the authority of the OECD and the power of numbers and statistics, one may say that this may also be seen as the power to define the purpose of education and set the political agenda.

Conclusions

International comparisons in education are important; they can introduce new perspectives, and they can provide inspiration and ideas for educators, researchers, and policymakers. However, international comparisons have a kind of Janus face; they can be understood and used in two contrasting ways. Such studies may be eye-openers to acknowledge and celebrate the great variety among youth, nations, and cultures on aspects of education and, as such, serve as a source of inspiration. But such studies, especially standardized comparative studies of educational achievement, like PISA, can be used normatively, creating pressure to oblige and fit to allegedly universal and common standards set by the authority of external specialists. In fact, PISA, in contrast to studies like PIRLS and TIMSS, is explicitly and intentionally normative.

PISA has become a driver for New Public Management of schools as well as for global governance and standardization of education (Ball, 2012; Münch, 2020). As indicated in this chapter, academics worldwide, and from several disciplines, have raised concerns about how PISA and the OECD are acting like a global ministry of education, overruling national and local priorities in education, often in alliance with commercial providers.

No test is better than the items of which it consists. The secrecy over most PISA items that appear on tests makes critique and scrutiny from the academic community, and even the public, difficult. Many of the published PISA items have been met with serious critique related to content, language, and relevance. Translations into the many different languages have only begun to be examined, but it is easy to find flaws and even substantive changes and mistranslations. More research is needed there. The problematic use of statistics and the lack of transparency also must be examined.

Similarly, there seems to be little attention to the fact that many of the results of PISA are at odds with what educators recommend as interventions to improve the quality of schools. Many politicians want to copy the PISA winners, but they don't fully understand the consequences; in order to copy the winners, policy-makers often prescribe measures that are the opposite of what these winners actually do. Moreover, PISA winners do very different things. Should we copy Finland or should we copy Shanghai and Singapore?

The reference to PISA to justify and legitimize educational reforms is widespread. With "creative" use of PISA-data, one may justify (or reject) almost any educational initiative or reform by cherry-picking results and model country. PISA is, in essence, part of a neoliberal, free-market political project—a perspective that often falls outside the agenda of the educational research community. A key aspect of the academic ethos is to provide a critical voice, and to question and challenge conventional wisdom. Given the great political and educational importance of PISA, there is a strong need for critical and independent research.

So What? Implications for School Policy and Leadership

For educators and school leaders, in particular, it is of paramount importance to understand the forces acting on the educational scene: globally, nationally, and locally. The OECD has, with PISA as an instrument, become a key actor in education at all these levels. The OECD's perspective is mainly reflected by the E in its acronym: Economy. The preparation of human resources to be active participants in the global economy is the organization's prime concern, and this is also how it presents its results. Worldwide, governments look to PISA results and rankings as objective indicators and predictors of a country's future competitiveness on the global scene. In this chapter, I have cast doubt on the soundness of such "common sense" interpretations of PISA data. We have also pointed to serious concerns about other aspects of the PISA test. School leaders should be aware of all these serious problems and the pitfalls in putting too much weight on PISA results.

The OECD boasts that PISA results have triggered educational policy reforms in nearly all participating countries (Breakspear, 2012). According to this analysis, the US ranking on PISA has not yet triggered reforms. This is likely because of the decentralized structure of power in US schools. However, as US education policy becomes increasingly standardized and centralized, the influence of PISA will probably increase. Rutkowski (2014) considered this issue and asserted that the development of "PISA for schools" may strongly increase the normative influence of PISA/OECD on US schools. When local schools are able to compare themselves with international PISA winners, such as Shanghai or Finland, one may expect a race to climb on this indicator.

Rutkowski et al. (2014/2015) addressed whether individual US schools should participate in PISA for Schools, where individual schools (or school districts) may compare and compete with other schools or even PISA-winning countries. The authors provided detailed arguments against such participation, based on technical perspectives of the test as well as educational arguments. A key argument is that the PISA tests are explicitly stating that they do not address school curricula or school knowledge. As instruments to monitor how schools live up to the mandates from national or local authorities, PISA should by definition be ruled out. Schools are bound by state-mandated curricula in the United States. I do not claim to know every detail of the inner workings of the US education system, but endorse the conclusion that the PISA-based Test for Schools program will serve no good purposes in US schools or schools in other countries.

Not only in the United States, but also worldwide, schools and the education arena in general become open markets for corporations to snag large contracts and large profits. In recent years, the testing industry has expanded and become global. Large sums of public money float into the pockets of these companies. Competition, privatization, and market-orientation are threatening the values that used to be the cornerstone of public education in many countries. School leaders and principals should take a stance in this battle over priorities and not become passive recipients of new ideas disguised as a means to increase quality and efficiency.

References

Addey, C., & Sellar, S. E. (2019). Is it worth it? Rationales for (non)participation in international large-scale learning assessments. Education Research and Foresight Working Papers Series, No. 24. Paris: UNESCO. https://en.unesco.org/node/268820.

Alexander, R. (2012). Moral panic, miracle cures and educational policy: What can we really learn from international comparison? *Scottish Educational Review*, 44(1), 4–21.

Arffman, I. (2010). Equivalence of translations in international reading literacy studies. *Scandinavian Journal of Educational Research*, 54(1), 37–59.

Ball, S. J. (2012). *Global education Inc: New policy networks and the neo-liberal imaginary*. Routledge.

Breakspear, S. (2012). *The policy impact of PISA: An exploration of the normative effects of international benchmarking in school system performance* (OECD Education Working Papers, No. 71). OECD Publications.

Breakspear, S. (2014). *How does PISA shape education policy making? Why how we measure learning determines what counts in education*. Centre for Strategic Education, Paper n8240.

Bybee, R., & McCrae, B. (2011). Scientific literacy and student attitudes: Perspectives from PISA 2006 science. *International Journal of Science Education*, 33(1), 7–26.

Engel, L., & David Rutkowski, D. (2019, March 28). Is PISA worth its cost? Some challenges facing cost-benefit analysis of ILSAs. Laboratory of International Assessment Studies blog series. https://bit.ly/2Wp3c9S.

Engel, L. C., & Rutkowski, D. (2018). Pay to play: What does PISA participation cost in the US? *Discourse: Studies in the Cultural Politics of Education*, 41(1), 1–13.

European Commission. (2007). *Science education now: A renewed pedagogy for the future of Europe (Rocard report)*. European Commission.

Grek, S. (2009). Governing by numbers: The PISA "effect" in Europe. *Journal of Education Policy*, 24(1), 23–37.

Helsvig, Kim (2017). *Reform og rutine. Kunnskapsdepartementet historie* [Reform and routine. The History of the Ministry of Education] (1945–2017). Pax.

Hopmann, S. T., Brinek, G., & Retzl, M. (Eds.). (2007). *PISA zufolge PISA [PISA according to PISA]*. LIT Verlag.

ICSU. (2011). *Report of the ICSU Ad-hoc review panel on science education*. International Council for Science. www.mathunion.org/fileadmin/ICMI/files/Other_activities/Reports/Report_on_Science_Education_final_pdf.pdf.

International Journal of Science Education. (2011). Special issue: Visual and spatial modes in science learning. *International Journal of Science Education*, 33(3).

Komatsu, H., & Rappleye, J. (2017). A new global policy regime founded on invalid statistics? Hanushek, Woessmann, PISA, and economic growth, *Comparative Education*, 53(2), 166–191.

Kjærnsli, M., & Lie, S. (2011). Students' preference for science careers: International comparisons based on PISA 2006. *International Journal of Science Education*, 33(1), 121–144.

Kjærnsli, M., Lie, S., Olsen, R. V., & Roe, A. (2007). *Tid for tunge løft. Norske elevers kompetanse i naturfag, lesing og matematikk i PISA 2006* [Time for heavy lifts: Norwegian students' competence in science, reading, and mathematics in PISA 2006]. Universitetsforlaget.

Kreiner, S., & Christensen, K. B. (2014). Analyses of model fit and robustness: A new look at the PISA scaling model underlying ranking of countries according to reading literacy. *Psychometrika*, 79(2), 210–231.

Loveless, T. (2009). *How well are American students learning?* [The 2008 Brown Center report on American education] (Vol. II, No. 3). Brookings Institution.

Lundgren, U. P. (2011). PISA as a political instrument: One history behind the formulating of the PISA programme. In M. A. Pereyra, H.-G. Kotthoff, & R. Cowen (Eds.), *PISA under examination: Changing knowledge, changing tests, and changing schools* (pp. 17–30). Sense Publishers.

Meyer, H.-D., & Benavot, A. (Eds). (2013). *PISA, power and policy: The emergence of global educational governance.* Symposium Books.

Møller, J., & Skedsmo, G. (2013). Modernising education: New public management reform in the Norwegian education system. *Journal of Educational Administration and History,* 45(4), 336–353.

Münch, R. (2020). *Governing the school under three decades of neoliberal reform from educracy to the education-industrial complex.* Routledge Research in Education Policy and Politics.

OECD. (1999). *Measuring student knowledge and skills: A new framework for assessment.* OECD Publications.

OECD. (2001). *Knowledge and skills for life: First results from PISA 2000.* OECD Publications.

OECD. (2005). *PISA 2003 Technical Report.* OECD Publishing.

OECD. (2006). *Assessing scientific, reading and mathematical literacy: A framework for PISA 2006.* OECD Publications.

OECD. (2008). *OECD economic surveys: Norway 2008.* OECD Publications.

OECD. (2009). *PISA 2006 technical report.* OECD Publications. www.oecd.org/pisa/pisaproducts/42025182.pdf.

OECD. (2010a). *(Hanushek and Woessman) The high cost of low educational performance: The long run economic impact of improving PISA outcomes.* www.oecd.org/pisa/44417824.pdf.

OECD. (2010b). *PISA 2009 results: What makes a school successful? Resources, policies and practices* (Vol. IV). OECD Publications.

OECD. (2010b). *PISA computer-based assessment of student skills in science.* OECD Publications.

OECD. (2013). *PISA 2012 assessment and analytical framework: Mathematics, reading, science, problem solving and financial literacy.* OECD Publications.

OECD. (2016). *PISA 2015 Results (Volume II): Policies and practices for successful schools.* OECD Publishing.

OECD. (2017). *Starting Strong 2017: Key OECD Indicators on Early Childhood Education and Care.* OECD Publishing. http://dx.doi.org/10.1787/9789264276116-en.

OECD. (2018). "Running in hot weather" (released PISA 2015 item). www.oecd.org/pisa/test/PISA%202015%20MS%20-%20Released%20Item%20Descriptions%20Final_English.pdf.

OECD. (2019a). *PISA 2018 results. What students know and can do (Volume I).* OECD Publishing.

OECD. (2019b). *PISA 2018 Assessment and Analytical Framework.* OECD Publishing.

OECD. (2020a). *PISA 2024 Background Document for tenders.* OECD Publishing. www.oecd.org/pisa/pisaproducts/PISA-2024-Background-Document.pdf.

OECD. (2020b). *PISA-based test for schools.* www.oecd.org/PISA/pisa-for-schools/pisa-based-test-for-schools-assessment.htm visited 8 November 2012.

OECD. (2020c). *PISA 2025 tender details for bidders.* www.oecd.org/pisa/pisaproducts/pisa-2025-call-for-tender-documents-for-bidders.htm.

OECD. (2021, in press). *PISA 2018 technical report).* OECD Publications. www.oecd.org/pisa/data/pisa2018technicalreport/.

Popkewitz, T. (2011). PISA: Numbers, standardizing conduct, and the alchemy of school subjects. In M. A. Pereyra, H.-G. Kotthoff, & R. Cowen (Eds.), *PISA under examination: Changing knowledge, changing tests, and changing schools* (pp. 31–46). Sense Publishers.

Rutkowski, D. (2014). The OECD and the local: PISA-based test for schools in the USA [Online]. *Discourse: Studies in the Cultural Politics of Education,* 36(5), 1–17.

Rutkowski, D., Rutkowski, L., & Plucker, J. A. (2014/2015). Should individual U.S. schools participate in PISA? *Phi Delta Kappan*, 96(4), 68–73.

Rutkowski, L., & Rutkowski, D. (2016). A call for a more measured approach to reporting and interpreting PISA results. *Educational Researcher*, 45, 252–257.

Sahlberg, P. (2015). *Finnish lessons 2.0: What can the world learn from educational change in Finland?* (2nd ed.). Teachers College Press.

Schleicher, A. (2013). Use data to build better schools. TEDGlobal, video. https://www.ted.com/talks/andreas_schleicher_use_data_to_build_better_schools/transcript?language=en. andreas_schleicher_use_data_to_build_better_schools?language=en.

Schleicher, A. (2018). *World class: How to build a 21st-century school system, strong performers and successful reformers in education.* OECD Publishing. http://dx.doi.org/10.1787/4789264300002-en.

Sjøberg, S. (2019). PISA: A success story? Global educational governance by standardization, rankings, comparisons and "successful" examples. In L. Langer & T. Brüsemeister (Eds.) *Handbuch Educational Governance-Theorien* (pp. 653–690). Springer VS.

Sjøberg, S. (2018). The power and paradoxes of PISA: Should we sacrifice Inquiry-Based Science Education (IBSE) to climb on the rankings? *NorDiNa*, 14(2), 186–202. www.journals.uio.no/index.php/nordina/article/view/6185/0.

Tienken, C. H. (2008). Rankings of international achievement test performance and economic strength: Correlation or conjecture? *International Journal of Education Policy and Leadership*, 3(4), 1–15.

Zhao, Y. (2017). What works may hurt: Side effects in education. *Journal of Educational Change*, 18, 1–19.

Zhao, Y. (2020, May). Two decades of havoc: A synthesis of criticism against PISA. *Journal of Educational Change*, 21, 245–266.

7
STUDENTS AS THE MISSING ACTOR IN EDUCATION REFORM

Yong Zhao and Jim Watterston

COVID-19 highlighted what is arguably one of the biggest problems in education: students' lacking self-determination capabilities such as self-regulation and goal setting. The virus shuttered millions of schools for over a billion students worldwide (Gigova & Howard, 2020; United Nations, 2020). When schools were closed, education was delivered in various forms of remote learning. For most schools, however, the biggest change and challenge with remote learning was that all students were not under the direct control of teachers. Students therefore, had a lot more freedom and, conversely, the potential for disengagement, than when they attended school in person. How well they proactively managed their freedom was one key to effective learning during the pandemic.

It seems that some students working in an external environment failed to take advantage of their freedom. Judging from reports compiled during the global pandemic, the overall effectiveness of remote learning experiences was limited (Hamid et al., 2020; Mukhtar et al., 2020). "Teachers, administrators, and parents have worked hard to keep learning alive; nevertheless, these efforts are not likely to provide the quality of education that's delivered in the classroom" (Dorn et al., 2020).

Self-determination

Students' capabilities for self-determination are an important factor to the quality of education experiences (Wehmeyer & Zhao, 2020). Simply stated, self-determined learners must be able to make the right choices and decide to invest their time and energy into the selections they have made. Learning is ultimately the business of the learner, who should be able to decide what to learn, when to learn, how to learn, where to learn, and with whom they want to learn. When the learner is

DOI: 10.4324/9781003108511-7

placed in a class supervised by a teacher who follows a predetermined curriculum, there is little room for students to exercise self-determination. As a result, many students lack the capabilities to make the right decisions when afforded the opportunity.

When schools use remote learning, the possibility for exercising self-autonomy is drastically increased. In fact, all students must exercise self-determination because their teachers are no longer there checking on them, managing them, and teaching them directly. Even when schools attempt to replicate their face-to-face model online with synchronous teaching, students can evade listening to the teacher with many different strategies that may not be available in the classroom. As a result, the degree to which students actively engage in the remote learning opportunities offered by the school is almost entirely up to each individual student. But since students have not necessarily developed the capabilities for self-determination during their school-based education, many of them naturally do not do well with the newly acquired freedom. Consequently, the quality of their remote learning experiences suffers.

Capabilities for self-determination are not just needed during an emergency situation when schools are closed. Self-determination is needed for all children to succeed in the future (Wehmeyer & Zhao, 2020; Zhao, 2012, 2018c). The uncertain world that is rapidly changing due to advances in technology and globalization needs individuals who are able to make the right decisions, solve the right problems, and pursue lifelong learning (Schwab, 2015; World Economic Forum, 2016). In this article, we discuss how schools can cultivate the capabilities for self-determination.

The Neglected Owner of Learning

Children should be the owners and co-designers of their learning (Zhao, 2012, 2018c) but they are rarely involved in major decisions and choices about their own education. When they are at a certain age, they must go to school and attend for a predetermined number of years. When they are in school, they have very little room to make decisions of their own. The curriculum is predetermined. They are told where to go and what courses to take. Teachers tell students what they need to learn and how they must demonstrate their learning. Students receive homework, which typically reinforces the content and skills taught in classes. Some teachers may give students the opportunity to make some choices during the school day, but the choices are of limited nature. For example, a teacher may allow students to choose formats of homework or when to turn in their homework. When children reach high school, they may have the ability to choose a few elective courses, but the choices by and large are limited as much of the high school curriculum is prescribed to align with standardized graduation requirements.

Attending school, in essence, is about compliance. School policy has rarely supported students' participation in decisions regarding the most important aspects of learning such as what to learn, when and where to learn, and how to learn since the foundation of modern schools for the public. Neither, for the most-part, has school policy enabled students to be part of the decision-making body about their learning environment—the campus, the facilities, the equipment, and the library. Students are generally not allowed to make decisions about their own learning, nor are they usually allowed to make decisions about the class or the school. They are more or less made to comply and conform.

In a broader sense, although education reforms are technically about improving education for children, children rarely play an active role in making the reforms or the target of reforms. First, it is rare that students are invited by policymakers to participate in making decisions regarding the educational changes to take place. Policymakers may consult a few select students, but, by and large, major policies aimed at changing schools and enhancing learning do not have serious input from students. Second, reform efforts around the world have been mostly aimed at changing curriculum, improving the quality of teachers and school leaders, and standardizing assessment. Rarely are there any policy level efforts that provide opportunities for students to impact their education in a meaningful way.

Schools generally disable students as owners of their learning. When students start school, they bring an innate curiosity and have their unique dreams and passions, strengths and weaknesses (Zhao, 2016, 2018c). As soon as their school trajectory continues, however, a great majority of students lose sight of their dreams and passions as they are conscripted to follow what the education policy and their local school has decided for them. They have to give up on what they may be good at or passionate about in order to spend the bulk of their time on the school curriculum. Students are not cultivated to make decisions, to explore uncertainties, or to follow their interests, strengths, and passions. Students must essentially suppress their agency about learning as well as the opportunity to develop capabilities for self-determination.

Returning the Ownership

There may have been many reasons for students not to make decisions about learning and learning environments in the past but the time has come for students to become owners of their learning (Engel, 2011; Levin & Engel, 2016; Zhao, 2011). Educational technology has advanced to the point that students now have access to knowledge and experts on their own, without being confined to the classroom (Aragon et al., 2019; Bonk, 2009; Bonk et al., 2015; Zhao, 2018a). Thus, teachers are no longer the only source of expertise. Today if a student wants to learn something, he or she can typically find online resources and experts to teach them.

More importantly, technology redefined which skills and knowledge are valuable (Brynjolfsson & McAfee, 2014; Goldin & Katz, 2008; Pink, 2006; Zhao, 2018d). An entirely new and broad range of skills and capabilities have been proposed as essential for students to thrive in the current world (Duckworth & Yeager, 2015; Trilling & Fadel, 2009; Wagner, 2008, 2012; Zhao, 2012; Zhao et al., 2019). Although commonly assigned the term 21st century skills, these new abilities include entrepreneurship, creativity, curiosity, collaboration, critical thinking, communication, and a number of others, but the new skills and capabilities are overwhelmingly focused on uniqueness and humanity (Tienken, 2017, Zhao, 2018b, 2018c). That is, students need to develop unique, signature capabilities based on their strengths and passions so as to avoid being displaced by artificial intelligence (Zhao, 2018c). To live successfully in the Age of Smart Machines, individuals will need to become more human and unique (Fried, 2018).

Furthermore, the fate of education reforms over the past few decades tells us that students must become partners of change (Zhao, 2011). Education reforms have been ongoing for decades and significant policy innovations have been implemented in many countries (Schleicher, 2018; Tyack & Cuban, 1995) but across many jurisdictions there are minimal meaningful systemic outcomes evident, even as those outcomes pertain to standardized test scores. International and national assessments have not shown markedly significant gains in terms of overall averages and the reduction of gaps among different subgroups of students. In the United States, for example, aggregate student performance on the National Assessment of Educational Progress (NAEP) have shown little improvement over the past few decades (Zhao, 2018e), although all subgroups have advanced since the inception of the NAEP.

The new skills required of students have rarely been assessed and in many cases remain untaught in schools. One of the biggest reasons for the failure of reforms is the lack of attention to students, to their passions and interests, to their overall engagement and agency, and to their involvement in reforms. It is difficult to expect meaningful outcomes without serious involvement of students in educational changes that directly impact them (Zhao, 2011).

We argue that education policy must have a deeper engagement with students about their own learning. One way to engage students more deeply is to highlight their role as part of the ownership of learning. Instead of taking charge on behalf of the students, education policy should empower teachers to consider changing their roles from instructing and managing students toward coaching, facilitating, motivating, and organizing (Zhao, 2018a). Schools should also consider transitioning into learning communities where students can become the architects of their own learning choices and pathways (Zhao, 2018b, 2018c). Students should have consistent opportunities and support to develop self-determination capabilities (Wehmeyer & Zhao, 2020).

Student as Owners of Learning

Students, as human beings, should have the right to self-determination (United Nations, 1989). Equally important, the capacity for self-determination in learning matters a great deal to help support their education. Moreover, self-determined learners are lifelong learners because they know how to capably make decisions and regulate their own actions. Furthermore, self-determined learners make education better for others when they are contributing members of the school community and the education system (Wehmeyer & Zhao, 2020).

Ultimately, self-determination is about making decisions, making smart decisions on things that matter. Although there are ways to help students cultivate the capacities for self-determination and self-regulation (Wehmeyer & Zhao, 2020), the most important thing education policy and educators can do is to teach students how to make important decisions and provide consistent opportunities for them to make those types of decisions. The nature of the opportunities can vary based on students' age and maturity, but the overall idea is for students to be engaged in making decisions that matter and have consequences. There are many important decisions a student can make, but one of the most important is about what to learn.

Personalizing Learning as Making Decisions about Learning

Personalized learning (Kallick & Zmuda, 2017; Kallio & Halverson, 2020; Xie et al., 2019) has many different meanings but the traditional and most frequent is that the learner follows a computer-based system that provides different pathways of learning based on the learner's response. In this chapter we use the term in a very different way. In fact, we are not using the term "personalized learning" from a teacher's perspective. Instead, we use the word "personalize" to mean that students should be given the opportunity to create their own learning pathways. In other words, personalization is actioned by the learner rather than to the learner by someone else.

To personalize learning is to give students the opportunity to make significant and consequential decisions about their own learning. There are many things that matter in one's learning, but a most significant element is what to learn. In traditional schools, what to learn has been completely programmed by education policy and the school curriculum, which typically follows a system, national, or state provided curriculum, or any form of education system such as the International Baccalaureate (IB), usually predominately decided by bureaucrats. Students in most schools have a minimal role in deciding what to learn other than what has been predetermined for them by others without their input.

Thus, the first thing to do is to enable students to own their curriculum. Instead of having one curriculum for all students, schools can move to have one curriculum for each student in the school. That is, every student has a unique personalized curriculum. The curriculum can have three components: government or system mandated curriculum, school mandated curriculum, and personal curriculum decided by the student (Zhao, 2021).

To develop a personalized curriculum requires governments or systems to minimize their mandated curriculum so as to create space for students' personal curriculum. The government/system curriculum should just be about what a society or system absolutely values its future citizens to know and be able to do. The personal curriculum builds on students' strengths and passions to develop their unique set of skills and abilities, which would make them successful in the future.

Where developing personalized curriculum may initially be too much for educators in a school, there are a number of steps that schools can take to move to that direction. First, educators can develop a strengths portfolio for each and every student. The portfolio can include what students have been learning in the required curriculum but also what students choose to learn based on their strengths and passions outside the classes. In other words, without necessarily changing the student activities and school curriculum, the school can at least legitimize students' work outside the prescribed curriculum. The portfolio should be co-developed with students but managed by students. To construct the portfolio each semester, students are invited to develop and choose areas they may be strong or passionate about and how they may continue to enhance their strengths and develop their passions.

Second, to move a step further, educators can review their curriculum and decide if they need to spend all the time on what is mandated. Quite often, they will find that the curriculum does not actually require all of their time to teach the subjects effectively. There is tremendous variation in terms of the amount of time spent on academic pursuits across various education systems in the world (OECD, 2016, 2019). In this case, educators could shrink the curriculum and find a limited amount of time, perhaps 10% of each week, for students to pursue their strengths and passions. Some schools have implemented this as Genius Hours or Passion Projects. In this way, students are given more possibility to personalize their learning and develop greater engagement. The percentage of time can gradually increase as students and staff get more used to this model.

Third, educators might also discover that the existing curricula actually contain room for students to personalize their learning. That is, it is quite possible that some of the courses are not as restricted as have been thought and students can make decisions about the content of those courses, or even whether to take those courses. It is likely that students already know the content of some courses and thus can be excused from the courses. It is also possible that students can come up with their own content to substitute for the prescribed content.

Eventually, students can completely personalize their learning. Besides the model of personalized curriculum with three components (government mandate, school mandate, and personal), another model of personalizing learning is when students make decisions about what to learn completely on their own. That is, there is no required course for any student, although the school may offer a range of diverse courses. In this model, teachers, students, and guardians/parents discuss what students would do and then create personal pathways for each student.

Students in essence manage their own learning while consulting adults for support (teachers and parents/caregivers).

What, When, Where, How, and Why?

Besides enabling students to make decisions on what to learn, educators can also support students in developing capabilities for self-determination in a number of other areas concerning learning. In schools, there can be many other decision-making points for students. They can decide on how to learn, when to learn, and from/with whom they want to learn. These aspects of learning have traditionally been predetermined but they do not have to be. For example, once a student decides on a topic of learning, she can then choose how to learn it. Some may choose to consult with a teacher, others may decide to attend a class, and still others may decide to learn through research on their own, with consultation with the teacher and online resources.

Likewise, students can make decisions about when and where learning can take place. In traditional schools, where learning can take place is predetermined to be typically in the classroom or some labs. But we know that learning does not have to take place in the classroom. As we now have experienced during COVID-19, a learner can do so at home, outside school, or in a library. Similarly, learning does not have to take place during predetermined times and the learner should be able to learn anytime.

There are many other ways to support students making their own decisions about what to learn. The overarching idea is to create space for students. Whether they are as young as kindergartners or high school students, they have a natural interest in pursuing their own learning, and seeking opportunities for self-determination. However, as they spend more time in schools, they gradually lose that interest or they learn that schools are not places for self-determination (Wehmeyer & Zhao, 2020). Students can become dependent on what has been decided for them. This is why when working with older students, it may take a while to re-develop that desire for self-determination.

Sharing Responsibilities and Making Decisions about Learning Environments

Another area where educators can support students to make decisions is the learning environment. A school is a community of learning. Every student should be treated as an equal member of the community, as should the adults and parents. Although their responsibilities and expertise differ, all students should have an equal opportunity to have a voice over the operations of the community. Democratic Schools have long practiced a model where students take responsibilities for the governance and operation of schools (Chertoff, 2012; Greenberg et al., 2005; Neil, 1960).

> While democratic schools vary greatly, the basic concept is the same. When it comes to governing the school—whether it's deciding what lessons will be taught or setting curfew—the decision-making rule is "one person, one vote."
>
> *(Chertoff, 2012)*

The idea that each person has a vote and the vote of a teacher is the same as a vote of a student, regardless of his age, matters a great deal because in most schools the number of teachers is smaller than the number of students. The decisions students can make are wide ranging regarding the social, cognitive, and physical aspects of a school (Zhao, 2012, 2018c). The social aspect of school life has to do with rules that govern how the community operates such as expectations of relationships between students and faculty. It is also about whether certain actions are allowed or not in the community. For example, should all students be required to attend all courses or can they choose to self study required courses? The social aspect can also include such details as how decisions are made for the school, who plays what role in the community, as well as how to make the community better.

The cognitive or academic aspect of schools where students can make decisions includes the academic environment such as curriculum, course schedules, assessments, and faculty. Students can be involved in making decisions about rules related to the entire curriculum of the school. They should be involved in decisions on what to teach and who is to teach each semester. This arrangement looks extremely difficult for traditional schools that have applied a standardized set of curricula to all students but democratic schools have already been doing so for a long time (Greenberg et al., 2005; Neil, 1960; Stanford, 2008). For example, at Subbury Valley School, one of the leading democratic schools, students each semester vote for what courses the school should offer. In other schools, students have been proposing and offering courses they wish to teach others.

The physical aspect is the school's facilities, libraries, the campus and any other parts of the built environment. Students can be given the opportunity to make decisions about maintenance and improvements of the physical aspect of their school precinct. For example, they can divide the labor of maintaining campus cleanliness, growing gardens, or managing the library. They can also be involved in making decisions about library acquisitions and purchases of technology.

Being able to make decisions about the learning environment and the school community, is crucial for students to learn about agency and self-determination. Enacting this decision-making role places students in important and consequential positions. Their decisions matter to themselves and others. Educators do not have to open all aspects to students but they can and should start somewhere. It is very important that educators engage students as early as possible in this practice so that students not only experience opportunities to develop leadership and self-determination capabilities but also learn about how their decisions affect other people.

Participating in Social Movements: Making Decisions Beyond Schools

There is another place where students can make decisions and make a difference. Consider Greta Thunberg, who started a global movement when she was 15 years old. She started by skipping school to protest outside the Swedish Parliament in August 2018. She held a sign that read Skolstrejk för klimatet (School Strike for Climate). She started by herself at first, then another person joined her, then some more, then hundreds, then thousands, and millions all over the world. The story of her as *Time* magazine's 2019 Person of the Year says:

> In the 16 months since, she has addressed heads of state at the U.N., met with the Pope, sparred with the President of the United States and inspired 4 million people to join the global climate strike on September 20, 2019, in what was the largest climate demonstration in human history.
>
> *(Alter et al., 2020)*

Whatever the eventual impact may become, she has done as much as anyone in the world in recent times to address the issue of climate change. The impact of Thunberg cannot be overstated. In less than two years, according to the *Time* magazine article:

> [S]he has succeeded in creating a global attitudinal shift, transforming millions of vague, middle-of-the-night anxieties into a worldwide movement calling for urgent change. She has offered a moral clarion call to those who are willing to act, and hurled shame on those who are not.
>
> *(Alter et al., 2020)*

Thunberg has persuaded political leaders to make previously fumbled commitments. She has successfully focused the world's attention on environmental issues that young activists have been protesting for years. She has inspired hundreds of thousands of teenage "Gretas" to skip school to lead their peers in climate strikes around the world. Thunberg represents the spirit of youth today. Her huge influence globally illustrates a number of significant issues that differentiate today's youth from those in the past. She has the great tools that were unavailable years ago. Social media is key to Thunberg's success. Tools such as Twitter, Facebook, Instagram, and WhatsApp help Thunberg reach a global audience in a matter of minutes. The size of the global audience is in the billions and the composition is as diverse as the human population.

When her actions reached them, some people in the audience resonated with the message and took actions to start climate strikes. This is significant because when a person has an idea, the idea may not resonate with many people in a local community. This is the case for Thunberg. Although her teachers and classmates in her school may be sympathetic with her, they did not support her skipping school to strike. They did not join her, but her message reached out to people beyond her immediate community and some people, a small percentage, participated. A small percentage of a very large population can be a lot of people, enough not to be ignored. The tools that carried Thunberg's message were not in existence 20 years ago.

The social media tools and other Internet-enabled technologies have already created different generations of youth. Generation Z and Generation Alpha grew up when digital technologies were generally available. They were born after the Web revolutions in the early 1990s. When the first among them grew up, social media tools and smart devices were already in the making and quickly became accessible. Survey data in 2019 found that today's teens spend more time on social media than in schools (Rideout & Robb, 2019; Zhao, in press). This means that the youth of today are much more connected to the outside world, much more influenced and more likely to take actions to influence the broad world than previous generations.

The possibility for today's youth to participate in or lead activities that have a global impact beyond their schools is much greater and at lower cost than 20 years ago. There are many issues affecting today's youth—climate change, environmental degradation, global economics, intercultural capabilities, gender, politics, pandemics, migration, and mental health to name but a few. They care passionately about these issues as well. Their issues are global and local. They touch everyone in the local community as well as the global community. Thus, it is necessary for education policy to allow educators the space necessary to create opportunities for students to participate and lead global and local activities to address these issues.

Educators can create courses within schools that are global by enrolling students from different countries to address specific issues, for example. These courses can be focused on one global issue but students from different countries work together to address the learning tasks. Students can play different roles and create different products in this course. They can also serve as mutual tutors to share information they have gathered locally with each other. They can further take the course outside the school and create global events happening in their local communities.

Educators can also support students to organize action groups with students in their local communities and across the globe to address global issues they have agreed upon. These groups can collaborate with adults or organize on their own. Likewise, students in schools can organize global meetings, both face-to-face and online. These events can draw students from various countries together to have short-term discussions focusing on specific issues.

When students are engaged in these activities, they exercise their right to self-determination. They learn about self-regulation. They learn about their interests and their capabilities. They learn to be responsible. They learn to interact and communicate with people from different cultures. They learn about freedom, influence, and responsibilities.

Conclusions

The school closures and associated remote learning caused by COVID-19 was a huge and unprecedented reality (United Nations, 2020). The United Nations Secretary General called it a "generational catastrophe" (Gigova & Howard, 2020). Reopening schools was the predominant solution to the problem, but returning to the pre-COVID school paradigm does not necessarily make education better. In fact, simply going "back" to school can just perpetuate the problems that schools and education policy have long been criticized for by students and other stakeholders. Some were not happy with the way education was delivered before COVID-19. Schools have not automatically become better just because they were closed or operating on remote schedules for months at a time. It is a natural reaction for school staff, after working above and beyond normal hours and conditions while schools were shut, to retreat back to the safety of the past as schools reopen. For the sake of our students, educators must not let that happen.

The real problem is not the lack of face-to-face teaching. It is the lack of student self-determination and self-regulation. In other words, the problem with student learning or lack thereof when schools are closed was largely due to the fact that students did not have the opportunity to develop the mindset and skills to become architects of their own learning. As a result, they have not developed the capacity for managing their own time, for passionately seeking knowledge, and for actively and responsibly owning their learning and learning environments. We have ensured that the dominant model is that the students have to be managed by teachers, checked on by teachers, and instructed by teachers all the time.

The lack of self-determination and self-regulation is not a new phenomenon. It had been in existence before the COVID-19 global pandemic. There have been plenty of efforts to reform and improve education. Apart from the bottom-up efforts of educators, education researchers, and stakeholders to introduce small-scale adjustments, policymakers and governments around the world have launched massive top-down reforms to improve education (Schleicher, 2018; Zhao, 2015; Zhao & Gearin, 2018). The results of the reforms have been largely disappointing, without significantly transforming education for the future world. The reforms have not led to more engagement, more positive social and psychological experiences, or more confident and happy students in schools (OECD, 2017; Zhao, 2018e).

There have also been serious interests in better preparing children for the changed and changing world. Many governments have introduced 21st century skills or similar capabilities such as global competency and entrepreneurial thinking into their curricula (Australian Curriculum Assessment and Reporting Authority, 2010; The European Parliament & The Council of the European Union, 2006; Zhao, 2015). But the majority of schools offer the same education experiences for all children. As a result, as Tony Wagner, a well-known thought leader in education, points out in his book *The Global Achievement Gap: Why Even Our Best Schools Don't Teach the New Survival Skills Our Children Need—And What We Can Do About It* there is a global achievement gap, the gap between what schools teach and what the world needs, because even our best schools do not teach the new survival skills (Wagner, 2008).

The key to realizing the new paradigm of education is student ownership. As owners, they take control of what they want to learn and how they want to learn. They also own their education environment. They make decisions about whom they want to work with. They also make decisions about how to organize and manage their learning as a community. Having ownership is perhaps the most important factor that can lead to significant improvement in education, as pointed out by Susan Engel in her *New York Times* piece about the Independent Project, a student run school within a school:

> The students in the Independent Project are remarkable but not because they are exceptionally motivated or unusually talented. They are remarkable because they demonstrate the kinds of learning and personal growth that are possible when teenagers feel ownership of their high school experience, when they learn things that matter to them and when they learn together.
>
> (Engel, 2011)

Accepting that students are the owners of their education is to recognize and respect students' inalienable right to self-determination. Students, however young they may be, are human beings. And human beings have the right to self-determination, including self-determination over their own education. It is unfortunate that this right has been taken away from children, ironically in the name of giving them an education. For the sake of a better education for all children and a better world for everyone, we need to return this right to our children.

References

Alter, C., Haynes, S., & Worland, J. (2020). *Time* 2019 Person of the Year: Greta Thunberg. *Time*. https://time.com/person-of-the-year-2019-greta-thunberg/.

Aragon, C. R., Davis, K., & Fiesler, C. (2019). *Writers in the secret garden: Fanfiction, youth, and new forms of mentoring*. The MIT Press.

Australian Curriculum Assessment and Reporting Authority. (2010). *A curriculum for all young Australians*. www.acara.edu.au/verve/_resources/Information_Sheet_A_curriculum_for_all_young_Australians.pdf.

Bonk, C. J. (2009). *The world is open: how Web technology is revolutionizing education* (1st ed.). Jossey-Bass.

Bonk, C. J., Lee, M. M., Reeves, T. C., & Reynolds, T. H. (Eds.). (2015). *MOOCs and open education around the world*. Routledge.

Brynjolfsson, E., & McAfee, A. (2014). *The second machine age: work, progress, and prosperity in a time of brilliant technologies* (1st ed.). W. W. Norton & Company.

Chertoff, E. (2012, December 12). No teachers, no class, no homework: Would you send your kids here? *The Atlantic*. www.theatlantic.com/national/archive/2012/12/no-teachers-no-class-no-homework-would-you-send-your-kids-here/265354/.

Dorn, E., Hancock, B., Sarakatsannis, J., & Viruleg, E. (2020, June 1). COVID-19 and student learning in the United States: The hurt could last a lifetime. *McKinsey*. www.mckinsey.com/industries/public-and-social-sector/our-insights/covid-19-and-student-learning-in-the-united-states-the-hurt-could-last-a-lifetime.

Duckworth, A. L., & Yeager, D. S. (2015). Measurement matters: Assessing personal qualities other than cognitive ability for educational purposes. *Educational Researcher*, 44(4), 237–251.

Engel, S. (2011, March 15). Let kids rule the school. *New York Times*. www.nytimes.com/2011/03/15/opinion/15engel.html?_r=0.

Fried, I. (2018, Nov 19). Tim Cook discusses staying human in an AI world. www.axios.com/tim-cook-apple-artificial-intelligence-human-ec98a548-0a2f-4a7a-bd65-b4d25395bc27.html.

Gigova, R., & Howard, J. (2020, August 4). We're facing a "generational catastrophe" in education, UN warns. CNN. www.cnn.com/2020/08/04/world/school-closures-catastrophe-un-covid-19-intl/index.html.

Goldin, C., & Katz, L. F. (2008). *The race between education and technology*. Harvard University Press.

Greenberg, D., Sadofsky, M., & Lempka, J. (2005). *The pursuit of happiness: The lives of Sudbury Valley alumni*. Sudbury School Press.

Hamid, R., Sentryo, I., & Hasan, S. (2020). Online learning and its problems in the Covid-19 emergency period. *Jurnal Prima Edukasia*, 8(1), 86–95.

Kallick, B., & Zmuda, A. (2017). *Students at the center: Personalized learning with habits of mind*. ASCD.

Kallio, J. M., & Halverson, R. (2020). Distributed leadership for personalized learning. *Journal of Research on Technology in Education*, 52(3), 371–390.

Levin, S., & Engel, S. (2016). *A school of our own: The story of the first student-run high school and a new vision for American education*. The New Press.

Mukhtar, K., Javed, K., Arooj, M., & Sethi, A. (2020). Advantages, limitations and recommendations for online learning during COVID-19 pandemic era. *Pakistan Journal of Medical Sciences*, 36(COVID19-1S4), S27–S31.

Neil, A. S. (1960). *Summerhill: A radical approach to child rearing*. Hart Publishing.

OECD. (2016). *PISA 2015 results (Volume I): Excellence and equity in education*. http://dx.doi.org/10.1787/9789264266490-en.

OECD. (2017). *PISA 2015 results: Students' well-being*. www.keepeek.com/Digital-Asset-Management/oecd/education/pisa-2015-results-volume-iii_9789264273856-en-.Wk1WGrQ-fOQ#page1.

OECD. (2019). *PISA 2018 results (Volume III): What school life means for students' lives*. https://doi.org/10.1787/acd78851-en.

Pink, D. H. (2006). *A whole new mind: Why right-brainers will rule the future*. Riverhead.

Rideout, V., & Robb, M. B. (2019). *The common sense census: Media use by tweens and teens, 2019*. Common Sense Media.

Schleicher, A. (2018). *World class: How to build a 21st-century school system*. Paris: OECD.

Schwab, K. (2015). The fourth industrial revolution: What it means and how to respond. *Foreign Affairs* (December 12). www.foreignaffairs.com/articles/2015-12-12/fourth-industrial-revolution.

Stanford, P. (2008, January 24). Summerhill: Inside England's most controversial private school. *The Independent*. www.independent.co.uk/news/education/schools/summerhill-inside-englands-most-controversial-private-school-772976.html.

The European Parliament & The Council of the European Union. (2006, December 12). *Recommendation of the European Parliament And of the Council of the European Union on Key Competences for Lifelong Learning*. http://eur-lex.europa.eu/LexUriServ/site/en/oj/2006/l_394/l_39420061230en00100018.pdf.

Tienken, C. H. (2017). *Defying standardization: Creating curriculum for an uncertain future*. Rowman & Littlefield.

Trilling, B., & Fadel, C. (2009). *21st century skills: Learning for life in our times*. John Wiley & Sons.

Tyack, D. B., & Cuban, L. (1995). *Tinkering toward utopia: A century of public school reform*. Harvard University Press.

United Nations. (1989). *Convention on the Rights of the Child*. The United Nations. www2.ohchr.org/english/law/crc.htm.

United Nations. (2020, August). *Policy brief: Education during COVID-19 and beyond*. United Nations. www.un.org/development/desa/dspd/wp-content/uploads/sites/22/2020/08/sg_policy_brief_covid-19_and_education_august_2020.pdf.

Wagner, T. (2008). *The global achievement gap: Why even our best schools don't teach the new survival skills our children need—and what we can do about it*. Basic Books.

Wagner, T. (2012). *Creating innovators: The making of young people who will change the world*. Scribner.

Wehmeyer, M., & Zhao, Y. (2020). *Teaching students to become self-determined learners*. ASCD.

World Economic Forum. (2016). *The future of jobs: Employment, skills and workforce strategy for the fourth industrial revolution*. World Economic Forum. www3.weforum.org/docs/WEF_Future_of_Jobs.pdf.

Xie, H., Chu, H-C., Hwang, G-J., & Wang, C-C. (2019). Trends and development in technology-enhanced adaptive/personalized learning: A systematic review of journal publications from 2007 to 2017. *Computers & Education*, 140, 103599.

Zhao, Y. (2011). Students as change partners: A proposal for educational change in the age of globalization. *Journal of Educational Change*, 12(2), 267–279. doi:10.1007/s10833-011-9159-9.

Zhao, Y. (2012). *World class learners: Educating creative and entrepreneurial students*. Corwin.

Zhao, Y. (2015). *Lessons that matter: What we should learn from Asian school systems*. www.mitchellinstitute.org.au/reports/lessons-that-matter-what-should-we-learn-from-asias-school-systems/.

Zhao, Y. (2016). From deficiency to strength: Shifting the mindset about education inequality. *Journal of Social Issues*, 72(4), 716–735.

Zhao, Y. (2018a). The changing context of teaching and implications for teacher education. *Peabody Journal of Education*, 93, 1–14.

Zhao, Y. (2018b). Personalizable education for greatness. *Kappa Delta Pi Record*, 54(3), 109–115.

Zhao, Y. (2018c). *Reach for greatness: Personalizable education for all children*. Corwin.

Zhao, Y. (2018d). The rise of the useless: The case for talent diversity. *Journal of Science Education and Technology*, 28, 62–68.

Zhao, Y. (2018e). *What works may hurt: Side effects in education.* Teachers College Press.

Zhao, Y. (2021). *Learners without borders.* Corwin.

Zhao, Y. (in press). Social learning and learning to be social: From online instruction to online education. *American Journal of Education.*

Zhao, Y., & Gearin, B. (Eds.). (2018). *Imagining the future of global education: Dreams and nightmares.* Routledge.

Zhao, Y., Wehmeyer, M., Basham, J., & Hansen, D. (2019). Tackling the wicked problem of measuring what matters: Framing the questions. *ECNU Review of Education*, 2(3), 262–278.

8

"WE COME FROM EVERYWHERE"

Innovating Bi/Multilingual Principal Preparation Programs

Soribel Genao

In 2015, the New York State Board of Regents approved changes to the Commissioner's Regulations regarding Bilingual Education and English as a New Language (ENL) programs. The modifications to Part 154 enforced substantial requirements on school districts and educators regarding the instruction, assessment, program placement, and services for English Language Learners/Multilingual Learners (ELLs/MLLs) (NYSUT, 2020).

The modifications also required educators to take part in new professional learning requirements in the effort to provide English learners with opportunities to achieve the same educational goals and standards established for all students (NYSUT, 2020). As mentioned in the NYSUT (2020) report *A Look at the Ramifications of* Part 154 *Changes to ELL Education*, although well-intentioned, some unintended negative consequences of the ramifications have been noted, including the fact that many school and district leadership preparation programs do not focus on how to effectively lead in bi/multilingual communities.

Admittedly, the task of creating a bi/multilingual-centered education leadership program using a social justice lens has not been easy. Understanding that although the results from countless research studies on principal preparation programs and social justice leadership have provided examples of best practices, there continues to be a need to focus on leadership in bi/multilingual schools and communities (Genao, 2020).

An initial attempt to assist the New York State Education Department's project to lead an innovative approach to address the issues involved establishing a pilot program dedicated to preparing local leaders to become global thinkers and leaders by focusing on bi/multilingual communities. The academic preparation, while exhibiting broad social justice understandings, was impacted by universal

DOI: 10.4324/9781003108511-8

understandings of how the state mandated policies impact all stakeholders in the school community (Genao, 2020). The program, while an incremental step in preparing education leadership candidates to become bi/multilingual leaders, had a larger goal to assist New York City's school leaders in their effort to effectively educate ELL/MLL students in the face of decreasing numbers of bilingual education programs (Menken & Solorza, 2015).

PK-12 Education Policy Peril

The New York State Commissioner's Regulations govern the programs for the education of ELLs/MLLs in New York State (NYS). Under CR 154–2.3(d) (2), each school district in which the sum of each school's annual estimate of enrollment of ELLs equals 20 or more ELLs of the same grade level, all of whom have a home language other than English, shall provide a sufficient number of bilingual education (BE) programs in the district the following school year. This was an important mandate whereby teachers, principals, superintendents, teacher education programs, and officials had to work in conjunction to make bilingual education a reality. As a part of NYS's need to meet the needs of ELLs/MLLs, the New York City College created a pilot program with the aims to provide educators' support via professional development for NYS certified teachers and the establishment of a school leader preparation program that included the coursework and experience necessary to complete a Masters of Educational Leadership with a Bilingual Extension Certificate.

During the pilot program, one cohort was established at the New York City College consisting of 16 teacher candidates enrolled in the joint (School Building/School District Leadership and Bilingual Extension) SBL+BIL program. All candidates completed their courses in the Educational Leadership program.

Purpose

This chapter emphasizes how the Commissioner's Regulation Part 154 (CR Part 154), which establishes the legal requirements for the education of ELLs in New York State, lacks acknowledgment of why principal preparation programs should be ready to educate and lead this population of students, schools, and communities. Based on the empirical research conducted in New York City, findings show that teachers who are prepared to lead in multilingual communities expose how future school administrators apply influence in shaping school communities' understanding of policy and the inclusive eminence of teaching and learning that an emergent bilingual (also identified as ELLs) student gets. Although school leaders are essential in fostering academic achievement in multilingual communities, it was glaring that few future administrators understood the importance of serving emergent bilingual students. Not unique to

New York, the preparation of future administrators to become instructional and bilingual leaders is not a requirement.

Need for bi/multilingual preparation programs

Uncritical focus on academic language can overshadow the importance of culturally sustaining pedagogies in diverse contexts. This is especially true for marginalized students *and* teachers of color in an increasingly global and multicultural society (Paris, 2012). Price (2015) also found that the interactions between principals and teachers related to teachers' perceptions of student engagement, which was mediated by trust in teachers and administrative support. Direct relationships between principal–teacher interactions and latent beliefs of trust and support are confirmed. Direct relationships between latent beliefs and perceptions of academic and school engagement are also confirmed. There is a relationship between principal–teacher interactions and teacher perceptions of student engagement, but the mediating effect of latent beliefs of trust and support accounts for much of the direct association.

These collaborative efforts are important for prospective school leaders to learn how to support teachers and cultivate trust as instructional leaders. The efforts should also be experienced and practiced while ensuring integration of support and advocacy of all students and families.

Understanding the critical need for supporting teachers working with bi/multilingual students, the urgency of preparing school leaders was a call to action. The goal of the Masters of Science in Education in Educational Leadership with an emphasis in Bilingual Education relied on the resources developed in NYS to support aspiring and current administrators and principals.

The program supported the vision of providing leadership in education for all children, especially ELLs/MLLs that enhanced the training of potential candidates as they become curriculum coordinators, assistant principals, principals, assistant superintendents, and superintendents who plan to work in districts and schools with substantial populations of ELLs/MLLs. The degree program and bilingual certificate was an asset to those interested in supervising/managing programs for ELLs/MLLs in both Bilingual Education and ENL programs at the district level. Developing this new integrated MSEd program in Education Leadership also qualified the candidates to sit for the New York State Teacher Certification Examinations (NYSTCE),which is a NYS requirement for certification prior to becoming a school building leader.

Understanding that every principal preparation program is different, with its own curriculum, requirements, mandates, and needs, it is also important to understand how to prepare prospective education leaders who will be leading schools with bi/multilingual populations. For schools and communities with bi/multilingual populations, the needs to be addressed extend beyond academics (Genao, 2020). The pilot program exposed the importance of intersecting the bilingual/multilingual leadership and social justice leadership. The intersection created better understanding of fundamental concepts of social justice beginning with a determination of how to balance equal treatment of individuals with the need for special treatment of those who have less (Bolivar, 2012).

Impact of Part 154 and Principal Leadership Programs

The language of Part 154 in the regulations consents to expansive understanding. This is especially the case when principals who are not always prepared to lead bi/multilingual schools exert power in New York to determine the instruction and pedagogical approaches provided to students required by city and state policy to receive ESL and/or bilingual education. Since this is also an added cost for districts to hire talent that are credentialed and experienced, the irregularity of training future administration leads to efficiency that is not always effective. Accordingly, this issue is mirrored in the quality of support teachers can provide to the student population and how teachers are evaluated with the demands of high-stakes accountability. The relationship with their ENL colleagues has been negatively affected by fears from standardized testing pressures, and, as a result, a true collaborative environment has not been forged. At the student level, ELLs/MLLs at the middle to higher levels of English language proficiency lost contact time in stand-alone ENL classrooms when the units of study were revamped. This transition directly impacts student achievement as evidenced by New York State English as a Second Language score, student growth scores, and English Language Proficiency (ELP) accountability, ELL/MLL graduation data and dropout rates. It also influences measures of teaching practices for ENL and classroom teachers as part of the Annual Professional Performance Review (APPR) of teachers.

The two-year pilot program, while showing evidence of success, was discontinued by the NYSED's new administration. The official reason given for discontinuance was that the NYSED officers did not agree with the need for such training because other institutions were pursuing educational leadership programs without the bilingual extension. In essence, not enough institutions were requesting this kind of program support for future leaders.

Deconstruct the Policy Peril

Ladson-Billings (1995) defined *culturally relevant teaching* as a pedagogy of opposition, not unlike critical pedagogy but specifically committed to the collective, not merely individual empowerment. Culturally relevant pedagogy rests on three criteria or propositions: students must (a) experience academic success; (b) develop and/or maintain cultural competence, and (c) develop a critical consciousness through which they challenge the social order's status quo. To accomplish the second criterion, teachers must respect, try to understand, and implement students' history, culture, and values into the curriculum.

Accomplishing the criteria is usually supported by culturally responsive school leaders. Culturally responsive leadership provides a way for educational leaders to theorize their work, develop agency, take action, and build school-wide capacity on issues of equity, diversity, and social justice (Lopez, 2015). In creating a culturally responsive school, leaders must start the process in themselves and lead by example. They would be seeking to find a balance between student performance and school climate if they are to create a successful community within their schools (Morales & Morales, 2020). To establish a better school culture and climate, leaders determine how to help parents feel more welcomed so they can become actively involved. Culturally responsive leadership highlights the ability of the school leader to engage students, parents, families, and communities in culturally appropriate ways (Khalifa et al., 2016). Given that the teaching force is predominantly White (Bireda & Chait, 2011), educators must rely on literature and statistics to help re-evaluate teacher and leader preparation programs to be more culturally responsive (Genao, 2016). This is particularly the case in New York City.

Educating New York City's bi/multilingual children and families has long been part of the city's history (Garcia 1997; 2010). The expansion of bilingual education and ENL programs continued an aggressive push under the de Blasio mayoral administration to meet a pledge to the state to offer more options for students who are learning English by adding almost 50 bilingual education programs, in a move that could help better integrate schools and boost learning for students learning English as a new language (Martinez, 2018; Viega, 2018). In 2018, 13.5% of the 1,135,334 students are ELLs in New York City (NYCDOE, 2019). However, New York State education administrators continued reporting shortages in special education and bilingual/ELL teachers (Cross, 2016). Although the disparity between teachers who are certified to teach the population is wide, the disparity between administrators and students is even wider. Principals, who are called upon to determine their school's language policy, have not received any formal preparation to do so. New York, like most states, does not require any coursework addressing the education of emergent bilinguals for the certification of administrators (Menken & Solorza, 2015).

Almost 20 million people currently live in the New York metro area who speak over 800 languages (Conrad, 2020). Yet, even with so many languages spoken within student communities, the most recent annual report states that there continues to be an expansion in incoming populations and emergent language learners (New York City Department of Education, 2019) without a mirroring increase in administrators prepared for these communities. New York City is home to the highest percentage of MLLs in the state at 63% (LEAD, 2019). In fact, there are 1,866 schools within the New York City Department of Education as of September 2019, and 1,126,501 students in the NYC school system of which 13.2% are ELLs (NYCDOE, 2020). In New York City 19% of bilingual education teachers were not certified in bilingual education, compared to 10.2% on the state level (Donachie,

2018). These data are particularly indicative of the need to prepare future administrators of schools offering bilingual education programs, given the restrictive policy contexts (Genao, 2020; Menken & Solorza, 2015).

Based on information from the New York State Education Department (2014), an aspiring educational leadership candidate must be an effective educator of diverse students and ELLs. S/he must utilize "knowledge of diversity within the school and the community to address the needs of all students, to create a sense of community among students, and to promote students' appreciation of and respect for all students in their diversity" (p. 3) and recognize the "characteristics, strengths, and needs of English Language Learners and effectively use this knowledge to assist in developing their language and literacy skills and promoting their achievement of learning standards in all content areas" (p. 4). Because it was imperative, a reflective work plan was put in place to support the pilot program. The plan consisted of seven mechanisms to prepare for the Masters degree in Educational Leadership and bilingual extension with an emphasis on ELLs/MLLs, as follows:

1. implementing a sequence of courses, field-based experiences, and supervised internships to produce highly qualified bilingual school leadership professionals possessing the knowledge, skills, dispositions, and competencies to prepare education leaders in education and state policy at the community, school, district, and state level. Specifically, teacher candidates would develop knowledge and skills to work with bilingual populations and support all school staff working with multilingual learners, and promote systemic supports for dual and transitional bilingual programs. The accepted students took a pre-test survey targeting their basic leadership knowledge of the Professional Standards for Educational Leadership (National Policy Board for Educational Administration, 2015) at the beginning of their program in order to determine baseline information on these important new standards that guide the work in school leadership.
2. retaining, mentoring, and graduating a cohort of bilingual professionals through intensive supports, including professional mentoring and coaching, peer mentoring, ongoing extended field experiences, and professional development activities to promote reflective problem-solving skills, self-efficacy, and career satisfaction. The aim is to ensure candidates' successful impacts on ELLs/MLLs' academic, behavioral, and social outcomes.
3. providing units and curricula that support the candidates' development of leadership skills and knowledge to be utilized with diverse learners in various school and district settings. Many of these performance indicators are also reflected in the NYSTCE Educating All Students exam which is under the rubric of educating diverse learners and student populations.
4. offering a combination of distance education via online classes will allow the Educational Leadership program to be accessed by New York State certified teacher candidates and administrators.

5. providing field experience opportunities for education leaders that offer practical experience in mentoring and supporting prospective bilingual teachers while focusing on the understanding and implementation of the Common Core State Standards, and Danielson Framework (2013) on evaluation, a practical tool for districts to assess all aspects of planning and professional responsibilities along with classroom teaching and streamlined observations that focus on classroom practice.
6. integrating curricula with clinical experience during the Guided Field Experience course by supporting prospective teacher candidates in preparing their portfolios while simultaneously giving educational leadership candidates the opportunity to extend their practice by conducting evaluations of prospective teachers using the Danielson Framework for Teaching, a set of reflective rubrics for teachers, used in some states as a teacher evaluation instrument.
7. establishing developmentally appropriate field expectations that will also incite the democratization of knowledge production in schools and development of culturally relevant and sustaining pedagogies as critical imperatives toward educational justice. The collaborative clusters must explicitly address these critical imperatives toward educational justice. Thus, proposing that explicit attention to culturally responsive and sustaining pedagogies can effectively frame such professional collaboration and growth among stakeholders in PreK-12.

Considering the program's pilot recognition, changes were made to the curriculum, yet were aligned with the NYSED mandates, the need for culturally responsive pedagogy and leadership and the intended commitment and deliverables of training qualified educators who work with bi/multilingual populations in New York State and seek permanent certification as a SBL.

The measurable objectives and deliverables presented to NYSED are outlined in Table 8.1:

TABLE 8.1 Pilot Objectives and Deliverables

Objective	Deliverable	Analysis and Method
Establish guidelines for coursework for year one and year two for clinically rich and/or mentored experiences	Professional development and training identified, scheduled, and completed	Resources applied toward development of new courses and to identify instructional materials for purchase
	Course syllabi, assignments, critical readings, and evaluations developed	New and revised course syllabi, assignments, readings, and evaluations developed and approved for implementation
	State approval of new program	New program approved & registered with NYSED

(Continued)

Table 8.1 (Cont.)

Objective	Deliverable	Analysis and Method
	Secure electronic data storage and central clearinghouse for trusted resources	Project's Blackboard Organization is developed and populated with resources
	Storage system and central clearinghouse for trusted resources	
	Instructional materials identified and purchased	Materials purchased and securely stored for students' access
Create a website to publicize the programs and share relevant information with NYSED, Regional Bilingual Education Resource Networks (RBERNs), potential participants, school districts, and other stakeholders	Development of information of project goals, mission, vision, and recruitment information	Information promoting and marketing the recruitment of candidates and criteria with application deadline and requirements
Engage in outreach to the public, partnering school districts, Boards of Cooperative Educational Services (BOCES) to identify and recruit qualified candidates	Sites and their respective administrative contacts identified, networking/relationship building activities initiated, and partnerships established	Sufficient number of schools serving ELLs with bilingual populations, staffed by certified ESL teachers with professional experience and bilingual certification secured to recruit candidates in ongoing extended field experience component
Establish guidelines for participants and assurance that participants are committed to program for duration	Number of screened, accepted, and rejected applicants	Review of transcripts, letters of recommendation, and personal statements
Report to NYSED on candidate progress, completion, and certification rates		
Develop and maintain a record of participating students throughout the grant-contract period	Evaluation of candidates' GPAs, instructors' feedback, and course key assignments	Review final course grades and cumulative GPAs, instructor feedback, and field linked and other course artifacts (Professional Developments or PDs)
How are candidates performing in courses, courses linked to field experiences, and program level assessments?	Evaluation of candidates' GPAs, instructors' feedback, and course key assignments	Review final course grades and cumulative GPAs, instructor feedback, and field linked and other course artifacts (PDs)

(*Continued*)

136   Soribel Genao

Table 8.1 (Cont.)

Objective	Deliverable	Analysis and Method
	90% of instructors' assessment of candidates' performance on key assignments are at "acceptable" or higher levels across elements assessed	Review individual performance assessment on key assignments and course artifacts electronically stored
How are candidates performing on the NY State School Building Leaders Assessments and the Bilingual Education Assessments?	Match or exceed EL candidates' history of pass rates	Review data compiled to examine candidates' performance across sub-areas and correlate this with course performance
How many candidates completed (graduated in) the program from the cohort?	At minimum, 80% of candidates complete the program and graduate	Review data compiled to determine total number of project completers and total number certified by NYSED

Throughout this pilot program, the candidates:

- learned about the three significant models of organization behavior as these models relate to education. A number of theories are advanced that serve to illustrate these models in the practice of educational administration in bilingual communities;
- learned how to educate future school leaders working in bilingual communities diversifying equitable curriculum design models, interpret school-level curricula, initiate needs analyses plan and implement with staff a framework for instruction, align curriculum with anticipated outcomes, monitor social and technological developments as they affect curriculum, and adjust curriculum content as needs and conditions change;
- examined school finance and budgeting practices in bilingual public elementary and secondary schools in New York State. The course guided candidates in an examination of financial allocation issues. Candidates learned how to calculate and analyze school-level revenue and expenditure budgetary data and relate fiscal decisions towards producing increased student performance outcomes;
- differentiated between the bilingual education communities and general education communities;
- learned how to navigate a variety of supervisory and administrative relationships within the bilingual and general education setting. These methods of navigation consisted of psychology, sociology, and educational developments that draw upon human behaviors and working collaboratively;
- utilized activities that were designed to connect with bilingual communities:

- learned and utilized mapping in order to have a better understanding of how ethnic, racial, and socio-economic geography impact the administrative methods of bilingual communities in New York State, New York City, and the respective countries in which candidates live and work;
- gained knowledge from collaborating with parents, community-based organizations, other schools within the districts, businesses in the community and external partners.

To the extent of meeting the primary goal of this project that identified highly qualified bi/multilingual future administrators, the knowledge, skills, and dispositions to meet program completions were constantly assessed via rubrics, observations, and feedback to students.

Implications and Taking Action

In policy and practice, the curriculum included in the pilot program described in this chapter has implications for the development of structures that support Educational Leadership candidates as they prepare for leadership roles in school and to take their licensure exam. The program curriculum provides leadership candidates the opportunity to extend their practice by conducting evaluations using the Charlotte Danielson Framework for Teaching (FFT), receiving feedback from faculty and invited superintendents, and helped to foster critical examination of how prepared candidates felt to lead via self-assessments and reflection simulations and activities beyond the curriculum.

The various job-embedded activities in the pilot program allowed for assessment of valued psychosocial and attitudinal characteristics such as teamwork, which has been touted as one of the critical skills that define workforce readiness in the 21st century (Basu & Barton, 2007; Casner-Lotto & Barrington, 2006). The outcomes of the program included an increase of career opportunities, preparation for the workforce, success in team environments, and better understanding and improvement of their teamwork skills (and related competencies). The preparation of the candidates also promoted the creation of pedagogical spaces in which candidates were able to engage in dialogue and receive critique with other candidates as well as teacher educators regarding these mandated frameworks and assessments.

A more comprehensive analysis of the outcomes revealed that candidates who were prepared in the pilot model (n=15) differed from those in the traditional model (n=15) in four important ways:

- Increased their knowledge and practical skills regarding immigration policies and impact (the ordinal (linear) chi-square = 8.20, $p < 0.01$)
- Positive attitudes toward the School Building Leadership Exams were related to greater satisfaction with the new program ($r = .502$, $p < .05$)

- EL candidates in the pilot program felt more confident regarding the role of standards and accountability in promoting quality and equity in education and attitudes about assessment than traditional candidates;
- EL candidates in the pilot program were less apprehensive about exam requirements, and found that feedback sessions and simulations helped clarify their understanding of how immigration policies, race, and class impact student, teacher, and leadership performance;

Feedback sessions in which EL candidates had access to the feedback on their peers' work and how to deal with difficult conversations and scenarios seemed to improve students' self-reported understanding of exam tasks limitations in that the data was gathered via self-report assessment based on the 10 PSEL and was descriptive in nature and not causal.

Additional outcomes from the program based on changes after the first year included:

- The students in the pilot program increased in each of the 10 PSEL standards.
- The pilot perceived that they grew in every one of the standards and overall, e.g., standard #1(Mission, Vision, and Core Value) from 4.1 to 9.2 as a mean score.
- In comparing the pilot cohort to the traditional EL cohort, as expected, they improved in every standard but one, standard #8 (Meaningful Engagement of Families and Community) from 7.6 to 7.3, a slight decrease.
- The pilot cohort exceeded the regular EDL cohort in nine of the ten standards with the exception of standard 9 (Operations and Management) by a very slight amount—7.8 to 7.9
- The written observations after the survey reinforced the Likert scale results. The mean GPA for the bi/multilingual cohort during the academic year was higher than for the traditional EL program.

Supporting the scopes of measurement, with the requirement of New York State English Language Arts and Math state assessment, leaders continue to be concerned with the achievement gap between English as a New Language students compared to students whose first language is in English. With the high-stakes exams, leaders are more concerned about the data. In order for school to disrupt injustice, it is crucial to have morally committed effective leaders with a clear vision who can "break the silence" (Fine, 1994) by using their voices as leaders to narrate how they worked to disrupt injustice through their distinct strategies. (Theoharis, 2010) and, most importantly, perseverance. It is also not only the work of the principal but the teamwork and collaboration of the whole school that can make schools just and equitable.

In reflecting on the findings, the importance of and support from the NYSED were emphasized. As the demographics of our nation's population continue to increase and the socio-political electoral climates transition, the critical mandate to support and sponsor principal preparation programs is essential. Future administrators will not only be better prepared, but will have diverse knowledge of the needs for bi/multilingual communities.

Recommendations

In support of the literature and outcomes of the pilot program, the importance of principal preparation programs focusing on bi/multilingual students and communities should be an essential facet of Part 154. In comparing students from the traditional EL program with the pilot program, it was clear that the confidence in preparedness was due to the focus and agenda around intersecting social justice with culturally responsive pedagogy and leadership. If the purpose of policy is for effective change, then there should be an added focus on the impact of principal preparation programs focused on diversity with an equity and inclusion lens.

Likewise, the accountabilities of administrators serving bi/multilingual communities are not the same as those administrators not serving that population of students. The outcomes of the pilot program supports the recommendation for preparing future administrators by revamping programs with a focus on bi/ multilingual education. Further, this same approach can be scaled throughout the state as a whole. The negative socio-political climate toward immigrants has had significant negative consequences for bi/multilingual communities. Simultaneously, districts and schools should be more intentional about cultivating innovative approaches that assist school leaders and future administrators with professional development that focuses on bi/multilingual communities. Also, as the findings indicate, the cohort in the pilot program demonstrated the importance of Part 154's emphasis on the impact of principal preparation programs' requirement to focus on bi/multilingual communities.

References

Basu, S. J., & Barton, A. C. (2007). Developing a sustained interest in science among urban minority youth. *Journal of Research in Science Teaching*, 44(3), 466–489.

Bireda, S., & Chait, R. (2011). Increasing teacher diversity: Strategies to improve the teacher workforce. Center for American Progress. https://cdn.americanprogress.org/wp content/uploads/issues/2011/11/pdf/chait_diversity.pdf.

Bolívar, A. (2012). Melhorar os processos e os resultados educativos. O que nos ensina a. investigação. Vila Nova de Gaia: Fundação Manuel Leão. https://fmleao.pt/ficheiros/Melhorar/Melhorar-a-escola.pdf#page=109.

Casner-Lotto, J., & Barrington, L. (2006). Are they really ready to work? Employers' perspectives on the basic knowledge and applied skills of new entrants to the 21st century US workforce. Partnership for 21st Century Skills. 1 Massachusetts Avenue NW Suite 700, Washington, DC 20001.

Conrad, K. (2020). How many languages are spoken in the New York area. www.worldatlas.com/articles/how-many-languages-are-spoken-in-nyc.html.

Cross, F. (2016, August). Teacher shortage areas: Nationwide listing 1990–1991 through 2016–2017. U.S. Department of Education, Office of Postsecondary Education. www2.ed.gov/about/offices/list/ope/pol/tsa.doc.

Danielson, C. (2013). The framework for teaching evaluation instrument, 2013 instructionally focused edition. www.nctq.org/dmsView/2013_FfTEvalInstrument_Web_v1_2_20140825.

Donachie, P. (2018, October). Will the city's new schools contract reduce the unequal impact of teacher turnover?https://citylimits.org/2018/10/18/will-the-citys-new-schools-contract-reduce-the-unequal-impact-of-teacher-turnover/.

Fine, M. (1994). Dis-stance and other stances: Negotiations of power inside feminist research. In A. Gitlin (Ed.) *Power and method: Political activism and educational research* (pp. 13–35). Routledge.

García, O. (1997). New York's multilingualism: World languages and their role in a U.S. city. In O. García, & J. A. Fishman (Eds.), *The multilingual apple: Languages in New York City* (pp. 3–50). Mouton.

García, O. (2010). Bilingualism in education in the multilingual apple: The future of the past. *Journal of Multilingual Education Research*, 1(1), 5.

Genao, S. (2016). Culturally responsive pedagogy: Reflections on mentoring by educational leadership candidates. *Issues in Educational Research*, 26(3), 431.

Genao, S. (2020). Meeting the needs for bi/multilingual education leadership preparation. (Re). Building bi/multilingual leaders for socially just communities, 1. www.infoagepub.com/products/Rebuilding-Bi-Multilingual-Leaders-for-Socially-Just-Communities.

Khalifa, M. A., Gooden, M. A., & Davis, J. E. (2016). Culturally responsive school leadership. *Review of Educational Research*, 86(4), 1272–1311.

Ladson-Billings, G. (1995). But that's just good teaching! The case for culturally relevant pedagogy. *Theory Into Practice*, 34(3), 159–165.

Latino Education Advocacy Directors. (2019). *Leaders investing in our future: A multilingual learner policy agenda for New York State*. www.latinoedleaders.org/resources/2020/7/5/investing-in-our-future.

Lopez, A. E. (2015). Navigating cultural borders in diverse contexts: building capacity through culturally responsive leadership and critical praxis. *Multicultural Education Review*, 7(3), 171–184.

Martínez, R. A. (2018). Beyond the English learner label: Recognizing the richness of bi/multilingual students' linguistic repertoires. *The Reading Teacher*, 71(5), 515–522.

Menken, K., & Solorza, C. (2013). Where have all the bilingual programs gone?!: Why prepared school leaders are essential for bilingual education. *Journal of Multilingual Education Research*, 4(1), 3.

Menken, K., & Solorza, C. (2015). Principals as linchpins in bilingual education: The need for prepared school leaders. *International Journal of Bilingual Education and Bilingualism*, 18(6), 676–697.

Morales, L., & Morales, O. (2020). Aligning curriculum for culturally responsive leadership. (Re) Building bi/multilingual leaders for socially just communities, 31. www.infoagepub.com/products/Rebuilding-Bi-Multilingual-Leaders-for-Socially-Just-Communities.

National Policy Board for Educational Administration. (2015). *Professional standards for educational leaders 2015*. www.npbea.org/psel/.

New York City Department of Education. (2019). *2018–2019 English Language Learner Demographic Report New York City Department of Education Division of Multilingual Learners.* https://infohub.nyced.org/docs/default-source/default-document-library/ell-demographic-report.pdf.

New York State Education Department. (2014). *Educating all students test design and framework.* www.nystce.nesinc.com/PDFs/NY201_OBJ_FINAL.pdf.

New York State United Teachers (NYSUT). (2020). *A look at the ramifications of Part 154 changes to ELL education: Key recommendations for decision makers.* www.nysut.org/news/2020/august/part-154-ell.

Paris, D. (2012). Culturally sustaining pedagogy: A needed change in stance, terminology, and practice. Educational Researcher, 41(3), 93–97.

Price, H. E. (2015). Principals' social interactions with teachers: How principal–teacher social relations correlate with teachers' perceptions of student engagement. *Journal of Educational Administration,* 53(1), 116–139.

Theoharis, G. (2010). Sustaining social justice: Strategies urban principals develop to advance justice and equity while facing resistance. *International Journal of Urban Educational Leadership,* 4(1), 92–110.

Viega, C. (2018, May 3). New York City to add almost 50 bilingual programs, the latest in a push to help English learners. *Chalkbeat.* Retrieved: https://chalkbeat.org/posts/ny/2018/05/03/new-york-city-to-add-50-bilingual-programs-thelatest-in-a-push-to-help-english-learners/.

9
EVALUATING THE DIFFERENT SIDES OF EDUCATION POLICIES

A Practical Policy Analysis Framework for School Leaders

Christopher H. Tienken

Introduction

A few analysis tools exist that school leaders can use to unpack policies. Examples include the Strengths-Weaknesses-Opportunities-Threats (SWOT) and PRINCE framework for political analysis of a policy (O'Leary & Coplin, 1976). But, practical frameworks for analyzing the content of education policies and projecting their potential consequences before enacting them are lacking. A dearth of policy analysis frameworks explicitly takes into account the current neoliberal policy environment and its impact on educational equity within schools. The lack of an evidence-based, practical framework with an eye on neoliberalism from which to analyze the content of policies and predict potential consequences can put some school leaders in the position of supporting education policies that have long-term negative effects on students. Conversely, and also problematic for administrators is not recognizing and capitalizing on educationally positive aspects of policies that would benefit students.

In this chapter I propose a policy analysis framework that school leaders can use to conduct an initial scan of education policies at the school level. The framework is anchored in the progressivist education philosophy and draws upon over 100 years of education research evidence and principles of democracy, yet is meant for the busy school leader on the go. Seven reflective questions are provided, steering away from an academic treatise on policy evaluation.

The five-component framework ("SIDES") is a practical, yet evidence-based tool that school leaders can use to analyze multiple sides of an education policy. The framework focuses on some ways in which education policies influence students, instruction and curriculum, democratic principles, equity, and social justice within the school. The SIDES framework, as I coin it, derives empirical support from the

DOI: 10.4324/9781003108511-9

landmark research that forms what is known as the Curriculum Paradigm (Tanner & Tanner, 2007). For decades, researchers and practitioners have used the Curriculum Paradigm to predict the success or failure of education reforms.

Current Policy Landscape

National and state education policies in the United States are replete with examples of how neoliberal influences moved public education into a state of bifurcation, a dual system of education. I use the description Mullen et al. (2013) articulated to define neoliberalism as "the economic ideological stances of free-market competition, and the privatization of state social services" (p. 182). The market system that has come to occupy public education does not run on democratic principles, ethics, or principles of equity—it operates on economic self-interest. Neoliberal education policies are camouflaged in the language of efficiency and effectiveness, but the overriding objectives are elitism and profit. The outcomes of such policies often lead to education inequity.

The bifurcated system provides taxpayer-funded alternatives to public school for the elite by draining the budgets of public schools that serve approximately 56 million children in the country to pay for the options afforded to the elite. Public magnet schools, charter schools, vouchers and tax credits for private schools, and the creation of selective public school academies are examples of how the intersection of regulatory and redistributive policies enact a dual system of education through structures that separate public schools from the public.

Americans find themselves in a period of elite dominance in policymaking including policies that pertain to education. Gilens and Page (2014) suggested that the United States has been transformed from a representative democracy, known formally as a *Majoritarian Electoral Democracy*, to a form of government categorized as *Economic-Elite Domination*, in which policies reflect the desires of a minority of economic elites. Governments characterized by economic-elite domination are also known as plutocracies, or government by the wealthy. As Gilens and Page (2014) explained,

> In the United States, our findings indicate, the majority does not rule—at least not in the causal sense of actually determining policy outcomes. When a majority of citizens disagrees with economic elites or with organized interests, they generally lose.
>
> (p. 576)

In these times, a socially just education promises to reinvigorate interest in the type of representative democracy needed to produce an equitable society (Tienken, 2020b). As Hinchey and Konkol (2022, Chapter 3, this volume) wrote, "Policymakers who wish to support democratic reform need to recognize the deeply embedded political issue and defend against perversion of their intent when new policies are translated to classroom action" (p. 52). In order to promote equitable education, the needs and interests of the many must outweigh the interests of an economically elite minority.

Structured Inequity

The United States' locally controlled unitary public system, once based on egalitarian and democratic aims, has been recast, by for-profit business interests—termed by Mullen (2021) as *Public Education, Inc.*—into a dual system founded upon meritocracy and market economics. Policies and programs in the country born out of neoliberalism penetrate almost all aspects of public education in some form, becoming normalized in the American psyche (Tienken, 2021).

Education policies based on neoliberal principles obfuscate views of a robust unitary system of public education. Dewey (1916) advocated for a system in which the structure and function of public school served to increase educational equity for all students and prepare them to be informed, participatory members of a democratic society. Beyond the structurally oriented policies that split the unitary system into a dual system, regulatory policies entrench neoliberal principles within the dual system to guarantee its continuance.

Standardized Inequity

One-size-fits-all standardization of curriculum, teaching, and student assessment coalesce to form a toxic mixture of Social Darwinism and performativity in which education is viewed as a zero sum game in that some must lose for others to win. Social Darwinism is a concept that suggests only the strongest, best-adapted humans should excel in society (Bannister, 1989). Proponents of neoliberal education policy believe that only students perceived to be the strongest deserve access to equitable education opportunities and that all others must be made to lose in order to supply resources to the elite within an efficient neoliberal market system.

How is Social Darwinism visible? One can spot it through the uses of one-size-fits-all curricula standards, rigid teacher evaluation systems, and results from mandated standardized testing to make important decisions about children and teachers. For children, poor performance on a single state test can result in being (a) denied entrance into quality academic program tracks or schools, (b) retained at a grade level, (c) placed in low academic tracks, or (d) denied the opportunity to graduate high school. The ingrained public perception is that students who do not perform as expected on one state-mandated test do not merit higher quality opportunities. Based on their test results, the academically weakest are deemed undeserving of having access to elite education options (Tienken, 2021). Teachers can be penalized with poor classroom evaluation ratings for not implementing standards with fidelity, even when that curriculum clashes with the cognitive, social, and emotional developmental needs of their students. They can be subject to salary reductions, challenges to their tenure rights, or denial of merit pay if their students do not score well enough on mandated standardized tests.

Another potentially insidious result of standardization is the smothering of what Mullen (2017) termed the "creative disposition" (p. 4). She associated the creative dispositions with a sense of wonder in the classroom:

> Wonder fuels creativity-curious students to generate questions on their own. When they partake in activities that introduce them to inquiry as an intellectual habit, they are being cultivated to have multiple perspectives on an idea or issue. We can think of this as a creative disposition.
>
> (p. 4)

The creative disposition does not just materialize spontaneously in the classroom—it is cultivated by teachers who share the creative disposition and are able to enact it in their teaching by providing the space for students to experience and exercise their creative dispositions. Standardization is a barrier to creativity. In many cases, it kills creativity in classrooms because it breeds conformity of teaching, thinking, and demonstration of understanding through rigid prescriptions for student output.

Performativity

Much of the dual system of education is buttressed by education accountability policies that work in concert to perpetuate a culture of constant failure in the public system and the appearance of excellence in the elite system. Accountability policies are founded upon the theory of performativity. Lyotard (1984) explained that this theory revolves around the ability of a social system, and those who work within it, to achieve the external goals set for it in the most efficient manner. Built upon language such as *effective, distinguished, failing, proficient*, and *partially proficient*, education accountability systems seek to label and sort people into inanimate categories.

The ubiquitous use of standardized test scores is one prominent example of performativity in action. The test score is viewed as the efficient proxy for quality and effectiveness at each level of the accountability system. Failure to meet predefined levels of achievement can result in being labeled as ineffective and enduring sanctions placed upon educators and students. As Butler (1997) described, the assigning of labels is a key aspect of controlling behaviors and perceptions within a system, based on the performativity theory. Labeling an educator or a student as substandard in some way works to dehumanize people within a system, which makes it easier to then attack the system itself and impose policies that sanction the system and those within it. Conversely, labeling elite education options as effective and efficient works to deify those options in the minds of the public and insulate the elite options from the attacks faced by public schools. The deification of elite education options pollutes the public mindset, resulting in the normalization of redistributing funds from the public system to the dual system of elite options.

Dewey (1916) clarified some perils of embracing the dual system in which the wealthy elite subjugate the less wealthy to an inferior education:

> The more activity is restricted to a few definite lines—as it is when there are rigid class lines preventing adequate interplay of experiences—the more action tends to become routine on the part of the class at a disadvantage, and capricious, aimless, and explosive on the part of the class having the materially fortunate position.
>
> (p. 242)

Dewey's quote prophesized the situation presented by Coughlan (2022, Chapter 4, this volume) in which the White middle class and elite class wall themselves off from other races through formal and informal policies of segregation. As Coughlan stated, while *Brown v. Board of Education* is in the rearview mirror of American society, it is front and center in education policy because segregation is still entrenched in the public education system aided by neoliberal policymaking.

The public education system now finds itself victimized by what Sandel (2012) called the "commercialization effect," in which government policy replaced a public social system of education with a market-based system of education (p. 120). The commercialization effect of the legally mandated market system of education entrenches what Freire (2000) termed a Banking Model of education for many students in the public system.

The Banking Model is a metaphor for a form of education in which students are viewed as passive receptacles of information. Unfortunately, the passive view of learning exemplified by the Banking Model is the predominant view of learning put forth in most neoliberal policies. Neoliberal education policies commonly place students in roles in which they are responsible for little more than unquestionably accepting and regurgitating knowledge at a time and format decided upon by educators and policymakers. The commercialization effect objectifies students by assigning such labels to them as *college and career-ready, partially proficient*, and *at-risk*, based on standardized test results. Then, students are assigned to various neoliberal education products as interventions, based upon the standardized system, that trap and stigmatize them with academic labels.

Privileged students, most often from upper class White families, generally score higher on standardized tests than students from poverty and of color. Those who are privileged go on to receive academic accolades and access to the best education opportunities while marginalized students receive a more mechanistic education aimed at raising the testing scores that are biased against them (Rosner, 2003; Tienken, 2020a).

Is This Policy Good for Kids?

Neoliberal policies and programs enacted under the ambiguous banners of education reform or accountability are sometimes difficult for school leaders to understand and critique. The rationales put forth for neoliberal policies often include logical sounding language aimed at reforming some aspect of education. The appealing, seemingly progressive language used to justify the policies can make it difficult to argue against them (English, 2021). Who would debate more *rigorous* coursework that is standardized for students so they can all become *college-and-career ready* to better compete in the *global economy*? What could possibly be wrong with using standardized test scores to judge student achievement, teacher quality, principal quality, and school quality and determine whether a student can graduate high school or move to the next grade? Those tests are objective measures of a student's achievement and a teacher's skill, are they not?

On the surface, most of the reform rhetoric sounds appropriate and beneficial, and many education reform proposals have positive aspects. But the devil lurks somewhere below the surface, in the intricate details. Beyond the progressive-sounding policy titles and pious language live consequences that are rarely fully examined or explained to educators or the public. In many cases, educators come to know the details and consequences of education policies as they try to implement them. School leaders seldom have time to fully identify the long- and short-term consequences of policies to develop customized responses prior to implementation.

The SIDES Policy Analysis Framework

It is reasonable to expect school leaders to determine the potential efficacy of a policy so they can, as Dewey and Tufts (1908, p. 2) wrote, distinguish between whether the reform is ethically and educationally "right and wrong, good and bad" for students, educators, and the system. Education reform policies and programs do not operate in isolation. They are part of a larger societal ecosystem and generally have different sides or aspects to them. A school leader can use the SIDES framework to view specific aspects of education policies based on the five components previously introduced: (1) students, (2) instruction and curriculum, (3) democratic principles, (4) equity, and (5) social justice. School leaders can use the results of the analysis to determine which components are positive, negative, or neutral in their potential effects on students and teachers (see Figure 9.1). The results of their initial analysis can set the stage for school leaders to conduct a deeper dive or to begin action planning to address the negative effects, capitalize on the positive effects, and develop ways to transform neutral effects into positive ones.

Student Component. Neoliberal policies tend to put students in situations in which they are treated as passive learners, like receptacles for knowledge, as Freire (2000) described with his Banking Model of education. The first component of

148 Christopher H. Tienken

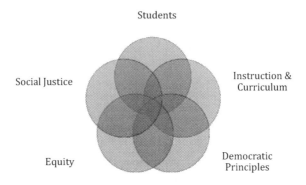

FIGURE 9.1 SIDES Policy Analysis Framework. This figure depicts five intersecting circles. Each circle represents one of the components of the SIDES policy analysis framework: (1) Students, (2) Instruction & Curriculum, (3) Democratic Principles, (4) Equity, (5) Social Justice.

the framework, *students*, is a lens leaders can use to analyze how well a policy aligns with the prevailing research on how students learn best.

Results from classic and recent studies coalesce around the theme of active learning as the answer to the question, how do students learn best? (Dewey, 1916; Kontra et al., 2015; Pirrone & Di Nuovo, 2014). The essence of active learning is that students learn best when engaged in learning opportunities and experiences that recognize them as active constructors of meaning who bring life and academic experiences, interests, passions, emotions, and prior collateral knowledge to the classroom (Dewey, 1916/2009; Tanner & Tanner, 2007). More students learn and are empowered to learn when they are treated as partners in the education process rather than absorbers and regurgitators of facts who perform basic skills upon request.

Results from landmark studies (e.g., Aikin, 1942) have demonstrated that students are not passive learners and blank slates upon which to imprint knowledge, empty vessels to fill with information, or sponges that learn best by soaking up facts. Simply put, students learn best when they actively participate in their own learning and make meaningful or useful connections between their prior knowledge and experiences and new knowledge and experiences (e.g., Merriman et al., 2020). Dewey (1916/2009) noted that educators must abandon the notion of education as the pouring of "knowledge into a mental and moral hole which awaits filling" (p. 39). Prior experiences of the student cannot be ignored or jettisoned from the learning environment because those experiences provide the potential bridges between their existing and new knowledge and skills.

School leaders can use the *student* lens of the framework to make efficient and practical evaluations of policies from the standpoint of how they view the learner:

active +, passive −, or neutral =, somewhere in between. Armed with that knowledge, school leaders can then go about engaging their staffs in democratic conversations about ways the educators in the building can bend the arc of a policy at the point of contact, the classroom, to increase the active learning that takes place.

School leaders can use this reflective question to guide their analysis of the *student* component of the framework: How well does the policy facilitate the student to be an active constructor of meaning who brings prior knowledge to the situation, and what further actions can we take as a school to create more opportunities for active learning? Leaders can answer with a +, −, or =.

Instruction and curriculum component. The second component speaks to how an educational situation should facilitate the learner in connecting prior experiences to the new content or skills and using those experiences as a bridge to more complex learning and experiences. In short, instruction and curriculum should actively seek to connect the content to the student in ways that promote active learning and increased understanding and control over future experiences (Dewey, 1916/2009).

Education policies and practices should capitalize on opportunities to connect content and students through developmentally appropriate common experiences, interests, passions, and emotions. The instructional strategies used must acknowledge the natural predilection of students towards active learning and allow them to exercise self-determination by having some voice and choice in how and what they learn (Fackler, 2020; Zhao & Watterston, 2022.

Historically, students achieve better academic, sociocivic, and personal development results when knowledge is organized into socially conscious, culturally relevant, problem-based, and project-based curricula activities (e.g., Dewey, 1916; Gijbels, Dochy, Van den Bossche, & Segers, 2005; Henriksen & Shack, 2020; Ladson-Billings, 1994). In most cases, the more customized the curricula around relevant problems and projects of interest to the students in the school, the more opportunities and multiple pathways they have to self-actualize their learning and achieve better results on academic and affective measures.

School leaders should view discipline-centered content, organized and taught in their individual silos (e.g., algebra, biology, and U.S. history) as something to be avoided. One problem with many curricular-based education reform policies is that the content, often standardized, is divorced from student experience, and cultures, and it is separated from other content areas. Policies that treat content as something separate and apart from lived experiences of students quickly become useless and forgotten in the minds of students. Dewey (1916) wrote, "But when the subject matter is not used in carrying forward impulses and habits to significant results, it is just something to be learned. The pupil's attitude to it is just that of having to learning it" (p. 169). Instruction quickly becomes mechanical when standardized curricular policies, enforced with standardized testing and teacher evaluation methods, are foisted upon teachers. Not only does curriculum and instruction become divorced from the lived experiences and active learning preferences of students when heavily standardized, it transforms their self-determination into learned helplessness in which they become habituated to the role of automaton (the Banking Model as per Freire, 2000).

Trapped in a standardized policy system, teachers can lose some of their altruistic motivation when also feeling like automatons, with few opportunities to use their educational imaginations. Because altruism is one of the most frequently cited motivations for teaching, school leaders should be on the lookout for how policies can crush teachers' altruistic motivation (Kunz et al., 2020). School leaders need to analyze the longer term consequences of policies from the viewpoint of how well polices support curriculum and instruction that foster active learning and connect content to the lived experiences of students and facilitate teacher creativity.

School leaders can use this lens of the framework (*instruction and curriculum*) to make efficient and practical analyses of policies from the standpoint of how they influence instruction and curriculum. Policies and programs that seek to script educator practice and student learning and assessment or otherwise intentionally or unintentionally restrict educators' ability to design, develop, and customize curriculum and connect it to student interest, needs, and backgrounds would be evaluated negatively, –, within the framework. Whereas policies that foster the organization of curriculum content, assessment, and instruction around socially conscious, culturally relevant, and interesting projects, problems, and/or scenarios would be evaluated as more positive, +. Policies that are ambivalent toward instruction and curriculum would be evaluated as being neutral, =, within this component.

Results from the analysis of this component can be used to engage staffs in democratic discussions about ways educators can reshape policy at the classroom level. Those discussions initiated or led by school leaders should focus on progressive ways to increase the organization of curriculum content, assessment, and instruction around socially conscious, culturally relevant, and interesting projects, problems, and/or scenarios to facilitate creative teaching, active learning, and meaningful connections between content and students.

School leaders can use this reflective question to guide their analysis of the Instruction and Curriculum component: How well does the policy in question facilitate the organization and teaching of curriculum content and its customization by the educators in the building to maximize creative instruction and the connecting of content to student experiences to foster active learning?

Democratic Principles. Democratic leadership and democratic education are some effective defenses against neoliberal domination of education and the overall erosion of democratic institutions. Ward (1883) first brought forth the importance of sociocivic education as one of the three fundamental functions of public school as part of what he called the three universal curriculums. An expansion of Ward's ideas and those of other progressive thinkers (e.g. Dewey, 1916) would later be published as the *Cardinal Principles of Secondary Education* (Commission on the Reorganization of Secondary Education, 1918).

The sociocivic aim called for public education to include experiences and knowledge to help students become informed, responsible, and participating citizens in a democracy and the global community. One historic role of public education has been that of the incubator of democratic thinking in the United States (Dewey, 1959). Public education has a history of uniting diverse peoples through exposure to the principles of democracy through a liberal education. This is how Dewey (1929) explained the importance of the sociocivic role of public education in nurturing a democracy:

> For the creation of a democratic society we need an educational system where the process of moral intellectual development is in practice as well as in theory a cooperative transaction of inquiry engaged in by free, independent human beings who treat ideas and the heritage of the past as means and methods for the further enrichment of life, quantitatively and qualitatively, who use the good attained for the discovery and establishment of something better.
>
> *(p. 84)*

School leaders can use this lens of the framework to make efficient and practical analyses of policies from the standpoint of how they influence sociocivic education and democratic leadership within the school building. Education policies that violate basic tenets of sociocivic learning and democratic leadership via top-down mandates that result in decreased shared decision making and increased meritocracy aimed at maintaining the advantages of the dominant culture pose an existential threat to democracy, in and out of the school building and would be evaluated negatively, –, within the framework.

Threats to sociocivic aims and democratic leadership need to be recognized by school leaders and they must work to overcome them or lessen their impact through acts of creative compliance (Tienken, 2020a). Likewise, policies that promote egalitarian practices and democratic principles such as shared decision making would be evaluated as more positive, +, and school leaders should seek ways to capitalize upon them. Policies that are ambivalent toward democratic education and democratic leadership would be evaluated as being neutral, =, within this component.

School leaders can use the evaluation of this component to engage their staff in democratic discussions about ways the educators in the building can increase sociocivic education and democratic leadership within the school. School leaders can use the following reflective question to guide their evaluation of the Democracy component: How well does the policy facilitate shared decision making and egalitarian principles in the school and what can we do to further democratic principles in the school?

Educational Equity. A common solution heard in education policy circles to improving educational equity and addressing the differences that exist in student achievement is to provide students with access to more resources. Scherrer (2014) termed this policy strategy as the "resource-based perspective" of education reform. Scherrer summed up the approach as a belief that,

> The effects of poverty can be buffered by giving students high-quality school-based resources (e.g., better teachers, and more of them). Scherrer identified an important weakness of the idea by stating that, "a resource-based perspective focuses on the first dimension of poverty—disparities in specific resources.
>
> *(p. 202)*

Access to high quality educational resources is one thing necessary for an equitable education experience. However, resources alone can't overcome the dampening effect that living in poverty or living without the support necessary to make full use of access to education opportunities has on learning.

Differences in student achievement and learning also exist in places where all students and teachers have access to the same type and amount of resources. Pascoe, Wood, Duffee, and Kuo (2016) explained that students from poverty and lower income strata experience anxiety, stress, trauma, food and housing insecurity, violence, and health insecurity at much higher rates than their well-off peers. They stated that evidence from more than 50 years of studies suggests that, regardless of the access of resources, "Poverty has direct negative effects on early brain development through the mechanism of toxic stress" (p. e3). Students living in poverty need more and different types of supports than their well-off peers to make full use of the resources provided to them. Simply providing Internet access and a complementary device will not bring educational equity to remote learning.

Scherrer (2014) urged policymakers and educators to shift their attention from a resource-based perspective to a "capabilities perspective" to begin to mitigate some of the negative effects of poverty, stating: "Specifically, a capabilities perspective focuses on the second dimension of poverty—ability to convert resources into their intended benefits" (p. 203). Through the lens of capabilities, as Scherrer explained, "The value of a proposed resource is judged to be lower when an individual does not have the capability to make use of the resource being presented to her" (p. 203).

The mere act of providing a student with a complementary digital device might have a limited impact if the student's Internet access is not strong enough to stream videos or download educational content. Likewise, removing barriers to higher level coursework in high school without also providing the supports necessary, like quality curriculum and instruction, tutoring, study skills, an organized and quiet place to do homework, food security, and quality health care will do little to increase educational equity. Teachers experience the "capabilities perspective" frequently during instruction in instances when all students have equal access to a device, Internet, textbook, pencils, and so forth when in school, yet some students perform in vastly different ways because of out-of-school factors that affect in-school performance.

School leaders can use this lens of the framework to make efficient and practical analyses of policies from the standpoint of how they influence educational equity within the school building, specifically in terms of access to and support for all levels of education opportunities for students. Education policies that violate basic tenets of equity, such as using standardized test results as the deciding factor for entrance into various levels of courses or education programs, or not providing the cognitive, social, and emotional supports necessary for all students to be successful, or the use of discipline programs that are overly punitive to students of poverty and color would be evaluated negatively, –, within the framework. Conversely, policies that seek to increase access and student support for high quality education opportunities and fair discipline policies would be evaluated positively, +, within the framework. Policies that neither harm nor help students would be evaluated as neutral, =.

School leaders need to be able to recognize policies that constrain or reduce educational equity and work to overcome them or lessen their impact through acts of creative compliance in which they subvert the implementation of negative aspects (Tienken, 2020a). Likewise, policies that seek to provide greater access and support for students to experience a rich and comprehensive education would be evaluated positively, +, within the framework. Policies that are ambivalent toward or do not address issues related to educational equity would be evaluated as neutral, =.

The results from the analysis of the equity component can be used by school leaders to engage their staffs in democratic discussions about ways the educators in the building reformulate, revise, or recast policy to increase educational equity for all students within the school.

School leaders can use the following reflective question to guide their evaluation of the Equity component: How well does the policy facilitate access and support to foster educational equity for all students and what can we do to increase equity for all?

Social Justice. Educational equity is one component of a larger domain that school leaders must address: social justice. Rawls' (1971) *A Theory of Justice* presents the foundation of thought in the United States underlying what is now called *social justice*. In its most basic sense, this theory associates justice with fairness. One way in which social justice emerges from the Theory of Justice is through the rules associated with public institutions. Rawls deemed an institution fair when its policies and practices advantage all members of a society, and in the case of education policy, a school community, not just some members. Institutional policies and practices must be fair to all concerned regardless of their race, gender, social economic status, sexual orientation, religion, political affiliations, and so forth.

White privilege—feelings of entitlement presumed by the dominant ethnic or racial group and economic ruling class, and overall empathetic blindness by some toward the plight of others—poses a resisting force to establishing and implementing socially just policies that increase institutional fairness. As Mullen (2020) wrote, "All too commonly, our lenses insulate us from questioning the status quo" (p. 9). If they seek to be agents of social justice, school leaders must shed their personal and institutional layers of insulation and question the status quo.

Neoliberal policies inherently include aspects of White privilege, entitlement, and empathetic blindness because they consistently advantage the already advantaged. Neoliberal policies redistribute public wealth, known as public services, to private coffers through the creation of dual systems built on a profit mindset. Mullen (2020) sounded the alarm about the neoliberal profit mindset's negative influence on social justice:

> The profit mindset, having overtaken the greater good mindset, transfers power from the public to the private sector, making education vulnerable to "market logic" that narrows and distorts meaning. A deep concern is that public education has turned into an economic sector with aggravated racial and income inequities and class divisions.
>
> (p. 41)

The profit mindset enables a redistribution of public services to the private market, to be sold like a commodity. The redistribution of public services to the private marketplace also redistributes power from the collective public to wealthy and powerful individuals and corporations, and it erodes institutional fairness, thereby undermining social justice.

School leaders can use this lens of the framework (*social justice*) to make efficient and practical analyses of policies from the standpoint of how they influence social justice through institutional fairness for students and educators within the school building. This component requires school leaders to consider who has power and voice within the school and who does not. It also requires that they determine the influence of corporate education interests on students and teachers (see Mullen, 2022, Chapter 1, this volume).

Policies that directly or indirectly reduce institutional fairness and/or favor or empower one group of people over another based on race, gender, sexual orientation, social economic status, etc. would be evaluated negatively, –. Similarly, policies that allow the interests of Public Education, Inc. (as per Mullen, 2022) to take precedence over the rights of students to an equitable and effective education and the rights of teachers to exercise their professional judgment to provide such an education would be evaluated negatively, –, within the framework. Conversely, policies that increase institutional fairness, democratize the power structure within the school, and eliminate, block, or at least limit the influence of Public Education, Inc. would be evaluated positively, +, within the framework. Policies that neither hinder nor foster social justice would be evaluated neutral, =.

School leaders can use the analysis of the *social justice* component to engage their staff in democratic discussions about ways educators can change the trajectory of negative policy aspects and capitalize on positive aspects of the policy to increase social justice for all within the school.

School leaders can use these three reflective questions to guide their evaluation of the *social justice* component: (1) How well does the policy foster institutional fairness and distribute power, and what can we do within the school to increase fairness and empower all people within the school? (2) In what ways does the policy hinder or facilitate social justice based on factors such as race, ethnicity, social economic status, religion, sexual orientation, etc. (3) In what ways does the policy directly or indirectly empower Public Education, Inc. within the school and what can we do to reduce its influence on students and teachers?

Now What?

School leaders can use the SIDES policy analysis framework independent of other frameworks like SWOT and PRINCE, or in addition to existing frameworks. The intended use of SIDES is for school leaders to be able to conduct an efficient scan of a policy, based on a brief set of criteria and reflective questions. School leaders can post the seven reflective questions in a common area or create a checklist/rating system for quick reference and use (see Table 9.1). Once familiar with the components, school leaders can quickly review a policy and derive important insights on its potential strengths and weaknesses in relation to the SIDES components.

School leadership requires complex thinking about complex problems in democratic arenas. Analyzing a policy is an important component of effective school leadership. But some school leaders might ask, what comes after the evaluation? What happens when policies are found to include many negatives? Then what should leaders do?

Recipes for effective school leadership do not exist. Leadership is not a paint-by-numbers endeavor. But leaders can arrive at next steps by carefully considering the answers to the reflective questions and engaging education staff, students, parents, and community members in democratic discussion and brainstorming. Democracy must be lived, not just read about.

The hollowing out of the public space, including public education, is one consequence of neoliberalism; dehumanizing children and educators is another. Educators are simultaneously the first line of defense and some of the first people in the neoliberal firing line. They see first hand, and early on, how neoliberal education policy treats educators and children as commodities, and how commodification can dehumanize and objectify people over time. Neoliberalism represents legalized economic violence against democracy and members of society. Egalitarianism and dignity are ideas like democracy. And, like democracy, egalitarianism and dignity must be defended and nurtured by educators at the local level to cultivate and preserve these values for future generations.

TABLE 9.1 SIDES Checklist and Rating System

Component	Reflective Questions, Ratings, and Notes
Student	How well does the policy facilitate the student to be an active constructor of meaning who brings prior knowledge to the situation, and what further actions can we take as a school to create more opportunities for active learning? Rating: + − = Notes:
Instruction and Curriculum	How well does the policy facilitate the organization and teaching of curriculum content to be customized by the educators in the building to maximize creative instruction and the connecting of content to student experiences to foster active learning? Rating: + − = Notes:
Democratic Principles	How well does the policy facilitate shared decision making and egalitarian principles in the school and what can we do to further democratic principles in the school? Rating: + − = Notes:
Equity	How well does the policy facilitate access and support to foster educational equity for all students and what can we do to increase equity for all? Rating: + − = Notes:
Social Justice	How well does the policy foster institutional fairness and distribute Power, and what can we do to increase fairness and empower all people within the school? Rating: + − = Notes: In what ways does the policy hinder or facilitate social justice based on factors such as race, ethnicity, social economic status, religion, sexual orientation, etc.? Rating: + − = Notes: In what ways does the policy directly or indirectly empower Public Education, Inc. and what can we do to reduce its influence on students and teachers? Rating: + − = Notes:

Note. The source of "Public Education, Inc." is Mullen (2021).

Author Note

Portions of this chapter are adapted from three published sources by Tienken (2020), with permission:

Cracking the code of education reform: Creative compliance and ethical leadership. Thousand Oaks, CA: Corwin.

Democratic education: What would Dewey say? *Kappa Delta Pi Record, 56*(1), 35–41.

The not so subtle inequity of remote learning. *Kappa Delta Pi Record, 56*, 151–153.

References

Aikin, W. M. (1942). *The story of the eight-year study*. Harper.

Bannister, R. (1989). *Social Darwinism: Science and myth in Anglo-American social thought*. Temple University Press.

Butler, J. (1997). *Excitable Speech: the politics of the performative*. Routledge.

Commission on the Reorganization of Secondary Education. (1918). *Cardinal Principles of Secondary Education*. U.S. Bureau of Education, Bulletin No. 35.

Coughlan, R. W. (2022). Brown versus Board did not work: Finding a new pathway to educational justice. In C. H. Tienken and C. A. Mullen (Eds.), *The Risky Business of Education Policy* (pp. 57–71). Routledge & Kappa Delta Pi.

Dewey, J. (1959). Introduction to the uses of resources in education. In M. S. (Ed.), *Dewey on Education* (p. 31). Teachers College Press.

Dewey, J. (1929). *The sources of science of education*. Liveright.

Dewey, J. (2009/1916). *Democracy and education: An introduction to the philosophy of education*. Readaclassic.

Dewey, J. (1916). *Democracy and education*. Macmillan.

Dewey, J., & Tufts, J. H. (1908). *Ethics*. H. Holt & Co.

English, F. (2022, this volume). Neoliberalism as a policy ventriloquist. In C. H. Tienken and C. A. Mullen (Eds.), *The Risky Business of Education Policy* (pp. 23–39). Routledge & Kappa Delta Pi.

Fackler, A. K. (2020). How do we teach science the Dewey way? *Kappa Delta Pi Record, 56*, 148–160.

Freire, P. (2000). *Pedagogy of the oppressed* (30th ed.). Continuum.

Gijbels, D., Dochy, F., Van den Bossche, P., & Segers, M. (2005). Effects of problem-based learning: A meta-analysis from the angle of assessment. *Review of Educational Research, 75*(1), 27–61.

Gilens, M., & Page, B. I. (2014). Testing theories of American politics: Elites, interest groups, and average citizens. *Perspectives on Politics, 12*(3), 564–581.

Henriksen, D., & Shack, K. (2020). Creativity-focused mindfulness for student wellbeing. *Kappa Delta Pi Record, 56*, 170–175.

Hinchey, P. H., & Konkol, P. J. (2022). Threats to meaningful reform of civics education. In C. H. Tienken and C. A. Mullen (Eds.), *The Risky Business of Education Policy* (pp. 39–56). Routledge & Kappa Delta Pi.

Kontra, C., Lyons, D. J., Fischer, S. M., & Bellock, S. L. (2015). Physical experience enhances science learning. *Psychological Science, 26*(6), 737–749.

Kunz, J., Hubbard, K., Beverly, L., Cloyd, M., & Bancroft, A. (2020). What motivates stem students to try teacher recruiting programs? *Kappa Delta Pi Record, 56*, 154–159.

Ladson-Billings, G. (1994). *The dreamkeepers: Successful teachers of African American children*. Jossey-Bass.

Lyotard, J. F. (1984). *The postmodern condition: A report on knowledge*. Theory and History of Literature, 10. Manchester University Press.

Merriman, W., Gonzàles-Toro, C. M., & Cherubini, J. (2020). Physical activity in the classroom. *Kappa Delta Pi Record, 56*, 164–169.

Mullen, C. A. (2022). Corporate networks' grip on the public school sector and education policy. In C. H. Tienken and C. A. Mullen (Eds.), *The Risky Business of Education Policy* (pp. 1–22). Routledge & Kappa Delta Pi.

Mullen, C. A. (2020). *Canadian Indigenous literature and art: Decolonizing education culture and society*. Brill.

Mullen, C. A. (2017). *Creativity and education in China: Paradox and possibilities for an era of accountability*. Routledge.

Mullen, C. A., Samier, E. A., Brindley, S., English, F. W., & Carr, N. K. (2013). An epistemic frame analysis of neoliberal culture and politics in the US, UK, and the UAE. *Interchange: A Quarterly Review of Education*, 43(3), 187–228.

O'Leary, M. K., & Coplin, W. D. (1976). Teaching political strategy skills with PRINCE. *Policy Analysis*, 2(1), 145–160.

Pascoe, J. M., Wood, D. L., Duffee, J. H., & Kuo, A. (2016). Mediators and adverse effects of child poverty in the United States. *Pediatrics*, 137(4), e1–e17. https://doi.org/10.1542/peds.2016-0340.

Pirrone, C., & Di Nuovo, S. (2014). Can playing and imagining aid in learning mathematics? An experimental study of the relationships among building block play, mental imagery, and arithmetic skills. *Applied Psychological Bulletin*, 62, 30–39.

Rawls, J. (1971). *A theory of justice*. Harvard University Press.

Rosner, J. (2003, April 14). On White preference. *The Nation*, p. 24.

Sandel, M. (2012). *What money can't buy: The moral limits of markets*. Farrar, Straus & Giroux.

Scherrer, J. (2014). The role of the intellectual in eliminating the effects of poverty: A response to Tierney. *Educational Researcher*, 43(4), 201–207.

Tanner, D., & Tanner, L. N. (2007). *Curriculum development: Theory into practice* (4th ed.). Pearson.

Tienken, C. H. (2021). *The School reform landscape 2.0: More fraud, myth, and lies*. Rowman & Littlefield.

Tienken, C. H. (2020a). *Cracking the code of education reform: Creative compliance and ethical leadership*. Corwin.

Tienken, C. H. (2020b). Democratic education: What would Dewey say? *Kappa Delta Pi Record*, 56(1), 35–41.

Ward, L. F. (1883). *Dynamic sociology or applied social science*. Vol. II. D. Appleton & Company.

Zhao, Y., & Watterston, J. (2022, this volume). Students as the missing actor in education reform. In C. H. Tienken and C. A. Mullen (Eds.), *The Risky Business of Education Policy* (pp. 113–127). Routledge & Kappa Delta Pi.

CONTRIBUTOR BIOGRAPHIES

Editors

Christopher H. Tienken, EdD, is Associate Professor of Education Leadership, Management, and Policy. He is the author of more than 90 publications whose recent books include *Cracking the Code of Education Reform: Creative Compliance and Ethical Leadership*, published by Corwin Press and *The School Reform Landscape Reloaded: More Fraud, Myth, and Lies*, published by Rowman & Littlefield. His 2017 book *Defying Standardization: Creating Curriculum for an Uncertain Future* (Rowman & Littlefield) received the Outstanding Book Award from the Society of Professors of Education. He was selected as the National Researcher in Residence by the American Association of School Administrators in 2020.

Carol A. Mullen, PhD, is Professor of Educational Leadership and Policy Studies at Virginia Tech, Blacksburg, Virginia, and a Fulbright scholar alumnus. She teaches graduate courses in education policy, qualitative research, etc. In addition to 28 academic books, she has authored over 240 journal articles and book chapters, and 17 guest-edited special issues of journals. Her 2020 book *Canadian Indigenous Literature and Art* (Brill) received the Outstanding Book Award from the Society of Professors of Education (SPE). Other major recognitions include the University of Toronto's Excellence Award; Virginia Tech's Alumni Award for Excellence in International Research and, earlier, Alumni Award for Excellence in Research, the Living Legend Award from the International Council of Professors of Educational Leadership (ICPEL); and the Jay D. Scribner Mentoring Award from the University Council for Educational Administration. She currently serves as President of the SPE and is Past President of the ICPEL.

DOI: 10.4324/9781003108511-10

Contributors

Ryan W. Coughlan, PhD, is Assistant Professor of Education in Molloy College's Educational Leadership for Diverse Learning Communities EdD program. He uses geospatial statistical methods to study school zoning practices, school segregation patterns, educational outcomes, and social bonds between neighborhoods and schools.

Fenwick W. English, PhD, is Professor and Department Chair of Educational Leadership at Teachers College, Ball State University. He is Past President of the University Council of Educational Administration in 2006–2007 and the International Council of Professors of Educational Leadership (formerly NCPEA) 2011–2012 from which he received the Living Legend Award in 2013. His major research interest is in the epistemology of professional practice. He authored or co-authored over 40 books including *The Leadership Identity Journey: An Artful Reflection* (2014) with Carol A. Mullen and William A. Kealy.

Soribel Genao, PhD, is Associate Professor of Educational Leadership and Provost Diversity Fellow at CUNY Queens College. Her research has focused on examining the inclusive, equitable and diverse systemic issues in and reform of urban schools while assessing administrative, educative, and community collaborations that facilitate more positive academic and behavioral outcomes such as student retention in marginalized communities.

Patricia H. Hinchey, EdD is Professor Emerita of Education at Penn State and a Fellow of the National Education Policy Center. She holds a doctorate from Teachers College, Columbia University, has conducted professional development for K-12 and university faculty nationally and internationally, and authored or co-authored numerous books and articles.

Pamela J. Konkol, PhD is Professor of educational foundations, social policy, and research at Concordia University Chicago and the Executive Director of the American Educational Studies Association. She holds a doctorate in Policy Studies in Urban Education and a Master of Education degree in Curriculum Studies from the University of Illinois at Chicago.

Morna McDermott McNulty, PhD, is Professor in the College of Education at Towson University and an artist, writer, and educator. She authored *Blood's Will* (2018), and co-produced the film *Voices of Baltimore: Life Under Segregation* (2017). She has been working in, and with, arts integration for public education for over 20 years. She received her doctorate, focused on arts-based research, from the University of Virginia in 2001.

Julia Sass Rubin, PhD, is Associate Professor at the Edward J. Bloustein School of Planning and Public Policy at Rutgers University and an Associate Visiting Professor at the School of Public and Internal Affairs at Princeton University.

Svein Sjøberg, PhD, is Professor Emeritus of science education at Oslo University, Norway. He has worked internationally with science education for national and international authorities such as the Organization for Economic Co-operation and Development, the United Nations Educational, School and Cultural Organization, the World Bank, and the European Union. He has numerous honorary professorships and doctorates and has won several prizes for his research as well as science communication and outreach. His current concern is the ethical, social, political, and cultural aspects of education from an international perspective.

Jim Watterston, PhD, is Dean and Enterprise Professor at the Melbourne Graduate School of Education, University of Melbourne. He has been a teacher and principal in primary and secondary schools, and Regional Director and the Deputy Secretary of the Victorian Education Department, and Director General. In addition to appointments to many educationally related Boards, he served as the National President for the Australian Council for Education Leaders and is an influential advocate for the education sector. His distinguished contribution to education has been acknowledged nationally and internationally with awards from professional bodies and educational institutions, including the highly prestigious Order of the Palmes Académiques (Chevalier) by the French Government in 2014.

Mark Weber, PhD, is the Special Analyst for Education Policy and the New Jersey Policy Perspective; a Lecturer in Education Policy at the Graduate School of Education at Rutgers, The State University of New Jersey; and a teacher in the Warren Township Schools in New Jersey.

Yong Zhao, PhD, is Foundation Distinguished Professor in the School of Education at University of Kansas and Professor in Educational Leadership at Melbourne Graduate School of Education, University of Melbourne.

INDEX

Note: **Bold** page numbers refer to tables; *Italic* page numbers refer to figures.

academic performance 73, 75, 79
academics, critique from 106
accountability 101, 131; corporate 2; education 145; policies 5; system 145; test-driven 93
Achieve, Inc. 9–10, 16
action civic programs 43, 51
actions 13–14, 23, 33, 60, 64, 122
advocacy 17, 48, 76, 78–9, 130
African Americans 32; housing purchase program for 66
ALEC *see* American Legislative Exchange Council (ALEC)
American Bar survey 2019 41
American exceptionalism 53
American Legislative Exchange Council (ALEC) 2
Annenberg Civics Knowledge Survey 41
Annual Professional Performance Review (APPR) of teachers 131
anti-bias training 67
anti-Blackness 19–20, 62–4
Apple, M. W. 14–16
Arffman, I. 98
attitudes 103–4; negative 103–4
authentic texts 89, 96–8
authoritarian approach 50
authoritarian patriotism 50

Baby PISA 106
Ball, S. J. 10, 13–14
Banking Model of education 146–8
bankrupting democracy 15
Bennett, W. J. 7, 9
BE programs *see* bilingual education (BE) programs
Berliner, D. C. 2, 6–7, 14
bifurcated system 143
big science 100
bilingual education (BE) programs 128–33
bilingual/multilingual leadership 130–1
bi/multilingual communities 128, 139
bi/multilingual preparation programs 130–1
Black Lives Matter (BLM) movement 19, 52–3
Black people 61–3, 81; struggles and greatness of 62–3
Black–White achievement gap 60
Block, J. 34
Bogotch, I. 4
Bottia, M. 60
Bourdieu, P. 26, 28, 33
Brass, J. 12–13
Brown, C. 41–2
Brown v. Board of Education 57–9, 146; purpose of 58; school integration *see* school integration; Supreme Courts ruling in 66
Buckley, J. 75

Bush, George H. W. 25
business philanthropists 78
Butler, J. 145

Campaign for the Civic Mission of Schools 42
Cassidy, J. 25
cataclysmic proportions 13
CCSS *see* Common Core State Standards (CCSS)
Center for Educational Equity 44
charter schools 72–4, 76; challenges of reproducing 74–5; competition 76–9; demographics 81–2; educational quality 74–5; financial impact of 81; growth of 79–80; impacts of 72, 79–82; parental school selection 75–6; proliferation 79–80; regulations of 78; segregation in 81–2; students in 73; White students 82
Chicago Federation of Teachers in 1898 49
children: Black 62–3; educational prospects of 57; as human capital 100–2
citizenship education 42–4, 49–50
civic education 40–3, 45, 47, 51, 53; practices in citizenship education 43; safeguards 41; taking action 53–4; threats to improvement 43–4; American education 50–3; meaningful experiences 45–7; respect and value young people 44–5; teacher professionalism 47–50; tipping point 41–3
civics: engagement 45; lessons 47
classroom: action 52; code of conduct 48; diversification 67; evaluation ratings 144–5; strategies 47–8; teachers 50
climate change 45, 121–2
color: students of 68; teachers of 68 *see also* Black children
The Color of Law (Rothstein) 66
commercialization effect 146
commodification 1–3, 16, 155
Common Core State Standards (CCSS) 2, 6, 9, 13, 17–18; certification tests 18; corporate views of accountability 18; influence 8; megacorporations supports 7–8; ploys and bedfellows 10–12; single market for 7–8; tests 8
community control of schools 63
competition 76–9, 109, 143; creating 72; free-market 1; market logic of 14; open 27–8
conformity 30, 145
conjecture 27, 32–3

Conner, J. 46
contemporary ideas 47
Coronavirus Aid, Relief, and Economic Security (CARES) Act 78
corporate identifications 13
corporate intervention, messages of 5
corporate networking 1, 10, 18–20
corporate sector 33
corporate titans 10, 13
corporations 1–7, 94, 109, 154
corporatization 15, 19, 35
correlation 96, 98, 103
Coughlan, R. W. 146
court-monitored desegregation 58
creative disposition 145
creativity 46, 60, 116, 145, 150; government policies and watchdogs work against 30–1
critical pedagogy 131
critical race theory 17
Cuban, L. 17
cultural bias 97
curriculum 48, 60, 77, 97, 114, 137; component 149–50; form of 7; implementation of 67; one-size-fits-all standardization of 144; and pedagogy 67; school 114; for students 117; universal 150

de facto segregation 63
dehydration 98–9
de jure segregation 63–4
democratic/democracy 2, 16, 155; component 151; corporate thinning of 14–15; education 150–1; governance 15; hallmark of 7; institutions 40–1, 150; leadership 150–1; patriotism 50; principles of 151; processes 43; rights and responsibilities 41; schools 119–20
demographics 59–60, 75, 79, 81–2
desegregation 57–8; court-monitored 58; residential 65, 67; school *see* school desegregation; thwart 64
Dewey, J. 44, 144, 146–7
Diamond, A. J. 23
Diamond, J. B. 65
dignity 155
discrimination 96; housing 64
DisCrit Theory 36
district community schools 75
district public schools 75–9, 81
diversity 12, 52, 58–60, 132–3
DoDEA 3, 8
Dolan, C. 34

dominant discourse 33–4
dominant groups 14, 16
Douglass Horsford, S. 24

economic development 91, 101
economic exchange 28–9
economic fatalism 23
Economic Injury Disaster Loan (EIDL) program 78
economic liberalism 28
educational/education 2, 13, 40, 91, 116, 142–4, 153; case of 153; community 43; current policy landscape 143–4; details and consequences of 147; dual system of 145; environment 10, 12; equity 142, 151–3; importance of 100–1; influential agencies in 9; justice 58, 65; leadership 36, 128–9, 133; legacy 49; market appropriations of 19; military families for 3; multiple sides of 142–3; neoliberal policies and programs 147; performativity 145–6; policymakers/policymaking 88–9; problems in 113; quality of 74–5, 82, 88; reform 33; resources, distribution of 62; and self-governance 6; SIDES policy analysis framework 147–55; standardized inequity 144–5; structured inequity 144; systems 13, 91; technology 115; value system 5 *see also* schools
education reform 113, 115–16; neglected owner of learning 114–15; participating in social movements 121–3; personalizing learning as making decisions about learning 117–19; policies 147; proposals 147; returning ownership 115–16; self-determination 113–14; sharing responsibilities and making decisions 119–21; student as owners of learning 116–17
educators 37, 65, 103–4, 120–2
effective learning 113
egalitarianism 155
Eisenhower, D. D. 3–4, 6
Elementary and Secondary School Emergency Relief Fund 78
ELLs/MLLs *see* English Language Learners/Multilingual Learners (ELLs/MLLs)
ELP accountability *see* English Language Proficiency (ELP) accountability
Engel, L. C. 89
English Language Arts 12, 79; standardized tests 60

English Language Learners/Multilingual Learners (ELLs/MLLs) 77, 128–9, 133; bi/multilingual preparation programs 130–1; emphasis on 133–4; implications and taking action 137–9; Part 154 and principal leadership programs 131; PK-12 education policy peril 129; policy peril 131–7; purpose 129–30; recommendations 139; substantial populations of 130
English Language Proficiency (ELP) accountability 87, 131
enquiry-based teaching 105
equity investors 8
equivalence of translation 98
Erickson, J. 46
Etzioni, A. 41

failing school 14, 36
Fairclough, N. 33
fair testing 89
fear 29, 63, 98
Federal Housing Administration programs 66
finances 79–81
financial literacy 91
financial vulnerability 35
Firestone, W. A. 17
food distribution 31
Franklin, B. 42
Frankson, J. E. 32
free market 25; capitalism 24; competition, economic ideological stances of 1; conjecture 32–3; ideology 31
free public education 31, 94
Freire, P. 146–8
Friedman, M. 27–31
Friedman, R. 27–9
Furstenberg, F. 35

garage tinkerers 31
Gates and Broad Foundations 8
Gates, Bill 6
gender differences 104
GERM (Global Educational Reform Management) discourse 34
gifted and talented programs 65
Gilens, M. 143
Giroux, H. 15, 26
Glass, G. V. 2, 6–7, 14
global climate 121
global community 122, 151
global economy 91, 109, 147

Index

globalization 88; free-market thinking and 93–4; neoliberal 94
global market economy 95
good citizen 50
government policies 63–5, 146
government-sanctioned residential segregation 66
GPA *see* grade point average (GPA)
grade point average (GPA) 77, 138
Great Recession of 2008 33

Habermas, J. 16
Hamowy, R. 25, 32
Han, E. S. 79
Hanushek economic modeling 101
Hayek, F. 25–6, 29, 31–2
Heintz, J. 4
Hess, F. M. 51
heterogeneous grouping 65
Hinchey, P. H. H. 143
Hispanic students 81
Hopkins, J. 35
housing discrimination 64
Human Capital Theory 100–2
humanity 116
human nature 40
human resources, development of 100–1

IB *see* International Baccalaureate (IB)
IBSE *see* inquiry-based science education (IBSE)
ICT *see* Information and Communication Technology (ICT)
independent thinking 12
individual biases 63–5
individual freedom 31
individual rights, theory of 32
influential decision makers 6
Information and Communication Technology (ICT) 105
information laws 78
informing policy-making process 93
innovative domains 99–100
inquiry-based science education (IBSE) 104
inquiry-based teaching 104–5
in-school elections 46
institutional fairness 153–6
instruction 149–50
integration 66; benefits and drawbacks of 58; documented benefits of 60; patterns of 66
interest in science 103
International Baccalaureate (IB) 117

International Journal of Science Education 103
IRT *see* Item Response Theory (IRT)
Item Response Theory (IRT) 100
item text 97–9

Jabbar, H. 76–7
Jefferson, T. 40
Johnson, R. C. 61
jurisdictional challengers 79
justice-oriented values of public education 6

Kahne, J. 42
Keefe, J. 79
Kjærnsli, M. 105
knowledge 148; domains 95
Konkol, P. J. 143
Kreiner, S. 100

labour's bargaining power 23
Ladson-Billings, G. 131
languages 97–9; Scandinavian 98
learning 116–18; aspects of 119; environment 115, 119; ownership of 114–16; personalizing 117–19
Lewis, A. E. 65
Lieberman, M. 29
linguistic gaming ploys 16–17
love-it-or-leave-it approach 50, 52
Lyotard, J. F. 145

managerialism: analysis of 34; definition of 34; ideology of 33; intersection with 33–6; neoliberalism and 35
market-based reforms 19
market logic 154; of competition 14
market/marketing/marketization 1–2, 94; domination 12; neoliberalism and 13–14; substantial resources to 76–7
Mason, P. 23–4
Mazzucato, M. 30
McFarland, D. 46
megacorporations 4, 7, 15, 17
metacorporations 16
Mickelson, R. A. 60, 82
military–industrial complex 3–4
misplaced power 4, 6
Mitchell, T. D. 46
modern corporations 7
modernization 28
Mommandi, W. 77
money-making markets 12

monopolies 28; method of creating 28
Mullen, C. A. 23, 143–5, 153–4
multilingual communities 128–9, 139
multi-state charter networks 73

NACC *see* National Action Civics Collaborative (NACC)
NAEP *see* National Assessment of Educational Progress (NAEP)
National Action Civics Collaborative (NACC) 51
National Assessment of Educational Progress (NAEP) 60, 116
national curriculum 8, 53; policies 92–3
National Education Progress 41
National Education Summit 1996 16
national schools systems, quality of 91
negative attitudes 89, 103–4
neighborhoods 37, 51, 59, 64
neoliberal/neoliberalism 1, 23–5, 144; as accidents 32; antagonism 31; business networks 10; consequence of 155; corporations 2; definition of 24–5; discourse of 37; doctrine 30; education policies 143–4, 146, 155; effects of 18; free market conjecture 32–3; globalization 94; ideology of 25, 29–30; enactment of 27; package 30; implementation of 26; intersection with managerialism 33–6; and managerialism 35; and marketization 13–14; nature of 26; neoliberal reforms 36–7; networks 15; pillars of belief 27; economic and political freedoms 27–8; government policies and watchdogs work against creativity 30–1; government's role 29–30; institutional services and relationships 31; political freedom, monopolies 28; professional associations and unions compromise economic exchange 28–9; social justice 31–2; policies 1, 147–8, 154; principle objective of 24; prophets of 25–7; public enemies 9; reforms 37; of public education 37; pushback against 36–7; as theory 24; thinking 32
New Public Management 93–4, 108
New York State English Language Arts 138
New York State Teacher Certification Examinations (NYSTCE) 130; pilot objectives and deliverables **134–6**, 136–7
The New York Times (Appelbaum) 26
Norwegian economy 97
NYC school system 132
NYSED **134–6**, 139
NYSTCE *see* New York State Teacher Certification Examinations (NYSTCE)

obedience 44, 50
OECD *see* Organisation for Economic Co-operation and Development (OECD)
Organisation for Economic Co-operation and Development (OECD) 88, 91; authority of 107; definitions and frameworks 90; indicators 107; and political advice 92; political aims of 88; Test for Schools 93
organized private interests 6
outside-in rewiring 5
overheating 98–9

Page, B. I. 143
parental school selection 75–6
partial monopolies 31
passivity 44
patriotic Americans 51–2
patriotic education 17, 52–3
patriotism 50; authoritarian concept of 51
Pazey, B. 36
Pearson Corporation 18
pedagogy of opposition 131
performativity 144–6
personalized learning 117–19
PIAAC 107
Pickett, K. 27
pilot program 128, 130–1; job-embedded activities in 137
PIRLS *see* Progress in International Reading Literacy Study (PIRLS)
PISA *see* Programme for International Student Assessment (PISA)
PISA for Development (PISA-D) 107
PK-12 students 49–50
police brutality 47
policy landscape 143–4
policymakers 42, 52
political docility 23
Political Economy Research Institute 4
political freedom 29
political landscape 24
post-recession austerity era 49
poverty 152
preferential regulatory environment 77–8
PRINCE 155; framework 142
principal preparation programs 128–30
principal–teacher interactions 130
private business corporation 35

private contractors 15
private management firms 2
private schools 76
private sector: donors 78–9; fiscal breakdown of 13; profits 13
privatization 94
privileged students 146
pro-American curriculum 52
problematic statistics 100
professionalism 12, 49
professional learning, requirements 128
Programme for International Student Assessment (PISA) 88; aims of 90; assessment framework 94; children as human capital 100–2; claims 90–1, 102; country rankings 100; creators 91; critique from academics 106; curriculum 95–6; data, analyses of 89–90; economical purposes of 91; educational reforms 93–4; education system 104; expanding and extending 106–7; framework 95–6; free-market thinking and globalization 93–4; fundamental weaknesses of 102; global influence of 106; innovative domain 99–100; item selection and test construction 96–7; item text, language, and translations 97–9; legitimize school reforms 93; on national curriculum policies 92–3; organizers for consideration 98; and political advice 92; politics and normative nature of 91–2; problematic aspects and intriguing results 102; and gender differences 104; and ICT 105–6; and inquiry-based teaching 104–5; interest and negative attitudes 103–4; resources and finance 102; problematic statistics and lack of transparency 100; project 91–2; purpose 88–90; rankings 91–2, 102; real life indicators 94–5; real life situation 99–100; reports 90–1; scores and rankings 91; social phenomenon 89; student background questionnaire in 105; subjects 104; techno-scientific machinery 89; testing 90–3, 95, 98; test situation 99–100
Progress in International Reading Literacy Study (PIRLS) 104
Prothero, A. 52
public education 2, 9, 14, 17–18, 48, 144, 151; corporate siege of 19; corporatization of 19; corruption of 15; destruction of 3; divestment in 49; and education policy 20; policy 41; provocative conception of 2; reforming 24; seizure of 19; system 146
Public Education, Inc. 2–4, 7, 19, 154–5
public funding 77
public schools 2–3, 6–7, 14–15, 59, 62, 73, 76, 145–6; corporate takeover of 4; district *see* district public schools; educators 18; fundamental functions of 150; military investments and real costs to 4; mission 19; sector and education policy: CCSS initiative 7–8; CCSS ploys and bedfellows 10–12; corporate thinning of democracy 14–15; empirical evidence 12; linguistic gaming ploys 16–17; military–industrialization 3–4; neoliberal business networks 10; neoliberalism and marketization 13–14; neoliberal public enemies 9; organizing for action 18–20; outside-in rewiring 5; private sector profits 13; public education 17–18; Public Education, Inc. 3; purpose of 1–3; shape 6–7; working flow chart 11; zapping school agency 5–6; sectors, corporate marketization on 19
public sectors 94
public services 26, 93–4; redistribution of 154
public space 1, 155
punishment 2, 67

racial/racism 17, 57, 61–4, 67–8; achievement gaps 57, 60; caste system 57–8; diversity 59–60; segregation 59, 75–6
Rasch modeling 100
Ravitch, D. 8, 14
Rawls, J. 153
real estate agents 64, 69
real life assertion 99
real life situations 89, 96–7, 99
religious institutions 59
remote learning 114; effectiveness of 113; forms of 113
representative democracy 40, 45, 143
residential desegregation 65, 67
residential segregation 63–4, 66; patterns of 63–4; structural problem of 66
resource-based perspective of education reform 152
responsive leadership 132
return on investment 61–2
Ridley, M. 80

Robertson, E. 48
robotic curricular circuitry 15
Rosenblatt, H. 24
Rothberg, I. C. 79–80
Rutkowski, D. 89

Sahlberg, P. 93–4
Sandel, M. 146
Savage, G. C. 13
Sawchuk, S. 42
Scandinavian languages 98
Scherrer, J. 151–2
Schleicher, A. 92–3
Schneider, M. 75
school desegregation 62–3, 65, 67; drawbacks of 62–3; programs 58
school integration 60; drawbacks of school desegregation 62–3; economic efficiency 61–2; educational benefits 60; government policies 63–4; individual biases 64; investment of 61–2; levels of 66; mechanisms for resisting 63; personal benefits 61; policies 63; societal benefits 61; state of 58–60; structures 65; tools for advancing 65–8
school leaders/leadership 148–9, 151, 153–5; importance of 49; shortsightedness of 5
schools 45, 64; academic performance 75; agency 5–6; based education 114; boards 65; charter *see* charter schools; choice 66, 76; civics instruction in 41; climate 54; cognitive or academic aspect of 120; community 54, 63, 153; competition among 77; corporate networking on 18; curriculum 114–15, 117–18; demographics composition 59, 75–6; effectiveness 101; equity 67; governance 43; marketing 77; market invasions of 5; personnel, diversification of 67–8; physical aspects of 120; policy 114–15; preference for 76; quality of 91; segregation 57, 64–6; shootings 47; structures 65; systems, professional staff in 17; transportation to 76; White supremacy culture in 58
science education 89, 104–5
SD *see* standard deviations (SD)
segregation 57, 64–6; patterns of 76
self-determination 113–14, 119; capabilities for 114–15, 119; capacity for 116–17
self-interest 13–14, 63
self-regulation 123

service learning 43, 45–6, 52
Shapiro, S. 41–2
shared decision making 151
Shields, C. M. 4
SIDES: checklist and rating system **156**; policy analysis framework 142–3, 147–55, *148*
social cynicism 23
Social Darwinism 144
social entrepreneurs 3
social functions 26
social justice 31–2, 153–5; agents of 154; component 155; leadership 128, 130–1; negative influence on 154; protest 6; understandings 128–9
social media 47, 121–2
social movements: building 17; participating in 121–3
social networks 64, 75
social practices, collection of 33
social solidarity, forms of 30
sociocivic education 150–1
sociocivic learning 151
sovereignty 15
special interest groups 2, 19
Spring, J. 34–5
stakeholders 1, 3, 5, 19, 42, 53, 65
standard deviations (SD) 74
standardization 6, 8, 108, 144–5
Starmanns, C.E. 46
state-led intervention 12
Stiglitz, J. 33
stimulus 97–8
Strengths-Weaknesses-Opportunities-Threats (SWOT) 142, 155
structured inequity 144
students 52, 113–14; achievement and learning 152; Black 62–3, 81; capabilities for self-determination 113–14; in charter schools 73; of color in low-level courses 67; democratic values in 45; engagement 130; Hispanic 81; as owners of learning 116–17; selection 77
SWOT *see* Strengths-Weaknesses-Opportunities-Threats (SWOT)
symbolic power 7–8

taxpaying citizens 1, 3, 5
teachers 49, 52; autonomy 49; evaluation, Value Added Model of 49; importance of 49; neutrality 48; professionalism 47–50; treatment of 75
technology 13, 30, 34, 93, 105, 115, 120

techno-science 100
Terrier, C. 79–80
The Terror of Neoliberalism (Giroux) 26
thwart desegregation 64
Tienken, C. H. 12, 101
TIMSS *see* Trends In Mathematics and Science Study (TIMSS)
traditional public schools 75, 79, 81; segregation in 73; segregation of 81–2
traditional public services 94
traditional schools 120
Trammell, L. 31
transformational leadership 18
translations 97–9, 108
transparency, lack of 100
Trends In Mathematics and Science Study (TIMSS) 97, 100–1, 104, 108
Trujillo, T. 24
Trump, D. 17–18, 45, 52
Tufts, J. H. 147

UCLA Civil Rights Project 58
UNESCO 89, 95
uniqueness 116
universal curriculums 96, 150

value diversity 61, 65
volunteer experiences 46

volunteerism 46

Ward, L. F. 150
Washington-based bullying tactics 10
Weber, M. A. 80
Weiner, E. J. 23
well-being 13–14, 17, 58
Welner, K. 77
Westheimer 48, 50, 53
Wexler, A. 7–8, 10, 14, 18
White Americans 62–4, 66
White-dominated schools 62–3
White flight instruments 75–6
White privilege 68, 153–4
White students 59, 62, 65, 67, 75–6, 82
White supremacy 19–20; culture of 57, 63; societal culture of 61
Wilkinson, R. 27
Will, M. 48
Woessman, R. 101
World Bank 34–5
World Economic Forum's Growth Competitiveness Index 101

youth participatory action research (YPAR) 43

Zhao, Y. 106
Zimmerman, J. 48

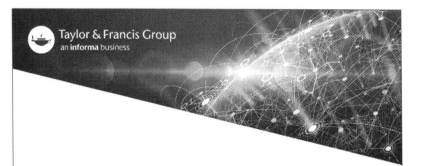

Printed in the United States
by Baker & Taylor Publisher Services